The Gus Van Sant Touch

ALSO BY JUSTIN VICARI

Mad Muses and the Early Surrealists (McFarland, 2012)

*Male Bisexuality in Current Cinema:
Images of Growth, Rebellion and Survival* (McFarland, 2011)

The Gus Van Sant Touch
A Thematic Study — Drugstore Cowboy, Milk *and Beyond*

JUSTIN VICARI

McFarland & Company, Inc., Publishers
Jefferson, North Carolina, and London

LIBRARY OF CONGRESS CATALOGUING-IN-PUBLICATION DATA

Vicari, Justin, 1968–
 The Gus Van Sant touch : a thematic study — *Dugstore Cowboy, Milk* and beyond / Justin Vicari.
      p.   cm.
 Includes bibliographical references and index.

 ISBN 978-0-7864-7183-6
 softcover : acid free paper ∞

 1. Van Sant, Gus — Criticism and interpretation. I. Title.
 PN1998.3.V363V53 2013
 741.4302'33092 — dc23   2012033485
 [B]

BRITISH LIBRARY CATALOGUING DATA ARE AVAILABLE

© 2012 Justin Vicari. All rights reserved

No part of this book may be reproduced or transmitted in any form or by any means, electronic or mechanical, including photocopying or recording, or by any information storage and retrieval system, without permission in writing from the publisher.

On the cover: Gus Van Sant (Focus Features/Photofest, © Focus Features, photographer: Phil Bray); film element © 2012 Shutterstock

Manufactured in the United States of America

McFarland & Company, Inc., Publishers
 Box 611, Jefferson, North Carolina 28640
 www.mcfarlandpub.com

For Julia Lesage and Chuck Kleinhans

Table of Contents

Preface: My Own Private Academy Awards	1
Introduction: Filmmaking as Sampling	9

PART ONE : EXPERIENTIAL TEXTS 19
1. Van Sant and Intertextualty 20
2. Cloudscapes and Pietàs: Visual Intertextuality 50
3. Schizo-ing *Psycho*: Quotational Intertextuality 62
4. "Where's Dad?" Thematic Intertextuality 80
5. *Finding Forrester*: Postmodern Skin, or, The End of *Whose* History? 112

PART TWO : TIME NAMES 127
6. Van Sant and Queer Cinema 128
7. The Mirror in the Mirror: *Gerry* 146
8. Queering the Iconographies of Fashion and Militarism in *Even Cowgirls Get the Blues* and *Elephant* 159
9. Back from Interzone: Reading William Burroughs' Sexual Politics Through the Films of Van Sant 180
10. Secret Histories 201

Conclusion: Beyond "Private"	226
Chapter Notes	233
Works Cited	243
Index	247

Preface: My Own Private Academy Awards

Essential to avoid the deadly distractions: sentimentality which is secondhand affect, "made in Hollywood" self-glorification. — William Burroughs[1]

The Academy Awards — any televised ceremony, actually — always made me think of William Burroughs' Interzone, not so much a place as a buzz of molecules, a reality-transmission, that "overloaded switchboard sending insane messages and countermessages to the viscera."[2]

With Interzone this was at least partly explained by the fact that the Zone ran on drugs the way most cities ran on oil: it was an electronic mirage made all the more pungent by the cloudy reek of hallucinogens and narcotics hovering around, within and between many of Interzone's citizens in lieu of a collective "reality." It could be a place where audience and spectacle merge. Whereas Hollywood was, by contrast, merely hyperaware of the separation that existed between it and its audience "out there." The movies had always been a trap in that sense: if moviemakers truly were artists, primal dreamers, then they had some innate right to be or seem different from non-artists; if they were merely the dreams that others have dreamed, then their conduct could hardly claim much independence. And what if they were, most likely, a hybrid of both? We were all still engaged in trying to classify that hybrid, to test how much and what kinds of reality it could safely bear.

A virtual place, a television broadcast that imagined it had come to life, whatever Interzone felt that it lacked in reality it always tried to make up for in an intensification of its own "space-time." Burroughs: "The meaning of Interzone, its space-time location is at a point where three-dimensional fact merges into dream, and dreams erupt into the real world,"[3] like a computer virus that imitates an actual site or program. By contrast, all Hollywood could do was "go live" once a year, and cross its fingers that the dreamers and the dreams remembered their places and stayed out of each other's way.

If all of this sounded science-fiction-y, it was meet to recall that the very physics of awards ceremonies traded in the weird physics of real time, of being live, of unfolding in some eternal, unreconstructed now: purgatorial and fleeting, deadly boring and sensationalistic, elitist and grubby at the same time, paranoid and meaningless, subversive and invisible. It was the "live" of some interminable Warhol take and also of combat footage — the point where earnest attention caved in to the fata morgana of a sort of induced déjà vu. For real time always contained this double agency: it was liberating, on one hand, to bring "freakery" down to the level of quotidian boredom, and at the same time it was a way of dissimulating systemic problems in a string of eternal "now"'s intently denying of contexts. Postmodernism needed to have it that way. Even right and wrong became meaningless, relative, irrelevant, the longer one was forced to contemplate them as barely registered non-gestures surrounded by nothingness.

It did not help that, today, time was colonized the way geographic space once used to be. We no longer needed to group diverse people beneath the same flag, language, religion or currency, when we could group them even more effectively beneath a shared idea of which unfolding events were live and real, a shared idea of what was and was not worth their time. The sun would set willy-nilly on flags, but never again on the twenty-four-hour news crawl and the great global chat-room. And that infinity of unfolding time took care of its own far better than the discernments of the former book culture ever did, since the old logic of exceptional events tended to shake out into clear-cut judgments and absolute values. Today, scandals, crimes, insults, revelations of gross corruption were not covered up, or finally dealt with, but simply jabbered through a gauntlet of polls, panels, equal-time coverage, op-ed spew, interviews and absurd reenactments, while the void watched greedily, grateful for something — anything — to fill it. In the end, one grew sick of issues long before they could ever be resolved. The winner in every public forum was meaninglessness, and the deepening schizophrenia (was it stoic or serene?) that came with holding both sides in one's head, both sides of every debate, both sides of every demographic.

So, even when it went live, television had a dull, rehearsed, embalming cast. "Live" was never live enough, I could barely recall the last time I was even mildly shocked by anything that had managed to slip the censor's *bleep*. I almost yearned for the coming of dead air, signifying some unaccountable snafu, the unspeakable being uttered, the way one waited for visceral counterproof of Gil Scott-Heron's insight about "the revolution" (such as it was anymore), that it would only take place in some "live" "real time" that the cameras would either miss or shun because it had not been scheduled in advance.

And again and again, Scott-Heron's formulation was proven right by its inescapable, depressing converse: *whatever was televised was not the revolution.* For nothing unspeakable interrupted the whole bland predigested stream of shows and commercials, running on time like trains in fascist countries. As if no one was allowed within one hundred feet of the cameras who was still capable of generating the kind of thought that would set off those censorious *bleeps*— or rather, as if prolonged exposure to the cameras themselves had created a drab, self-preserving species unable even to *conceive* a subversive observation. Speak No Evil smiled and winked at Hear No Evil while See No Evil politely looked half-away, looped on their endless advertiser's cycle, and if there were still cloistered viewers who became alarmed in reflexive, knee-jerk ways, it was only to demonstrate how the medium of TV had forever lost what small potential it had ever nurtured in itself to walk upon the sludgy waters and disturb the airwaves with something unexpected, something crazy and mystic and profound. For electronic mysticism had always ventured into quixotic battle with the small-minded forces of dogmatic literalism merely as part of its entrée into the spotlight, ever since Robert Johnson first plugged in his amp and had some people thinking he was a rare poet and others thinking he was Satan. Such points were always meant to be moot; the spotlight alone survived.

Yet, wasn't I still foolish enough to view live broadcast as holding out the remains of some implicit threat of *something*, at least one half-beat of transcendent, pinch-yourself silliness if nothing else? If only a streaker in the background, all flashing hair and pasty, sun-deprived skin — a breaking down if not quite a breaking through. For if Interzone, according to DJ Spooky, "could easily be seen as a metaphorical vision of what the Internet has become and a signpost on the road to what it will be in the future,"[4] then surely this is because the Zone itself is, as Gail-Nina Anderson writes, "that postcolonial, postmorality no man's land where to know the rules is to break them, where everyone has an angle, where it is the shadow rather than the light that defines."[5] Business subverts under a pretense of normalization; antinormalization makes its bid for business success (or something like it) and either sells out or implodes into those scrambled eggs that did not quite have the wherewithal to become "Yesterday." For some, it *was* such an easy game to play; for others, next to impossible. And between the commercial breaks, between the limos discharging their usual payloads into a demoralizing heat of microphone small-talk and oddly intense descriptions of what everyone was wearing — it was impossible to deny, while watching the 2008 Academy Awards, that business was still business, still *usual* if not quite sane.

Except for one fact that cheered me personally. One of my long-time cultural heroes, Gus Van Sant, had made a film, *Milk* (2007), which garnered eight nominations in all the major categories, including Best Director. An Oscar win for Van Sant (whom many of us already regard as our best director) would have been a reason to celebrate. In Harvey Milk and the rise of the gay rights movement, Van Sant had not only found one of his great subjects, but seemed to have been finally able to put into explicit words the kind of identity issues which his other films left partly hidden in enthrallingly ambiguous poetry. Not that there wasn't poetry and ambiguity in *Milk*, and not that the identity issues themselves were not fraught with more complexity, conflict and soul-searching than they usually are in lesser exercises in biographical cinema — but there was pragmatism, too, and a real streak of righteous and convincing pride, and all the things that Milk, the activist, the martyr, had stood for.

Van Sant had been trying to get his movie made since the early 1990s, so its eventual arrival was a tribute to his determination as much as anything else. It had been in pre-production, once, in 1993, and Van Sant had rented an apartment in Milk's Castro District in preparation for shooting. The film at that time was to have been based on *The Mayor of Castro Street*, Randy Shilts' biography of Milk. Too much interference from major Hollywood players, including the barnstorming Oliver Stone no less, understandably dampened Van Sant's enthusiasm. "The script lacked humanity," Van Sant said. "It was too much like a circus, a regular Hollywood script ... the film would have been a cliché."[6] He "quietly withdrew from the project, unwilling to direct the version of the script that Stone and his co-producers wished to make. It is indicative of Van Sant's independent spirit that he should opt out of a movie that would have featured a bigger star (Robin Williams had been mooted as Harvey Milk), demanded a much bigger investment and got a wider distribution (from Warner Bros.) than each of his previous films."[7]

Fifteen years' delay had only served to ripen, so to speak, the meaning of a Milk biopic. Indeed, one could only marvel at the finished film's utterly Brechtian timeliness, as if Van Sant and writer Dustin Lance Black had refracted today's headlines through forty years of gay activism — that is how much the references in *Milk* resonated with current left-wing and community concerns. Here was a portrait of the 70s Castro without a single bathhouse or popper; but when Milk finally wins a City Supervisor seat after four failed runs, we see a shower of falling chads superimposed over the San Francisco cityscape: the missing Florida chads from the 2000 presidential election had made those round bits of punched-out paper a ready symbol for the unheard voices in our democracy. In another scene, Harvey talks to the Teamsters' union about the threat of jobs being moved overseas, surely not as pressing a concern in the mid–70s as it has become today in the current anti-union, outsource-giddy U.S. economy. There is even a moment of outright pandering, slipped in virtually out of nowhere, when Milk praises firefighters — a de rigueur part of public discourse after 9/11.

And of course, it was not difficult to see in Anita Bryant a bouffant mirror of Sarah Palin, with a sack of acidic oranges substituting for the infamous shotgun. But, as if to cement both Bryant and Palin as twisted aberrations of faith rather than products of it, this version of the 70s gay world has God in it, too. What does Van Sant's Milk tell the desperate young gay, disowned by church and family and contemplating suicide? Not "God is dead, baby," but "God loves you." If Pier Paolo Pasolini offered a Marxist Jesus for the 60s, Van Sant would offer a religious Milk for the millennium.

Such outreach toward the middle (middle of the road, middle America, middle class) was more necessary than Van Sant's most radicalized followers were probably ready to accept. But the mainstream's down-low affair with gay sensibilities and issues has always served to demonstrate how some images can blur in the focused light of visibility. Getting it "wrong" is often half the price of getting it at all. Even after the anomalous *Brokeback Mountain* (2005) made some movie people very wealthy, Van Sant had called attention to the ongoing paucity of gay-themed film projects in Hollywood:

> I was actually surprised to find that there weren't many gay projects in the works in Hollywood when we started our movie [*Milk*]. I was always under the impression that there were a lot of them out there because of *Brokeback Mountain*, but I guess not. It definitely helped that our distributor, Focus Features, is the same studio that did *Brokeback Mountain*. I'm sure that they were encouraged by their own success with that film.[8]

It was a familiar pattern: perhaps because gays had been involved in cultural production all along, while being forced to remain in the closet, we tended to look toward cultural artifacts for redemption and validation — was it lodged somewhere in our collective DNA, for better or worse? A thorny rose if ever there was one. There were clearer and clearer reasons all the time why *Mala Noche* (1986), Van Sant's first feature, shot in one month for $25,000, had failed to get a distribution deal and still went largely unscreened in the U.S.: its gringo hero, happily fucked by young Mexicans who disdained to learn English, made for dicey politics in an era when minority acceptance seemed to hinge on "U.S.-right-or-wrong" mentalities, on wanting to see "*our* way of life" (whatever that may be) flourish unabated.

There were more openly gay members of the middle class than ever before, and Van Sant had guessed, correctly, that this new gay middle-class would be just as unamenable to films with large amounts of foreign dialogue and subtitles as the old hetero middle-class.[9] Still, it was one of the last dreams to die, the last of the angels we had to kick out along with our collective demons in order to become non-threatening and conformist enough to move into Any Neighborhood, USA, to marry, to adopt — the dream that, by being gay, we automatically carried some quotient of art and radical leftism in our very DNA. That angel kept dying, and dying hard. It remained to be seen if the material rewards that some of us have earned in exchange would prove worth it.

This crossroads-time of compromise and "brave new" assimilationism was a large part of why Van Sant continued to gain in importance. In two decades, he had come to stand for a host of longings for integrity, for commitment, for artistic touch and reach. Watching the Academy Awards in 2008, I wanted Van Sant to win not only for *Milk* but as a vindication of everything he had ever done. A private reel ran through my mental movieola: the fleshy shadows of *Mala Noche*, the perfect period details of *Drugstore Cowboy* (1989), the constant insights into chains of desire, chains of being, throughout the epic journeys of *My Own Private Idaho* (1991) and *Even Cowgirls Get the Blues* (1993) — all the daring, aching imagery of Van Sant's films which had accompanied my own journey into (gay) adulthood. I wondered how Van Sant would handle a win, he always seemed quiet and humble, not needing attention, not needing to show off; a last Western hero in a natty suit. Somehow I didn't know what I would make of a Van Sant victory until I found out what *he* would make of it.

Whenever the camera isolated Van Sant's face in audience shots, he looked like an eminent figure, attentive, beneficent, with that "understated power" which one observer has remarked about him: "God, what focus...."[10] He hardly moved in his chair, but his eyes seemed as concentrated on the theater stage as if he were looking through a viewfinder. He took photographs, he wrote, he played music, there seemed to be nothing artistic that he could not do to some extent; but it was finally as a filmmaker — a watcher and recorder of events in time and space — that Van Sant would always be remembered.

In his own victory speech, actor Sean Penn, star of *Milk*, spoke of the enormous trust he felt for Van Sant as a director: "There [are] no finer hands to be in than Gus Van Sant's." There was a reaction shot of Van Sant smiling, accepting the compliment, and it was nice to see that smile brought out by Penn. Van Sant had told an interviewer: "When I called [Penn] to see whether he would play the role in *Milk*, he took half a second to say yes. I guess he knew the elements were there."[11] The late River Phoenix also praised Van Sant's sensitivity toward actors: "Gus is very open to collaboration. He doesn't direct in a show-and-tell style but instead asks questions and brings it out of you like a good psychiatrist might. He allows you to be responsible for your role. Directors can be very frightened of collaborative things with actors."[12]

Phoenix's and Penn's words rang true, since who else but a trustworthy director could work so well with so many non-actors, first timers, young people; these are not skills that can be faked.

But then, it is always buzziest right before a crash, and during his speech Penn had also reminded us — as if channeling Milk's activism — about antigay protesters outside the Kodak Theater. He took us right into the hidden heart of Interzone:

> For those who saw the signs of hatred as our cars drove in tonight, I think that it is a good time for those who voted for the ban on gay marriage to sit and reflect and to anticipate their great shame and their shame in their grandchildren's eyes if they continue their way of support. We have got to have equal rights for everyone.

For a second Penn seemed to perform a Cagney-like hunching of his hips, as if needing to call on the sainted spirit of Hollywood's First King Pugnacious, in order to take on, as one man, the army of disapproval he seemed certain of having to face down.

A curtain, for a moment, lifted; and if it had been strange to see Gus Van Sant, always an exponent of natural lighting, patiently seated there amid the flashy glitz of the Oscars, it was not surprising at all that we were running on *their* treadmill, stuck between a minute's standing ovation and a furious lynch mob, we had been lauded, or tolerated, on only one level of American reality, there were a thousand other levels where disappointment waited, or worse. We would have to make do, to substitute, to pretend, yet again. We would have to tell ourselves, yet again, that it was beautiful, and right, to be despised — that we, too, had something fabulously large and rich and intangible and human as "God" in us. Every time the haters crucified us, they demonstrated that even the most non-believing of us — the gay sacrifices, the ones who had grown used to loss and insult — understood God better than the most zealous of *them*. (And whether we wanted to or not.)

That demoralizing realm of Interzone was in our face, and gone again. We had seen behind the curtain; we had seen too much. I felt, somehow, as though *I* had failed. But the real struggle remained where it had always been.

Introduction:
Filmmaking as Sampling

In place of a hermeneutics we need an erotics of art. — Susan Sontag[1]
Whatever it grants to vision and whatever its manner, a photograph is always invisible: it is not it that we see. — Roland Barthes[2]

River Phoenix has spoken, good-naturedly, of the famous campfire scene in Gus Van Sant's *My Own Private Idaho* as being "[similar to] the confession scene in *Stand by Me*. It's also similar to the scene in *Running on Empty*." These were two films which Phoenix had starred in prior to working with Van Sant. But for Phoenix these connections were not troubling in the least. "Gus did see both films," Phoenix went on to say, "so maybe he sampled them?"[3]

"Sampling" is a term from late 80s hip-hop and electronic music to denote when composers weave snippets or entire tracks from other songs into their own compositions. For young people, sampling never posed the problematic of non-originality or "stealing" which became a stumbling block for older generations committed to the idea of art as organic, made from whole cloth. Not that sampling was unheard of in the visual arts, at least since the early 20th century when painters and collagists freely incorporated signs, newspapers, and actual detritus into their works. There have even been examples of sampling in classical music — as when Gustav Mahler wrote the folk melody "Frère Jacques" into his first symphony.

Cinema is often thought of as being more complex, more constantly in search of Terra Incognita, but in reality images are the most common raw material of artistic sampling, since thought and sight have always been preternaturally linked, and since any image is always already a representation. Why reinvent serviceable wheels?

As Gianni Vattimo writes in *The End of Modernity*, this filmmaking-as-sampling is part of the constant, restless search for identity through pointed referencing which Heidegger recognized as the basis of (postmodern) art, in which "the thing comes to Being only as an aspect of a total project that, while it allows the thing to appear, also consumes it in a network of references. In [Heidegger's] *Sein und Zeit*, hermeneutic totality is established only in relation to the possibility of its not being there anymore. Each thing appears as itself (as what it is) only insofar as it dissolves into a circular reference to all other things."[4] This is not the same as a grounded dialectical relation, which would still possess a now-impossible "foundational totality"; rather, this "network of references" is characterized as a circle dance, and also as "the mirror-play of the world" in which things first appropriate themselves in their own right, only to be expropriated by other things, which finally results in a transpropriation — a new value arising from the reciprocal relation among two or more entities.[5]

I would suggest that the reason why Van Sant's contribution to this "circle dance" of appropriations avoids falling into the nihilism which Heidegger rejected (according to Vattimo),[6] is because at the heart of it is the project of creating a new Being in a state of un-grounding by attempting to locate oneself, somewhat subversively, within a larger cultural context. This Being has a classically social aspect, in spite of its postmodern resignation to what has been called "post-foundational thought."[7] Van Sant attaches Heideggerian, postmodern Being to a queerness which gives it purpose and a larger raison d'être which manages to transcend the loss of absolute meanings. The very act of ungrounding attaches itself to a kind of "founding" even as it radically alters both itself and the founding upon which it comments, in that "transpropriation."

Thus, by appropriating the image of a young heartthrob (Phoenix) from films of heterosexual childhood and family, for a film about young queerness (*My Own Private Idaho*), Van Sant is making a statement similar to Kenneth Anger's recycling of Mickey Rooney's Puck for a cameo in *Scorpio Rising* (1964). In addition to what critic Richard Dyer has called the "now-you-see-it-now-you-don't" aspect of queerness within mainstream cinema, there is an adjunct, a corollary: "It has always been there, whether anyone saw it or not."

It is intriguing that Phoenix would be open to the idea of filmmaking as sampling, that he would accept the premise that this kind of referencing (we will also see that it is a kind of intertexuality) would not only be acceptable for Van Sant, but utterly natural and inherently creative. Just as music sampling calls attention to the song as constructed work, and also one which is attempting to locate itself within the history of musical culture(s), so cinematic sampling partakes of the same postmodern concerns. A film is constructed less from "life" (the impractical ideal of raw, unmediated experience) than from other films, as many critics and filmmakers have already surmised.

Again, sampling scenes from other movies becomes a way of re-recognizing or recontextualizing a familiar (or beloved) body under different, perhaps more intimate or revealing circumstances. What the campfire scene in *My Own Private Idaho* adds to the other scenes which, in Phoenix's view, it samples is the element of gay longing between Phoenix's character Mike and his best friend Scott, the character played by Keanu Reeves. Here, again, the sampling becomes a none-too-secret fantasy subtext, as if to say to the viewer, "Whatever you thought those earlier scenes were 'about,' *this* is what they were really about," a kindred version of those subliminal cuts in *Scorpio Rising* in which homoerotic desire suddenly intrudes into an ostensibly non-sexual scene. (Anger, as the first important radical-queer artist in film, is a crucial touchstone for Van Sant's aesthetic and for the idea of subversive appropriation which I am tracing, here.) Thus, this kind of sampling enters into a dialectical cultural relation with other films, but not entirely for the purpose of critiquing them, usually more often for the purpose of celebrating the liberation of hidden and subversive energies.

In fact, going even farther, sampling in cinema speaks to that pure, headlong love of form and formal invention which Susan Sontag, in her landmark essay "Against Interpretation," seemed to define as an erotics of art, and not just because recontextualized *bodies* are involved. It is never exactly content that is sampled, quoted, reshuffled, although it may seem like content; rather, it is the sensuous contours, the resonance, the aura surrounding content, in other words, elements of form. Not what is seen or shown, but how it is seen and shown. Even "pure" content, if such a thing exists, becomes hyper-formal when sampled, or referenced intertextually, since the same content within a new narrative, a new work of art, cannot possess the same contextual function, and thus becomes a kind of trans-evocation of style.

This process is already inherent in the standard cinematic practice by which bodies are converted into images, and vice versa, images converted into "bodies," which is to say, presences and integral units of meaning which present themselves to us for emotional and aesthetic delectation. Here is where cinema as counterfeit fraud meets cinema as transcendent love; here is where the viewer asks to be lied to, so as to be able to go on loving, or asks to go on loving so as to be able to be lied to. The cinema is a hustler, as many gay filmmakers have noted (Fassbinder's "holy whore"); the hustler as character or body within the film translates into a metacinematic image. The hope of getting close to him is the hope of warming oneself at the movies.

William Burroughs writes about a shady, enterprising Interzone guide, a guy whose face mutates suddenly into "a gray screen, hustlers' faces moved across it."[8] And just as the "face-screen" contained memories and foreshadowings of other faces, other bodies, so memory roams freely among image-bodies, as it does among real ones. With images as with bodies, we are always

Elias (Elias McConnell), the student photographer in *Elephant* (2002), examines a reel of negatives in the school dark room. Photography is one of Van Sant's passions; many images of his films could be said to have the density, the "flashpoint," the rawness, of great photographs. Such images are also self-contained and largely resist being paraphrased in the language of conceptual interpretation: they exist on a sensual, nearly tactile level.

returning to what we love about the entire category itself whenever we contemplate what we love about the individual example, and, again, vice versa. I remember this or that man's body as attractive, but largely by way of remembering what I find attractive about the male body to begin with; particularities shade into abstracts. Sex and sexual attraction are much like art in that sense; memory performs that photographic trick of smoothing out complexities into a sort of single, isolated flashpoint. (No matter how "raw" the given photograph might be.)

These are untouchable images, sealed in the mind, available but also intangible, and hard to classify, the way photographs are according to Barthes: we no longer see the photograph for the image (subject) contained within it.[9] A photograph, any visual image, is a transparent net for the desire to do one's looking, in the first place; a finite, replaceable substitute for a vast, irreducible desire. The photographer Diane Arbus said something similar: "For me the subject of the picture is more important than the picture. And more complicated."[10] The subject lives in the spaces which the arbitrary framing cannot contain or account for.

Thus, the body as snapshot is always a reduction, a necessary framing to "crop out" having to see the subject himself again, or live with him and his problems, his quirks. In the short story "Nothing Ever Just Disappears," Sam D'Allesandro has his narrator describe meeting a new lover and not wanting to get too close to him: "I didn't want to know him as much as I wanted to be able to be around my image of him. I didn't want things to get too difficult."[11] For this commitment-shy narrator, named only S., the difficulty comes from too much comfort, but it all amounts to the same pain[12]: in the taxonomy of human emotions, and given a long enough timeline, everything eventually becomes grouped in the "pain" category. But with an image there is only the flashpoint. There are no categories. No interpretation. No "arrangement into a mental scheme of categories,"[13] one of those self-limiting, abnegating qualities of that hermeneutics which Sontag persuasively derided as "an open aggressiveness [toward art], an overt contempt for appearances."[14]

Eroticism is where we most flatter the surface of appearances; even if the act of sex can partake of intimate emotion, of knowing something of the content behind, or embedded in, the form. It is important to note, here, that in the case of Van Sant's films, eroticism is rarely tied directly to images of actual sex or even to sexuality. Indeed, *Restless* (2011), Van Sant's most recent film as I write, also his most beautiful and delicate, is pointedly a story of two young lovers, Annabel (Mia Wasikowska) and Enoch (Henry Hopper), who do not consummate until two-thirds of the way through the film, after they have spent numerous scenes talking and getting to know one another intimately. Moreover, Van Sant cuts away from showing the sex itself, like the gallant Enoch who refuses to discuss any details of the private act afterwards. This is also made clear in the resonant image of Enoch drawing a chalk outline around his and Annabel's bodies as they lie together on the ground holding hands: chastely, their heads and upper bodies are close together, allowing them to talk closely, while their lower bodies stretch apart from each other. Steeped in the Victorian — from Enoch's formal frock-coat to Annabel's love of Darwin, as well as their names, possibly derived from Poe and Tennyson — *Restless* is the fulfillment of Van Sant's long-standing project of bringing kindness, shyness and a kind of childlike decency to bear on issues of sexuality and death which we are used to seeing treated more inquisitively and sensationalistically.

This reticence ensures that nothing in the plots (content) of Van Sant's films is ever merely gratuitous, yet serves to indicate, on a formal level, a meta-aesthetic dimension of eroticism — in ravishing textures, in passages that play with slowed or sped-up time, in dreamlike discontinuities which under-

Restless (2011), the story of doomed young lovers Annabel (Mia Wasikowska) and Enoch (Henry Hopper), is so chaste and sweetly romantic that it seems to be the work of a precocious child steeped in Victoriana. An emphasis is placed on the couple's extended courtship of getting to know each other through intimate conversations long before they consummate, discreetly off-camera.

mine the hegemony of content. Van Sant has done nothing if not demonstrate that there are many, many ways to project sensuality besides clichéd iconographies or scenes of blunt sex. Frontality — the head-on approach to a subject — has an element of innate eroticism in Van Sant's films (as it does in some photographers' works) simply by its very bluntness; also the passage of time, not because it rebels against the constraints of everyday life but precisely because it follows, no matter what or whom, the same pattern of coordinates. Surrender is denoted, specifically surrender to the processes of art as if these were automatically romantic and sexual. Erotics *is* art; art lends grace, meaning and honor to the feeling of seducing and being seduced, just as again and again Van Sant (and his viewer) surrenders to the seduction of patterns, of visual and aural forms — the same surrender which Sontag called for — without questioning, without reaching for the mental equivalent of a chastity belt.

Naturally, we cannot allow ourselves to be seduced by everything, by anything and everything — some of the exclusivity of interpretive judgment, of cataloging and classifying, always remains, if only because not everything piques our interest to the same degree. But according to Sontag, interpretation(s) only add to the clutter in all of our minds. She insists that art has become as rare as real nature in our cities — in a further tweaking of urban ecological metaphors, she likens interpretation again and again to pollution, to the sheer "excess" of postindustrial culture[15] — and speaks to the same primal need for nature's restorative consolations, as if the thirsty man in a parable desert would bother to "interpret" the glass of water and not just drink it down, gratefully.

"What is important now is to recover our senses. We must learn to *see* more, to *hear* more, to *feel* more."[16] This injunction of Sontag's has been a ruling principle of my life. She had been channeling Nietzsche's insistence that now everything (even the ineffable and the spiritual) comes to us only through the palpable, the immanent world: "All credibility, all good conscience, all evidence of truth come only from the senses."[17] But Nietzsche was more ambivalent than Sontag about whether or not this immanence was as stable or productive as abstract reasoning: after all, the senses play tricks on us. As concrete as their evidence can be, it is not always reliable. Also, what the senses have to say can be dismissed more easily than an airtight rational argument; ironically, it is the rational (interpretive) to which we end up returning, anyway, in order to second-guess, dismiss or certify the inchoate evidence of our senses. Thus, patterns and repetitions not only render our random observations axiomatic, they formalize them in yet another way of playing down the instinct for interpretation. If I become ill once from eating unripe cherries, say, it is an unpleasant sensory experience; the second time, however, elevates my hunch to the law of scientific method, but also places me within a kind of déjà vu that is meta-aesthetic: a double exposure, a tapestry, a symphony, shades within shades — a flashback?

The 60s exploration of the senses went hand in hand, in general, with an interest in mind-altering drugs. Some of Van Sant's films speak to, and uphold, a certain psychedelic texturing or flavoring, if not the actual taking of drugs. His films almost want to become drugs, but in the same way that reality sometimes becomes a drug as well. And there is a literal, physiological level to this free-flowing, naturally-occurring "drugging" of consciousness by daily, real life. Finally, to be passively acted upon is the nature of the human organism. I think of how Bonanza Jellybean (Rain Phoenix) calls "drugged" a "stupid word," in *Even Cowgirls Get the Blues*, because everything in the world is constantly changing the chemical composition of everything else; a state of nature that is ongoing, interdependent and mutational. The worst drugs were ones that seemed to take us out of nature, and away from human solidarity, like the heroin in *Drugstore Cowboy* and *Last Days* (2005). "Not to mention" — my favorite quote from Walter Benjamin — "that most terrible drug — ourselves — which we take in solitude."[18] If it was true that *ourselves* are *the most terrible drug*, then could the converse be true? Could other people's living, physical bodies be the best and most beneficent drug, drawing us away from ego and isolation?[19]

At the same time, drugs queer love. It would seem odd, and perhaps unhealthy, if a heterosexual said that her intimacy with a male partner was "like a drug." Narcotics underscore the illicit, the uncanny, the thing dislocated from normative time and space. The narrator in Sam D'Allesandro's short story "Giovanni's Apartment" has taken codeine to get high on the night he happens to meet Giovanni, who picks him up on the street; under the stronger "effects" of Giovanni, he immediately forgets the drug, quits his job, and ends up moving into the apartment, which he does not leave for thirty-two straight days: "By then, he [Giovanni] was installed inside me — the ultimate drug, effectively filling my bloodstream, warm and soothing, the thing that I wanted and knew I wanted. I loved knowing for a change."[20] This story, which is like James Baldwin refracted through David Lynch, suggests that the pursuit of a kind of high is the only metaphor we have for romantic and sexual experiences that take place outside of normative heterosexual courtship and marriage; the moments, thrilling as they are, would not add up without a superadded structure of "addiction," however parlous and judgmental that word or concept seems to be. "Giovanni's Apartment" is a beautiful postmodern fable in which there is a "happily ever after" to be found in the surrender to addictive love; its fictional dynamic clicks, the way it usually doesn't in real life.

"Real art has the capacity to make us nervous,"[21] Sontag wrote — let's face it, like real attraction or real love. None of these is an act of hermeneutics, rather a more or less spontaneous, visceral reaction; after all, one does not interpret a body one loves: one drinks it down, admires or celebrates it, at most one might describe its lineaments and details. The work of art (no matter what it is) is a kind of body in that respect, and it usually contains the shapes of bodies, bodies translated into images or words — the way that Guillaume Apollinaire arranged the typography of his "calligramme" poems in the shapes of the objects about which he was writing.

If I seem to be referencing poetry and poetic language a lot, it is because I would say that Van Sant's films are primarily poetic. But, again, their metaphors are often sealed up in a sort of blatant intertexuality of things or people, which has to be pursued literally rather than metaphorically. Van Sant's filmed images present similar classificatory problems to Barthes' photographic images; indeed, unlike most films (both narrative and non-narrative ones alike), Van Sant's cannot be easily reduced to a description or analysis in words. They are about the moment in which one sees and hears something, and simultaneously feels something. Like poems, they can't really be expressed in ways other than

In *Even Cowgirls Get the Blues* (1993), Sissy Hankshaw (Uma Thurman) becomes the awkward center of sexual attention for a couple (Sean Young, left, and Crispin Glover, center) who pick her up in New York City. Sex sometimes has a manikin-like quality of stasis in Van Sant's films, as if he were saying that we tend to remember it less as a freely flowing movement than as a series of heightened if somewhat dammed-up snapshot-moments. Also, he has frequently depicted scenes of sex from the viewpoint of a third party who feels excluded from the coupling. At the same time, frontality, an inherently photographic approach, has an innate eroticism in Van Sant's films, precisely because the camera is being made to look so directly, so openly.

the words (images) which the poet already chose — words which come from, stimulate, and lead back to the senses.

This is not to say that Van Sant's films have no content or substance, no emotional depth. Far from it. There are ideas in his films as well as direct life and, I would say, an oddly compelling and wholly secular feeling for moments of sacredness within the stream of that direct life. (I mean "sacred" in a secular sense, one which speaks to the vitality and importance of human life. In *Even Cowgirls Get the Blues*, one of the mottos literally carved in stone at the Holy Man's encampment is, "I believe in everything, everything is sacred. I believe in nothing, everything is sacred." This motto affirms that the conception of sacredness transcends narrowly religious dogmas.) But again, the stream is not set apart: to the characters living through it, it simply *is* life, the way anyone's life would be, no matter how odd, absurd or tragically unbearable it might seem.

Again, like a poem, the emotions have been poured into a perfect vessel, which shapes and contains them — becomes identical with them. Analysis might best be served by pointing to the shape itself, as Sontag advised critics in general to do:

What kind of criticism, of commentary on the arts, is desirable today? ...
The aim of all commentary on art now should be to make works of art — and, by analogy, our own experience — more, rather than less, real to us. The function of criticism should be to show *how it is what it is,* even *that it is what it is,* rather than to show *what it means.*[22]

In fact, Van Sant seems to resist a densely hermeneutic approach, inviting instead the kind of immediate response that we have to attractive form, attractive bodies. He fulfills Sontag's famous anticipation of an "erotics of art" in which hermeneutic analysis is rendered bulky and irrelevant in favor of what she calls transparence, or "experiencing the luminousness of the thing in itself, of things being what they are."[23] What is at stake is the direct perception of people and objects, not what is hidden or abstracted behind that perception. Like Blake, like Huxley, like LSD and Jim Morrison, Van Sant wants to open the doors of perception.

Although the octane of the 60s wafts through Van Sant's films, there is no naïve faith that the right ideas, or even the right behaviors, will bring about a kind of revolutionary moment in and of themselves. His characters are not post–Godardian ideologues, not revolutionaries — with the notable exception of Bonanza Jellybean, Delores Del Ruby (Lorraine Bracco) and the other philosophizing cowgirls in *Even Cowgirls Get the Blues*—but romantic losers drifting between haphazard, bedraggled triumphs and crushing disappointments, ultimately destined to be swallowed up (to little purpose) in the rusty-toothed gears of the American machine. And even those cowgirls seem to drift away from dogmatic certainty after accomplishing their revolution at the Rubber Rose Ranch, allowing "complexity" and "paradox" to have the final say: after all, Van Sant ends that beautiful film by trying to count the stars in the sky over Oregon, way up there in transcendent, non-programmatic space, neither science nor religion but a kind of ecstatic sensory immersion in a world that grows wide-eyed with wonder at the thought of both.

— PART ONE —
EXPERIENTIAL TEXTS

In order to recuperate art as an experience of truth, the notion of truth ... must be replaced with a more comprehensive notion founded on the concept of Erfahrung, *that is, on experience as a modification that the subject undergoes when it encounters something that truly has relevance for it. It may then be said that art is an experience of truth if it is an authentic experience or, in other words, if the encounter with the work actually modifies the observer.* — Gianni Vattimo

1. Van Sant and Intertextuality

When Gus Van Sant contributed an appreciative tribute to the box set of Kenneth Anger's films on DVD, he wrote that "images of his films [are] in all the ones that I have made," to affirm Anger's abiding influence on other filmmakers' work and on his own. Intriguingly, Van Sant implies that influence, here, takes the form of a kind of direct quoting or homage in which entire images — as talismans and shared objects — are incorporated, collage-style, into new works:

> A pentagram in a mirror. A red velvet wall. An opium pipe. A jewel necklace. I have a feeling that my next film will have all these images, because I have become transfixed with the ones I have seen in Kenneth Anger's works.[1]

Already we feel as though we are in a room somewhere, surrounded by all of these things, seeing them, touching them. These images in question, as objects which "transfix" and demand to be translated or retranslated into another visual language, suggest more than mere images — they suggest bodies which a portrait photographer might be drawn to photographing, in an effort to comprehend, define, encapsulate, save and savor.[2] As "Anger images" reinscribed by Van Sant, they would be, in fact, intertextualities, but ones which contribute to a new understanding of what intertextuality is, since the references might not signify anything beyond the act of appreciation, of acknowledgment, of reaching into another's world and touching something that exists there; turning it over in one's hand, under one's eye, until it becomes part of one's own world.

Put otherwise, it would become intertexuality without the conceptual impedimenta which are often considered to be the raison d'être of intertexuality in the first place. Aesthetic theory, emerging from aesthetic practice, folds itself back into practice again, winking, wiser, without the need to show off what it has learned about itself. Or rather, offering that self-knowledge like a gift rather than a puzzle to be decoded. Sharing and identification are more important, here, than interpretation or even deconstruction. This form of intertextuality exists beyond interpretation if not against it. It points to, and embraces, form, rather than excavating some hidden value of content, or what Sontag calls "the X, the Y, the Z [of content], and so forth."[3]

Intertextuality in cinema becomes a way of registering aesthetic intention and a consistency of vision; and also of giving cinema something of the physical density of an actual world. It is experiential at heart, although it seems based wholly within the conceptual. It is a way of giving to art something of the tangibility and continuity of a real experience. Thus, Van Sant's early films blatantly cross-reference each other in specific moments, as if each film were part of an ongoing world that lived around, between and through the films themselves, and simultaneously inviting us, the viewers, to step into and inhabit this world — a model of the three-dimensional world as a kind of living diorama.[4] Johnny (Doug Cooyeate) from *Mala Noche* turns up briefly in *Drugstore Cowboy*, hanging out on a drug dealer's porch and playing a game with a knife. The house that Bob (Matt Dillon) hallucinates flying through an empty sky during one of his highs in *Drugstore Cowboy* comes crashing down in the middle of a prairie during Mike's blowjob at the start of *My Own Private Idaho*. William Burroughs plays Father Tom in *Drugstore Cowboy*, a survivor and a kind of terse Greek chorus, and then turns up again near the beginning of *Even Cowgirls Get the Blues*, muttering, "Ominous!" about the weather and crossing the street. And more than once, misfits turn to the dictionary to find out who they are in the world: the highlighted definition of "narcolepsy" which introduces Mike gets reprised as the moment, early in *Even Cowgirls Get the Blues*, when young Sissy Hankshaw (Treva Jeffryes) looks up "thumb" and finds that it can be a verb as well as a noun, thus setting her on her career as the world's best hitchhiker.

The later films also contain ever more abstruse cross-references. In *Finding Forrester* (2000), the 1930s song "Deep Night," used as a plaintive, fragile "anthem" of furtive gay fantasy in *My Own Private Idaho*, is played by a full-ballroom orchestra in the formal party scene where the tentative romance between Jamal (Rob Brown) and Claire (Anna Paquin) is threatened by racist disapproval. In *Gerry* (2002), a story is told about playing a Dungeons & Dragons–type role-playing game with someone named "Jerry"; in *Last Days*, this role-playing game comes again, with the rock star Jerry Garcia identified as the Dungeon Master. On an informational level, such a motif might seem next to meaningless; yet it has the teasing quality of any aesthetic recurrence, the awareness of a mind at work, a set of preoccupations. Kinships, both distant and immediate, are evoked by all of these intertextual cross-references, which are for the most part unadorned: they simply pop up, or spill over, from one film to the next. For this reason they elicit an ultimate kinship between the films and their viewer.

But this is only a sort of first dimension of intertextuality, the idea (not always entirely convincing) that those early films inhabit some postmodern Yoknapatawpha County of the mind. In fact, a further, even blunter interweaving takes place in the fact that nearly all of Van Sant's films take place in Portland, Oregon. Later Van Sant films involve more complex intertextualities with other filmmakers and their work, an increasing dilation of the director's perspective, becoming not only a world in himself but one which can contain other worlds within it. In intertextuality, generosity and selfishness, the conquered and the conquering, can be difficult to tell apart; but the symbiotic is always an ecological relationship, a two-way street, and this is Van Sant's great understanding of intertextuality. It does not automatically diffuse relational meaning in a postmodern sense; rather, it enhances that meaning.

I want to show that intertextuality is Van Sant's dominant aesthetic mode; however, again, the intertextual exchange itself is never impersonal or abstract, never merely conceptual or theoretical, but instead a radical act of witness in the name of solidarity, admiration, love, Eros. It is in fact part of Sontag's "erotics of art." This is why intertextuality can bear a special meaning in gay art: the multiple, intertextually-related artists corroborate each other's vision of reality; they become co-witnesses, as it were. Suddenly, where there had been only one testimony of desire (Anger's, for example), there are now two (Anger's and Van Sant's). Solidarity with another artist is one of the main uses of specifically queer intertextuality.

If we look at intertextuality through the lens of queerness, we find that it does not necessarily have to mean the classic Barthesian kamikaze mission, the "death of the author."[5] Rather, it can point to a kind of Zen-like lessening of authorial ego, a willingness for an author to take part in an interpenetrative dialogue with other authors, other texts. In some ways, this might even serve to augment the power of the author in non-traditional ways (think of a union collectively augmenting the power of individual laborers), particularly when it comes to issues of dismantling hierarchic canon formation at its most traditional, or making inroads into a culturally ordained language or value-system which has previously excluded minorities.

Queer intertextuality is also distinct from what I would designate as "queer montage." Anger, for instance, was a master of queer montage, one of his most famous juxtapositions being of Christ with a gay orgy in *Scorpio Rising*. Queer montage presupposes a queer mode of identification, a queer way of seeing: the deliberate attempt to reconcile, not what *might* naturally go together (as in the logical-syllogism approach of standard narratological montage) or even what *must be* explicated ideologically (as in Eisenstein's dialectical montage), but what *cannot be* reconciled, what has been radically and permanently sundered — what is verboten, taboo, to put together in the first place.

Queer montage also juxtaposes images and sounds which liberate the viewer's consciousness (often in relation to the overturning of norms). A powerful instance of queer montage, for me, occurs in Tim Hunter's masterpiece, *River's Edge* (1986). A sociopathic teen, John (Daniel Roebuck), has strangled a girl, Jamie (Danyi Deats), for "talkin' shit." In a later scene, he recounts the deed to a friend: we see a close-up of Jamie passively staring up at John, then a reverse-angle close-up of John staring down at Jamie, his hands around her throat. John says, in voiceover: "I had total control of her." Hunter then cuts to two other teen characters, Matt (Keanu Reeves) and Clarissa (Ione Skye Leitch), having sex in the park. The pattern of close-ups repeats, but Clarissa is on top of Matt, therefore in charge of the sex: we see a close-up of Matt on the ground, writhing passively, then a close-up of Clarissa, smiling down at Matt as she grinds on top of him, and over this shot of Clarissa, Hunter repeats John's line: "I had total control of her." This sex scene instantly reverses the gendered power lines which the murder scene had originally established and, in a sense, places Matt in the feminine role, as the one being "totally controlled," not only by Clarissa at this moment, but by the director who has staged and shot the scene, and even, by extension, the audience who can watch Matt's helpless orgiastic writhing voyeuristically. The symbolic-semantic queering of Matt as a "her" creates hope, within the plot, for the cycles of macho male addiction and violence to finally be broken (it is Matt who goes to the police to turn in John for Jamie's murder), while refusing, at the same time, to hypocritically imply that there can be sexual pleasure without some kind of symbolic "violence" and power, e.g., someone being on top and in "control" of someone else.

Van Sant is also a master of queer montage. One of the most obvious examples occurs near the beginning of *My Own Private Idaho*, where he juxtaposes a shot of wild salmon leaping upstream to spawn with the orgasm that the hustler Mike has while being fellated by a male client. The shiny salmon swimming in the rushing water suggest a visual metaphor for semen and sperm, and the fact that the salmon are an image from procreative nature (one of *the* classic images of procreation) causes the homosexual blowjob to be recontextualized as an act which possesses the same gravity and importance. If it does not exactly procreate by biological standards, the blowjob nonetheless *creates* on either side of the exchange, it fecundates, it spawns. Like Christ and the gay orgy in *Scorpio Rising*, procreation and gay oral sex become radical if unlikely equivalences.

Another example of queer montage, albeit more generally subversive than specifically queer in a homosexual sense, occurs in *Drugstore Cowboy*, where Van Sant includes a shot of a porcelain Virgin Mary statuette in a series of close-ups of drugs and drug paraphernalia, implying that narcotics addiction, in its cycles of suffering and redemption, its rituals, and its investment of everyday life with mythic, superstitious resonances, has an inherently religious quality. Also in *Drugstore Cowboy* there is a scene where Bob gets beaten up by his nemesis, Detective Gentry (James Remar). Two officers restrain Bob while Gentry punches him in the stomach; Bob doubles up, and as he raises his head, the camera (from Bob's viewpoint) focuses on the knot in Gentry's necktie. Without a word of commentary, this edit presents the almost subliminal idea that, contrary to our normative social assumptions, men who wear suits and ties are more likely to be violent than the scruffy junkies and thieves who are the film's anti-heroes. This is in keeping with *Drugstore Cowboy*'s antiestablishment sympathies. Both of these examples of queer montage are meant to be immediately and easily assimilated; they do not stop the diegtic flow and point outside of it, as examples of intertextuality do.

It happens that the queer montage from *Scorpio Rising*, in which Anger's juxtaposed images act coextensively to subversively re-imagine the world through their intercutting, is also an example of queer intertextuality, or appropriation, since the images of Christ come from a cheaply made religious film which Anger has claimed to have accidentally received in the mail.[6] Thus, we find the second main use of queer intertextuality, not only as a primary expression of solidarity with another queer artist (as when Van Sant pays homage to Anger) but an expression of generally subversive appropriation, raiding mainstream texts in order to turn them inside-out, so to speak, and make them testify to a queer perspective beyond and against their own literal meanings.

I Remember the Chateau Marmont in the 50s

In his work on intertextuality and film, Mikhail Iampolski calls attention to the nature of reality itself—shifting, dependent on naming, and needing corroborative witness, as it were: "Reality becomes the bearer of a meaning that cannot always itself be formulated.... Indeed, what is at stake is the creation of mystery as such, the affirmation that meaning, as it emerges, is an enigma."[7] Reality itself is called into question; it becomes a kind of text or textuality open to interpretation. As Burroughs writes: "Consciousness *is* a cut-up; life is a cut-up."[8] The cut-up artwork is a mirror of reality, not in spite of the fact that it is disjointed and mutational, but precisely because it is. As much as the various texts which it produces, consciousness is layered and labile, unreal, and bears meanings which must be broken down, made to betray themselves, and finally reconstituted anew. We learn, or perceive, by putting things together, after all, by suturing already sundered representations and meanings.

For most, however, this suturing is unconscious and obedient to what we might call the pre-scripted aspects of life. Thus, calling attention to the process of "cut-up/fold-in" in all its manifestations is an aspect of queerness, for which everyday "reality," as it is normatively constituted (e.g., as straight reality), has been oppressive and exclusionary. The queer mind, necessarily adept at living around and through this kind of routine self-questioning, is constantly *cutting* into the world around itself and also *folding* back into the world wherever it can. I would say that it has been a strong aspect of gay identity that we have had to learn an art of living which sees everything from two sides, as it were, or which sees the hidden, shadow side of acts and behaviors.

This has sometimes been misidentified as "paranoia." Freud was close to the truth when he established a link between homosexuality and paranoia (in the Schreber case and others), but he saw both conditions as negative symptoms to be corrected. Some paranoia (the kind that falls short of outright schizophrenic delusion) always measures the distance between one's own subjective reality and the dominant reality of one's surrounding world. "As Burroughs famously notes, 'Paranoia is just having the right information.'"[9] In particular, gay reality has always existed in the shadow of heterosexual reality, which stifles and undermines the former's claims to truth. Schreber "himself was the 'only real human still surviving,' and the few human forms he still saw, the doctor, the orderlies and patients, he explained as being 'miracled up, fleetingly improvised men.'... The end of the world is the projection of [Schreber's] internal catastrophe; his subjective world has come to an end since he [Schreber] withdrew his love from it."[10] This is true; however, in Schreber's dislocation and madness, in his isolation, he probably felt that the world had withdraw its love from *him*. Unwilling to seek external and sociopolitical explanations for internal psychical and emotional states, Freud sees the enmity and lack of love as being entirely contained within Schreber's being, and then expressed as a projection.[11] It is the same blaming of the homosexual which runs throughout Freud's work on paranoia, the same unwillingness to acknowledge that the various repressions, which lead to unhealthy projections, are conditioned by social stigmas more than by malfunctioning psyches — or rather, the malfunctioning psyches themselves are produced by stigmas.

Homosexual feelings have never been as free to be felt, or to be responded to in kind, as heterosexual ones; however, Freud's definition of "love" seems to imply a level playing field: "In delusions of persecution distortion consists in a transformation of affect: that which should have been felt internally as love is perceived as hate from without."[12] Freud applies a linguistic formula: "Indeed, I do not *love* him — I *hate* him, indeed — because **he persecutes me.**"[13] This would seem to imply, however, that if the homosexual did not repress his feelings of love a priori, and announced them to the man in question, saying, "I love you," the man would automatically love him back. Put otherwise, it is assumed that there could stand a happy, friendly world from which the paranoiac violently and incomprehensibly breaks. Freudian repression and paranoia place the cart before the horse, so to speak, on the assumption that the horse *would* pull the cart if only he were hitched up to it properly; but in terms of homosexual isolation within straight society, it is sometimes the case that there is no horse to begin with.

The problem, then, is not that a wish cannot be felt, but that it cannot be expressed or fulfilled. (Although in extreme cases, the wish, too, might be foreclosed upon by the wishing psyche — but this, too, by definition, implies the internalization of a pre-existing homophobia which is always already societal in nature.) But here is where intertextuality becomes a formal solution for the artist, a kind of willed vaulting over repression and paranoia. Intertextuality mitigates against the isolation of the unfulfilled wish. Intertextual art does not necessarily fulfill the wish expressed by a previous artist as reiterate it through the adoption of a second source's wish, in order to make the wish itself even stronger and clearer, even more understood — just as the difference between "paranoia" and a truth claim often lies in whether or not someone else backs up one's own account of what is happening.

In the sense that it places like with like, too, intertextuality can be seen as a kind of incipient queerness; also a gesture of breaking boundaries and appropriating what is off limits or forbidden. The appropriation itself becomes an act of liberation. The intertextual artist seems to say, "This re-expression of the canonical status quo is also, presto change-o, a queer expression." Thus, intertextuality has, in some senses, replaced the cock-eyed sarcasms of camp as a new, smarter, more streamlined mode of modern, urban, gay sensibility. It winks to the knowing, the way camp always did: "Well, of course Text A quotes from Text B — anyone can see that. And of course I am borrowing someone else's identity — someone else's costume, singing voice, hairstyle — but only in order to express myself." As with Burroughs and Andy Warhol, who both discredited the idea of originality, intertextuality presupposes a way for the excluded gay consciousness to feel as if it is a part of the world, woven in with the fabric of life — a comforting, contented feeling which has not always been automatic for gays. Moreover, gay art of all kinds has often taken place on a fault-line blurring reality and art, and so has gay reality as well: a reality, again, that was undernourished, not allowed to become quite fulsome or real, versus a fantasy life that drew on too-numerous, phantom images of stardom.

These queer images of stardom were for a long time (and often continue to be) images of mostly delusional passing: the nobody passing for famous, the monster passing for loved, and behind all this, the queer passing for straight. This is why there is another kind of gay cinema — and an application of Matthew Tinckom's interest in what the studios meant when they praised Vincente Minnelli for working "like a homosexual"[14] — driven largely by closeted gay actors from classic Hollywood, and what we now know about their true sexualities even as we watch their "straight acting." Generations of Hollywood insiders have known who was doing what with whom in the gay demimonde of the industry, but part of the entry fee at being employed within that industry was to keep quiet about it. The non-queer films of Anthony Perkins and Sal Mineo, to cite two actors who played straight but are known to have been gay, are now part of queer cinema; we are primed to seek out queer undertones in their work, and angered, as well, to realize how much they had to carefully suppress. Van Sant tells a story about meeting Perkins, late in the actor's life, when his well-publicized AIDS had caused him to become more open about the past, a sort of Cassandra in reverse, telling long-ago disasters of denial:

> We get to the front door of the restaurant, there's this yellow 1963 Rolls Royce convertible, the doorman has the door open, and Perkins says, "I remember the Chateau Marmont in the 50s, when you might go down for a swim, and you'd see Natalie Wood and James Dean sitting by the side of the pool laughing, those were really the days...." And then he bounded off towards this Roll Royce, and I thought, "It's like young Hollywood, he's driving off in his Rolls." And he walks past the Rolls and out onto the street. I'm walking down the street and I hear this beep beep, and it's Perkins, he's waving from this small mini-station wagon.[15]

"Young Hollywood" has always grown up fast, and aged quickly, in every era, but its gay denizens knew a special suppression even in a town given over to widespread lonely-at-the-top isolation. Van Sant had hoped to get Perkins to play the Countess in *Even Cowgirls Get the Blues*, the reclusive transvestite who owns the all-female Rubber Rose Ranch, but *that* kind of intertextuality with Old Hollywood may still be too far beyond the pale. The role ended up going to John Hurt, who had a history of "playing gay," and whose career coincided with more socially open times. Hollywood may never be quite ready to fully acknowledge its gay casualties.

Because intertextuality is an inherently queer process, in its use of imitations which more or less announce themselves as such, it insists that art is not based on difference (or originality) but a kind of mimicry, like Perkins playing straight roles, enforced at first and then becoming a sort of game, with its own artistry and aura, its own "insider" knowledge. At any rate, intertextuality ensures that the parts of a given artwork do not become smoothly and unrecognizably integrated. They stick out. The repressed returns. *Restless* casually massages a dizzying host of intertextual references and back-stories: *Harold and Maude*, *Love Story*, Yukio Mishima's ritual suicide, Erroll Morris'

Gates of Heaven, ornithological and entomological data, Araki's *Mysterious Skin*, Nico's love affair with the young Jackson Browne, and finally, the fantasy of what *Rebel Without a Cause* might have been like if Dennis Hopper had scored the title role instead of James Dean. And these are merely my own resonations, my own cultural G-spots, as it were; I allow that other viewers might "miss" some of these while picking up on completely different ones. Creativity itself becomes characterized as a repeated and repeatable process, pointing out the mechanical code within which things must operate, and this code's hopeful liberation through a surrender to its own lack of true freedom. Individualism is expressed, finally, through the recognition of one's place in a collective lexicon. Generations of the same image are pressed to perform the same duty or function, just as we could say that generations of queers have been pressed to fulfill other people's straight expectations. And just as intertextuality exposes artworks as shifting and interchangeable "parts," it also suggests the elements of queer identity which do not assimilate, and have never assimilated, to straight reality: erotics, desire and its appropriations, fantasy, viewpoint, the awareness of genders as labile or ridiculous or oppressive constructs, and the polymorphic, amorphous nature of identity itself.

I do not want to suggest that intertextuality in itself is equivalent to real political action, that it can substitute for a coherent program of civil rights. As Alan Sinfield argues in *Gay and After*:

> We have supposed too readily that to demonstrate indeterminacy in a dominant construct is to demonstrate its weakness and its vulnerability to subversion. That is optimistic.... It is easier than we once imagined to dislocate language and ideology; and harder to get such dislocations to make a practical difference.[16]

He is right; the dominant culture withstands merely aesthetic (and philosophical) assaults. As a gay artist, one can struggle for years with the tenor and texture of one's coming out, only to be told, when one finally creates one's magnum opus (one's sexual declaration of war, so to speak), that everything, ho-hum, has already been done; that one has overlooked the struggles of other minorities[17]; that one has only made an ambiguous or superfluous gesture — all criticisms which have been used to nullify the consciousness-work of gays.

Nonetheless, when I say that intertextuality is queer, I mean that gay art is so rarely made from "whole cloth," so to speak, but instead built up from disparate parts, homages, challenging references, barbed transvaluations, and, again, intertextual moments when two or more sources or artists are made to stand together in symbolic solidarity. In fact, this latter sense of solidarity differs markedly from Iampolski's insistence that successful intertextuality is always about concealing the quoted source, in order for the newly created text to seem organically original. Iampolski: "Intertextuality, then, works not only to establish precursors but also to deny them, a denial essential for any text to become 'strong.'... Now the intertext, which had served to conceal the initial borrowing, itself becomes a threat to the artist who had assimilated it in order to avoid appearing derivative."[18] But this would serve to relegate intertextuality — like queer sexuality — to an imprisoning closet of denial. (Iampolski's use of the word "strong" as an ideal value for artists and art resonates with traditional masculine, even macho, characteristics, a pervasive, even unconscious linking of art with male power and conquest which has typically demeaned the work of not only queer but female artists.) With openly queer intertextuality, the real danger would be, not exposure, but the exact opposite — that an artist or work hadn't "gotten it right" enough to be appropriated, thereby giving rise to the loneliness of texts that do not speak to each other instead of the solidarity of like-minded texts.

Plus, there are occasions when intertextuality is literally a kind of queering. Let us consider "Le Marais," the short film that Van Sant contributed to *Paris, Je T'Aime* (2006). In a very offhanded way — somewhat in the manner of a loose translation — this film reprises elements of Minnelli's *An American in Paris* (1951) within a dreamlike and explicitly gay context. (Minnelli's film could only insinuate implicit gayness in fairly broad ways, moments passed off as campy male bonding: a few scenes between Kelly and Oscar Levant; other scenes where Kelly duets and dances with other men.) In "Le Marais" Elie (Elias McConnell) is an American working in a Paris frameshop; one day he finds himself being hit on by an attractive customer, Gaspard (Gaspard Ulliel). Gaspard speaks romantically in an unbroken stream of French, similar to the love-struck spiel that Gene Kelly speaks to Leslie Caron when he finds her working in the *parfumerie*. Elie is circumspect; he maintains eye contact with Gaspard, invites him to sit down, at one point asks for a light for his smoke — but says nothing in reply to Gaspard's infatuated torrent of talk, which includes Gaspard volunteering his passionate musical tastes (Charlie Parker and Kurt Cobain), further suggesting that "Le Marais" is a kind of postmodern deconstruction of the musical. We might even say that Gaspard is "singing" to Elie, in the sense that songs in musicals often soliloquize romantic passion. But Van Sant doesn't really tip his hand until after Gaspard has left, when Elie confesses to his boss that he simply didn't understand what Gaspard was saying, the words were not in his phrasebook. By this, Elie is designated as the "American in Paris."

At the end, Elie is dressed in all-black clothes like the ones Kelly wears in *An American in Paris*' final ballet sequence, itself a quintessentially stylish outpouring of romantic loss and despair. Instead of dancing through a mental landscape that apostrophizes Paris, Elie simply runs headlong down the street;

and yet, his movement, particularly in its incongruousness (no one else on the street is running), can be seen as a kind of dance, however discoordinated. The use of a country song in the background, "Lonely Blue Boy," completes the idea that this is a deconstructed dance sequence, and also completes the picture of "Le Marais" as an intertextual deconstruction of the musical genre in general, and of *An American in Paris* in particular.

Music and songs have served various intertextual functions throughout Van Sant's work. Sometimes a song will function in a more or less straightforward way, as in the magnificent usage of Desmond Dekker's "Israelites" over the montage in *Drugstore Cowboy* that shows the junky crew on the road trying to stay one step ahead of the police; rousing and lovely, the song complements the energy of the editing and adds a conscious wistfulness to the characters' nomadic existence. These "criminals" (who essentially hurt no one but themselves) are briefly framed within a fantasy that they are a persecuted tribe seeking freedom and homeland. The sweetness of this montage, and the triumphant moments of luck and flight which occur within it, lingers in the film even after reality becomes less kind to the characters.

Other songs have a nearly Brechtian purpose, as in the way Madonna's "Cherish" plays under a pseudo-documentary scene in *My Own Private Idaho* in which young street hustlers discuss their trade. The catchy, bubblegum spirit of the song feels "off," and inexorable, against the hard-case stories being told, and the lyrics, in which the singer addresses a boy and promises to always cherish him, have a biting irony, especially when one of the hustlers recounts being raped by his first john. These boys are pointedly un-cherished, by the men who rent them and by the world at large. Yet, although the use of the song is an implicit mode of critique, it is also, on a more literal, basic level, exactly what it is, a love-song of praise, delivered with a certain affecting "heart" by Madonna. We identify with her pop devotion and we also identify with the hustlers' gritty abjection, even as we see that these two modes are separate and mainly incompatible. Oddly, and in a way that reveals the sureness of his instinct and touch, Van Sant manages to show us how the fantasy falls far short of the reality, but without forcing us to entirely damn or jettison the fantasy itself.

Put otherwise, there is something both naïve and complicating about the union of Madonna's "Cherish" with the flat, direct-to-camera address of these non-actors' hard-luck stories. Not only is her music sustaining of a kind of polished production value which Van Sant is not interested in replicating cinematically for this artless, off-the-cuff sequence; it serves, in a sweet, light-handed way, to undermine the expressed feelings of the hustlers. For example, we note that a blond hustler smirks and grins when he talks about being raped, and this disconcerting tic serves to reveal, spontaneously and unselfconsciously, a unique body language of adolescent discomfort, more authentic than the mechanically churning song, which nonetheless claims equal if not greater attention as a more socially certified "right of speech." The ambiguous smirk also upholds, inadvertently perhaps, an element of fantasy even in the face of reality itself: that prostitution is about *jouissance*, sexual enjoyment and excess. Madonna herself returned this ambiguous gesture, as an actress in Abel Ferrara's *Dangerous Game* (1993), when, during a scene in which she recounts being raped and specifically forced to perform oral sex, she licks her lips provocatively even as she says she was afraid and in pain during the event.

I am interested, here, in the formal presentation of these ambiguities, not their content, which is more difficult to assimilate; but it is primarily on an immediate, sensuous, formal level that we take in the "Cherish" scene from *My Own Private Idaho*: like a moment of life, it is defined by casual internal contradictions and instances of simultaneity that cannot be rationalized, and which, more importantly, would never occur again in exactly the same "random" pattern, just as actual hustlers, in their off hours, might stop into a café or bar where a romantic, Top-40 love song happened to be playing. ("Cherish" was Madonna's current single when *My Own Private Idaho* was being filmed.) It is part of Van Sant's larger interest — pursued without much fanfare or underscoring — in how the lives of individuals do not really intersect that much with the machinations of what can be characterized as "the culture industry" in spite of all our misgivings about its infecting influence. Mike in *My Own Private Idaho* has never heard of Sinead O'Connor; while the junkies in *Drugstore Cowboy* interpret TV shows and commercials like those superstitious "tea leaves" which David Bowie sings about in his song "1984," as indicators of good or bad fortune, rather than consuming the programming in a normative way. In *Last Days*, the rock star Blake (Michael Pitt) is too paralyzed by heroin to even notice how a popular R-&-B group is replacing his own band in the MTV-style countdown; even this successful member of the "industry" is essentially insensible to it because the chaotic noise inside his own head drowns out such distant messages.

Do You Miss Me, Miss Misery, Like You Say That You Do?

Van Sant's work has a kind of larger intertextuality with the songs of Elliott Smith, the brilliant Portland singer-songwriter whom Van Sant propelled onto a wider world stage by organizing *Good Will Hunting* (1997) around a number of Smith's songs, elegies for lost love, tortured youth, and the wages of addiction. Smith's plaintive, tense voice and insistent, nervy acoustic-guitar plucking helped cast that dangerously commercial film as surprising indie lo-fi, and made infinitely more believable the hero's gritty, unglamorous, skid-row origins. Smith's "Miss Misery" was nominated for a Best Song Oscar but lost out to the theme from *Titanic*. Smith was also a crucial link to Portland in that Boston-set film, since Van Sant — much like Fassbinder did with his native Munich, Bavaria, or John Waters with Baltimore — has focused nearly all of his films around a somewhat idiosyncratic, extreme and poetic interpretation of Northwestern U.S. regionalism.

I say this because Van Sant asserts the right of his Portland to be a teeming universe unto itself, with disparate sides, and because he does not flinch from its inevitably seedy sides. Like Phil Stanford's book *Portland Confidential: Sex, Crime, and Corruption in the Rose City*, an entertaining insider-tour modeled on Kenneth Anger's *Hollywood Babylon*, Van Sant seems to delight in revealing disorder within Portland's communities. He focuses on problems of racial and ethnic minorities, the poor, drug users, gays, hustlers, delinquent youth, taking Portland's buzzy pulse but also inviting us to see it as a trap, a dead end, even a kind of hell, for some. So staunch is he in being even-handed that, in *Elephant* (2003), he relocated the Columbine High School massacre from Littleton, Colorado, to Portland, thereby absorbing a tragedy that had dismayed and shamed citizens of Littleton into a piece of his own local, native "history," to be witnessed, probed and perhaps exorcised. Portland is, finally, the most labile of Van Sant's intertexts; it is anything he wants it to be, this is its magic for Van Sant and for his viewers, and David Thomson is correct in saying that in Van Sant's films it becomes like Paris,[19] a place whose very name conjures mythology and stirs the imagination.

And *Elephant* is yet another example of Van Sant's intertextuality on a formal level, in that the title is in direct homage to the 1988 Alan Clarke film of the same name, in which a series of brutal shootings is filmed with dispassionate, vérité-like interest. The shared title, *Elephant*, points to similarities between the two films — mainly the fact that they are about the prevalence of, and desensitization to, gun violence in current western societies — even as Van Sant veers away from his chosen intertext in other ways. For example, he provides some clues as to the motives of the shooters, as well as scenes of dialogue which introduce us to the eventual victims. In Clarke's film, no such background information is provided.

In this sense, intertextuality with a single source (Clarke's stark film) contains within it a multi-layered dialogue in which the new work becomes more than a quote or an imitation, but an attempt to evoke the aura of the earlier work in, again, a distinctly poetic way. In fact, the adoption of an existing title, or the use of another author's name in a title, is a common technique of postmodern poetry. For example, Ruth Krauss titles a short poem "Artaud,

Van Sant is a great collaborator with other artists. Here, he directs Matt Damon on the set of *Good Will Hunting* (1997), a film co-written by, and starring, the young actor. One could say that Van Sant and Damon have forged a long professional relationship, helping each other to realize the making of personal and sometimes quite avant-garde films within mainstream Hollywood. As this book is written, Van Sant's current directorial project is ***Promised Land*** (2013), also written by and starring Damon.

Reverdy and Myself"[20] even though the poem has nothing directly to do with either of the name-dropped writers; or Don Yorty titles a poem "For John Keats"[21] when his poem has only glancingly to do with Keats. Instead, we are meant to think about these other writers, and what they represent, as we approach the new poems; it is a shared ground crossed by lines of cultural force. Sometimes the implication is that the new poet is saying, "I have suffered, or I have achieved, in culturally recognizable, allegorical ways." Artaud's madness is my own; Keats' beauty is my own. More to the point, the titles become talismanic, and Van Sant's reference to Clarke in the title *Elephant* is similarly talismanic, meant to position him in relation to Clarke, to cue the viewer to be mindful of Clarke, and to create a node of identification that becomes both conceptual (in film-historical terms) and emotionally charged (the acknowledgment of Clarke's film establishes a friendly, insider intimacy between Van Sant and those in his audience who also admire Clarke's film).

What I am saying here — as well as its serious implications for ways of beginning to reconfigure postmodernist assumptions (something we will return to, throughout this book) — may be best defined by way of contrast. In Avital Ronell's fascinating book, *Stupidity*, which I take as being (among other things) an acerbic and lively debunking of the way in which obfuscation and incomprehension have been swallowed wholesale in the work of certain "untouchable" male philosophers, Ronell riffs upon the tropological semantics of Paul de Man appropriating a title, *The Concept of Irony*, from Kierkegaard. Suggesting that de Man's purpose was precisely to show that irony is not a concept, therefore to show up Kierkegaard and prove him wrong, Ronell inquires:

> Does the title that de Man picks up double only to negate an already ironic title that stands on and by its own error? What kind of a couple do Kierkegaard and de Man form here? ... Appropriating and repeating the gesture ... de Man rewrites the book on repetition but also produces an allegorical distance within what is presented as a moment of identity. [A]nd so [de Man] pick[s] up where [Kierkegaard fell down] ... It is fairly typical of de Man to name the winner but also, in the same gesture, to undermine the very possibility of winning within what nonetheless remains a contest.[22]

We recognize the same appropriation of a title ("The Concept of Irony") that occurs as well with Van Sant's *Elephant*, in which an affinity is meant to be established. And yet, in Ronell's reading of de Man, it is an anti-affinity, a mismatched, quizzical couple. Ronell reveals a great deal in her deployment of the "couple" trope, a queering device but one which sours on contact. Pointedly, de Man is not expressing affection for Kierkegaard, or more precisely Kierkegaard's thought, since physical being is irrelevant to this time-traveling exchange, but instead an "allegorical distance," and "a contest." Much like Iampolski, with his leeriness of artists rubbing off on each other too much, his insistence that master texts must completely efface their messy referential origins, de Man (as read by Ronell) is enacting a disavowal of influence, rather than a celebration of it. This view of postmodernist thought, and specifically of appropriation, stands in direct opposition to what I am tracing in the practice of Gus Van Sant, in which affinities are based on the sense of shared witness or experience, and in which the physical existence of a referent (as talisman, as fetish, as imitative homage) is honored. Also, in which the process of queering becomes either self-evident, reinforced by doubling, and for the most part celebratory.

No doubt Ronell is entirely right that male philosophers do engage in territorialism, a struggle for dominance (elsewhere in her book she likens academic theory to "a kind of masculinist rage, the last residue, to be kind, of a warrior impulse"[23]). But what I am seeing in the cinema of Van Sant is something which works against the nature of postmodernism to negate and snipe, to cancel out for the sake of doing so, and for the glory of one's own sharp intellect, like the ingestion of dead enemies' flesh by certain warriors. Instead of one-upmanship and a relentless defiling of the past, Van Sant's appropriations are motivated by something more like kindness or tenderness. Distances are bridged by shared allusions and referents; the idea of a mano-a-mano competition gets replaced by a sort of relay race, in which artists and thinkers from different eras end up on the same team rather than as combatants. There is a sense of acknowledging one's pioneering forebears, and including them in an ongoing progress, which, as I will attempt to show later, brings a certain glimmer from modernism's utopian aspirations into the otherwise murky, undermining and negating realm of the postmodern.

All the Best Cowboys Make Westerns

So Van Sant, in a sincere albeit not naïve way, has allowed himself and his films to *stand for* things. There are persistent links with the classical, the old-fashioned, the hallowedness of genre, coded, even ritualized behaviors. Van Sant's films, for all their discursive nonlinear open-endedness, want to hang upon familiar structuring the way a painter's blank canvas gets stretched upon a frame. Indeed, the canvas' "negative space" is defined and contained, as it were, within the reassuring dimensions of the frame itself. For example, I have always been intrigued by Van Sant's statement that all of his films are, in a sense, "westerns," in response to Graham Fuller's remark, in their famous 1993 interview, that "*Drugstore Cowboy* is a kind of Western." Van Sant replied:

> Well, all these stories are really modern Westerns because they're written in the West and take place there.... Only fifty years ago, Portland had dirt streets. The

people that live there are descendants of the original pioneers and of the Indians.... That kind of history is behind a lot of the characters in the films.[24]

In a humble, pragmatic way, the director attempts to ground Fuller's intuition in the factual: stories set in the west must be, of necessity, westerns. But Fuller seemed to be on a slightly different tack, which is that the *form* of Van Sant's films — and perhaps also their moral compass — derive strongly from the classic Hollywood western.

Some of this arises from the use of "group codes" in a number of Van Sant films. The Mexicans in *Mala Noche* have a kind of code which makes them wary, mocking or hostile toward gringos. In *Drugstore Cowboy*, there is a fascinatingly elaborate criminals' code, as well as a kind of junkie's code, which determines how large a share of the stolen drugs will go to each member of the gang based not only on how much they help in the robberies but their level of drug tolerance and experience; within this, there is a still more private code, heavily inflected by superstition and personal history, involving hats on beds and small dogs. Articulating various codes to outsiders becomes an initiatory rite of passage. Acceptance of the code betokens acceptance within the group, a constant motif of frontier life in western films, where outsiders and newcomers must be "bound in" with makeshift communities through heroic acts of shared sacrifice. So, too, an antiheroic heroism enters the "modern western" world: in both of these films, the heroes begin as self-interested outsiders and end up being broadened by their direct witness to suffering and death. They are rootless creatures who only discover that they have found a home for themselves when something painful "hits" them there.

Furthermore, teen codes are displayed in *To Die For* (1995), *Elephant* and *Paranoid Park* (2007), in which different kinds of communication or sexuality are reserved for one's peers, as opposed to the ones used with grown-ups. Some of the chaos that ensues in *To Die For* stems from the high-school students turning their sexual attentions toward an older woman, one who feels no obligation to respect or protect them. In *Paranoid Park*, Alex (Gabe Nevins) lies to his parents constantly, as a survival mechanism and sometimes seemingly as second nature; he also lies to the police. Whether out of cluelessness or apathy, these various adults never seem to demand that Alex should be anything other than shifty and unfocused. It is as if he is does not matter to the adults, or is invisible to them, therefore his lies to them fulfill the passive, problem-free identity that they expect him to have, and are more harmful to himself than to others. But Alex is aware that he cannot get away with lying to Macy (Lauren McKinney), the fellow teen who befriends him; deceiving her would be a violation of his social code, even worse than the accidental murder which he is covering up.

Likewise, in westerns, we often see characters living by similar codes, primarily honor codes. Good guys must defend women and children against outlaws; posses must be formed to dispense justice; even outlaws cross the line if they stab each other in the back. Thus, a constant sense of order takes shape underneath the diegetic layers of lawlessness and violence. Often the learning of these codes plays a vital role in boys becoming men, or in characters failing or succeeding to establish themselves as belonging within a given social order. The alternative to not belonging, in the Old West, is to have to face the wilderness alone, a poor prospect.

The honor codes of the western do not preempt rash, violent, or antisocial behaviors, however; in fact, in many ways, they demand and enforce such behaviors. Thus, *Elephant* can be considered as a very sophisticated updating of such "band of outlaw" movies as Sam Peckinpah's *The Wild Bunch* (1969). In *The Wild Bunch*, we are primed to root for the outlaws because they finally seem more human than the other outlaws and the bounty hunters who stand in their way. The intertexuality by which we can read *Elephant* in light of *The Wild Bunch* (and vice versa) proceeds through one very major shared characteristic — both films end in climactic gun massacres — and also through a host of more minor shared characteristics.

Peckinpah's natural sympathy is with the outlaw gang. He depicts the posses hunting the wild bunch very negatively, as ignorant rednecks squabbling among themselves. Likewise, the school jocks and popular kids who pick on Alex (Alex Frost) and Eric (Eric Deulen) are also unlikable, phony, hollow and shrill. The wild bunch's youngest member, C.L. (Bo Hopkins), is directly reminiscent of Eric's adolescent aggression: wild-eyed, C.L. sadistically baits his hostages, making them sing and then shooting them in the back after telling them to run away (as Eric does with the school principal). And like C.L., Eric is gunned down in the midst of his bravado.

Of course, the outlaw bunch have their internal squabbles, too, but they are essentially bound by their code, just as nothing threatens the bond between Alex and Eric, except perhaps the explosive fulfillment of their honor-vendetta, which will mean their own lives as well as the lives of those whom they kill. Just as Peckinpah shows Pike (William Holden) and Dutch (Ernest Borgnine), best friends, sleeping side by side under the stars, so Van Sant lingers on a tracking shot of Eric sleeping at Alex's feet the night before the massacre. Intercut shots of the night sky suggest that the two boys, although indoors in Alex's bedroom, are symbolically "camping out"—like Dutch and Pike, rugged outsiders, outlaws, without a sense of home. In both films, the buddies make a fatalistic pact, promising to go to the end of the line for each other against their sworn enemies, or, as Pike says, "people who just can't stand to be wrong." It is, in the end, pettiness rather than violence that most disturbs the bunch. What they despise is the same self-righteous vanity and pride, the same relentless, bullying face-saving that drives the inner social mechanisms of the high school, from the bulimic girls to the geeky librarian traumatized by having to wear shorts in gym class to the jealous bickering of a cute, popular couple. Male bonding emerges as a different, more honest kind of pride, in opposition to the others, facing and accepting death rather than denying it. "I wouldn't have it any other way," Dutch says when he and Pike make their fatal pact, meaning that, like the gay lovers in a Smiths song, he can think of no more heavenly way to die than at Pike's side. Like Alex and Eric, it is their honor to defend each other from a world that has kicked and "hunted" them, and it is this honor for which they finally die.

Van Sant even finds a way of paraphrasing the joking, raunchy "whorehouse" talk between members of the bunch, by having Alex try to distract and amuse Eric, while the boys are prepping for the massacre, by telling him a story about a house that puts out a sign which designates it as a place of prostitution. At this point, the boys have already been intimate with each other (in the shower scene), so their laughter at prostitution is meant both to designate *them* as worldly, no longer virginal, and also to draw a kind of exclusionary circle around their shared sexuality. Whatever it might be (and it is never defined, least of all by Alex and Eric themselves), it is not shameful or dirty such as prostitution might be. Put otherwise, the homosexuality that is repressed from *The Wild Bunch*'s male bonding, or deferred through the figures of readily available female prostitutes, is fully expressed between Alex and Eric.

Indeed, in both films, solidarity among men always trumps allegiances to women; again, similar to the scene where the bunch good-naturedly disparage the sister of one of their members, in order to assert that their first loyalty is to each other (and to the pact with death that they have made together), so Eric belches in front of Alex's mother and says that she smells bad. C.L. licks the ear of a dowager who called him "trash," a more extreme version of the way Eric berates Alex's mom, but not too far away from the way Eric dominates and humiliates the simpering school principal (whom Van Sant has cast as a fussy Eric Blore type). Too much respect for women or womanliness is akin to respect for the oppressive social order that would have these male outlaws live enslaved rather than die as free men.

There are also a lot of kids in *The Wild Bunch*, a running motif that becomes almost overly obvious. Kids are torturing stray scorpions in the opening scene when the bunch first rides in; two kids, caught in a shoot-out, hold each other in the middle of the mayhem; in the Mexican village kids are present at the drinking and dancing party around the campfire. Although the world of the wild west outlaws is very adult and tough, children bear it constant witness, in a way that is not presented as pathological but utterly normal, even joyous, part of the bacchanalia of a different era (and something which also resonates with the permissive 60s, when *The Wild Bunch* was made). Children are grinning, demented onlookers to the most extreme carnage. In *Elephant*, however, it is adults who warily bear witness to the comings and goings of strange, secretive young people; it is adults who, dismayed, get drawn into the violent maelstroms of the teens in a manner that seems blatantly unnatural to the more traditional order of things, whereby younger people are meant to learn from, and follow, their elders. In *The Wild Bunch*, kids learn the harsh but fair laws of social justice from watching adults; in *Elephant*, kids arbitrate their own justice, which has become more like pure and savage revenge, and the adults no longer have any relevant, much less didactic or controlling, position. This difference between justice and vengeance is an important one, and one of the saddest, most elegiac elements of Van Sant's film. Whatever crimes they do commit, the bunch does not tolerate personal revenge within its code, as when Angel (Jaime Sànchez) desires to avenge his father's murder and Pike tells him sternly, "Either you learn to live with it or we'll leave you here." They cannot afford the sloppiness that comes with passion; whereas Eric and Alex are entirely motivated by their passion for revenge, and have no plans to outlive its complete fulfillment.

In the end, Van Sant's kids are nihilistic in a way that Peckinpah's outlaws were not: for the outlaws hoped to live, and romantically squeezed every possible drop of pleasure out of life one day at a time, in case they died; while for Eric and Alex, death is a foregone conclusion, and everything they do beforehand is simply and grimly checked off a kind of list of things that they would like to try, or things that they feel they are supposed to do, before their inevitable deaths. In this, they anticipate the kamikaze pilot Hiroshi (Ryo Kase) and the doomed lovers Annabel and Enoch in *Restless*. Both *Elephant* and *Restless* are about the importance of being able to say goodbye, and the pain that occurs from not having this opportunity.

Yet life can never adequately contain, account for, or express the infinite mystery of death, its way of having the final word; just as no experience has the power to recall the outlaws or the school shooters back to life and away from the death that must claim them. *Elephant*'s intertexuality with westerns, especially *The Wild Bunch*, asserts this fact implicitly; likewise, it is after watching *Elephant* that we understand that the men of the wild bunch are really grizzled adolescents, older but not quite grown up, sharing solemn crushes on each other and guffawing uproariously at sex and gore. Westerns appeal to the innocent, childlike tendency to understand life best by standing apart from it and mocking its seriousness. Death is the crucible which literally prompts a necessary regression to childhood, in order to combat disturbing realities with radical innocence. At the end of *Restless*, Annabel's funeral buffet — a long smorgasbord of classic junk food and kids' treats — signifies not only her own peaceful acceptance of her death, but the (again Western-like) redemption of the young hero Enoch, whose loss of Annabel enables him to finally join some human community without sacrificing his own individualism.

Intertextuality and Mala Noche

There are even more complex instances of intertextuality in the films of Van Sant, where the film is not only engaged in a primary relation to one or two other texts, authors or genres (as "Le Marais" is with *An American in Paris*, or as *Elephant* is with Alan Clarke and Sam Peckinpah), but more polymorphously, as it were, in a nexus of relations and references. An example of this would be *Mala Noche*, Van Sant's first feature film. As a text, *Mala Noche* is composed of disparate elements from distinct, even readymade aesthetic backgrounds. Its primary intertextual relation is to a prose memoir by the gay, neo-beatnik Portland poet Walt Curtis. Passages from Curtis' work are used as voiceover, to provide lyrical counterpoint to, or commentary on, the action. This is what we defined before, with Kenneth Anger, as the solidarity of queer intertextuality, corroborating witnesses to desire.

Van Sant is true to the grit as well as the lyricism in Curtis' writing. Curtis himself proudly praises *Mala Noche* as "a true documentary,"[25] because Van Sant shot on real locations in the Old Town section of Portland, which had been home to prostitution and various underground lifestyles since the early 20th century, a section "confined to the North End ... north of Burnside and west of the Willamette River."[26] This is a second major area of intertextuality, although the "text" in question happens to be an actual, living neighborhood — life and reality themselves, again, being a kind of textuality. (Old Town, more romantically, is the place where Enoch finally finds the toy xylophone which he has been promising to get for Annabel in *Restless*.)

In general, Van Sant's films enter into an intertextual relation with the real, and it is not surprising that his interest in documentary filmmaking seems to be constantly growing. Documentaries have always held a special, if not always accurate, claim as experiential texts par excellence, substitutes for actual encounters. In *Mala Noche* film furnishes bare, bald proof of a reality (Portland's Old Town) which generally escapes recording. When he made *Psycho* (1998), Van Sant was pleased to discover the exact same phone pole along a California highway, near the town of Boorman, where Hitchcock shot the scene in which Marion Crane is questioned by a state trooper.[27] Although mediated by cinema, the real emerges as irrefutable proof of raw and authentic existence. Likewise, in *Elephant*, Van Sant filmed Alex taking a drink from a cup in the school cafeteria during the massacre because the same image appeared on surveillance camera footage from the actual massacre itself.[28] Some of *Last Days*' stylings derive from famous images of Kurt Cobain onstage (the oatmeal cardigan like the one which Cobain wore on *Unplugged in New York City*) and in death (the position of his body inside the garden shed). And just as celebrity icons already mediate between reality and fantasy, what we think we know about them and what we would like to know, so the real is already a readymade documentary of itself, which only needs to be imitated in order to come to life (as myth, as narrative) all over again.

But of course, conscious technique and artistry enter into this mimetic process. Curtis also praises *Mala Noche*'s cinematography: "John Campbell, the cinematographer, got some amazingly gorgeous chiaroscuro. Night in rundown hotels. The glint of light in eyes; glitter of raindrops falling through the arc of a streetlamp. Haunting classic stuff like that."[29] Indeed, *Mala Noche* replicates, more than most films, the way one really sees at night, which is to say half-blindly, in stark patterns, with sudden shapes moving into dim focus. We recognize this chiaroscuro from the high-contrast, fatalistic noir lighting of John Alton or Russell Metty — yet another piece of the film's intertextual puzzle. However, this would be an example of intertextuality's subversive use, since here Van Sant overturns the obligatory heterosexualism of the noir, recasting "femme fatale" as "garçon fatal."

Furthermore, part of the plot involves Walt (Tim Streeter) and his friends Johnny and Pepper (Ray Monge) getting hold of a Super-8 camera and taking home movies of themselves. These snippets of staged home movies, shot in grainy color, have yet another aesthetic: prankish and more spontaneous, a kind of "anti-cinema." (Home movies — shot by the actors of each other while improvising in character[30] — are also used in *Drugstore Cowboy*, to highlight the intimate ties among the main characters, and as a kind of innocent respite from the pursuit of drugs which drives them and the majority of the film's action.)

Just as the color home movies open up the black-and-white confines of *Mala Noche*'s cinematography, so they also serve to reveal unguarded personalities within the often brooding and self-conscious characters: in the home movies, the characters smile, clown and run around, the way people do who are filming each other off-the-cuff, trying to preserve a moment in time and make it special. However raw, the rest of the film's cinematography is composed, sometimes to replicate the oppressive feeling that minority groups and especially immigrants might have in being seen or watched (as in the scene where Pepper is cornered and shot by the police), whereas the home movies have a more idealized and relaxed feel, as befitting a situation in which the film's minorities (Mexicans, gays) are alone with each other and in charge of their own representation. Thus, there is also a recreation of kinship outside of heteronormative and Caucasian strictures.

There is further aesthetic corroboration for this queering of the home movie "genre," notably the films of Derek Jarman. Justin Wyatt writes that, through the use of actual and simulated home movies, "Jarman is able to construct both a personal history and a history of gay life ... beyond established media categories."[31] He continues: "Jarman encourages a defamiliarization of the home movie; the familiar is made unfamiliar given its placement with ... other material."[32] The blurring of fantasy with factual documentary, of the composed with the experimental (home movies already cross all of these lines), is an inherently queering process. As with Van Sant's constructed home movies in *Mala Noche* (and later *Drugstore Cowboy* and *My Own Private Idaho*), "home" is made doubly strange, first by being mediated through fragments of raw cinema, and secondly by being situated within a subversive or queer perspective, thereby interrogating "basic presuppositions, in effect asking what are 'proper' and 'expected' behaviors, and what are the implications of 'cultural membership'?"[33]

As if to give them a certain pride of place, Van Sant ends the film with more of these home movies, set to a raucous, thrashing, catchy punk song, "Rich Man Stream" by the Neo Boys, which seems to suggest that even the most tragic elements of the story we have just witnessed (Pepper's death; Walt's broken heart) are to be ultimately subsumed in the giddy energy of protest and the sheer abandon of rock 'n' roll. Punk becomes the film's final intertext, employed in much the same way that it will be in Gregg Araki's early films or James Robert Baker's landmark queer novel *Tim and Pete* (1995), as not only an assault on the mainstream straight world but a restoration of queer energy and the reconstitution of a marginalized world in jeopardy. In this sense, we are allowed to step outside *Mala Noche*'s diegetic space, at the end, to imagine a better world of sorts, in which the characters are all alive and happy together. This intertextuality with punk and home movies signals not only the presence of a hipster scene within the film, but one outside of it as well, since punk's historically confrontational spirit turns the viewer away from potentially gloomy introspection or depression, and sends him or her, if not out into the streets, then at least into the public realm of a club or bar.

All of these many intertextualities combine to create *Mala Noche* as a distinctly experiential text which points both toward the recent past and toward the future, and which makes us acknowledge its place within a cultural framework that includes gay/beat poetry, noir, slum life, punk, and the *mise en scène* of home movies. In nearly all of these cases, the original experience in question is one under some duress and therefore extreme. Indeed, what all of these various intertexts hold in common is that they are marginalized within the dominant culture and therefore subversive; we are not surprised to find them brought together, nor are we particularly surprised to find them being used mainly as signifiers to represent queerness. Through the use of these diverse cultural signifiers, we come to recognize queerness as something always already inscribed within the dominant culture. In this sense, Van Sant's use of intertextuality approximates what Barthes in *Writing Degree Zero* characterizes as "the perfection of some new Adamic world where language would no longer be alienated."[34] Put otherwise: where texts would become what I am calling *experiential*, at one with life rather than outside of it. Like knowledge according to Plato, we do not learn it but come to remember having

In *Drugstore Cowboy* (1989), Van Sant cast noted Beat author William Burroughs as Father Tom, an aging junkie who becomes temporary mentor to Bob (Matt Dillon). Burroughs was an aesthetic hero of Van Sant's, and famous writing technique of cutting up and collaging pre-existing texts can be seen as a direct harbinger of postmodernist techniques of decentralizing the privileged position of the author. Yet, Van Sant adopts such postmodernist techniques in his films, not for the po-mo purpose of revealing the world to be hopelessly relative and meaningless, but seemingly to stake out new, powerful claims for the human integrity of life, love and death: a search for wholeness which nonetheless acknowledges randomness and diffusion as a natural part of that search.

always known it, the memory of a cosmic existence prior to birth. So, in Van Sant's films, we are often reoriented in relation to simple, quotidian things as well as to the most complex of systems and human processes. Just as he sometimes uses enormous close-ups of isolated parts of objects (the corner of a five dollar bill on a store counter in *Mala Noche*, for example, or the wattage printed on the bottom of a glowing light bulb in *Drugstore Cowboy*)—making us ask, "What is it really?"—so the everyday is wrenched out of its straight, utilitarian context, and reality broken down in order to be reconstituted and redefined.

Van Sant, Burroughs, Barthes

One of my assumptions in this book is that Burroughs' famous "cut-up" technique of writing, also known as cut-up/fold-in, is a systematic form of intertextuality. The first cut-ups were made by Burroughs' friend and collaborator, the artist Brion Gysin, in 1959. Gysin cut a page of written text into four parts with a pair of scissors, rearranged the parts, read the new lines straight across, and transcribed them into a new text. Burroughs has described the cut-ups variously, sometimes as a quasi-mystical, even magic process; sometimes as an excavation of unconscious personal and collective knowledge; and sometimes as an aesthetic method similar to the surrealists' exquisite corpses, in which new meanings arise by chance through unexpected juxtapositions.[35]

In *The Burroughs File*, Burroughs gives a complete account of adapting the literary cut-up technique to tape recordings, editing a whole series of texts into each other like aural collage or montage. Burroughs began by recording a symphony from the radio on his Wollensack tape recorder, along with the sound of radio wave static, "most interesting sound on the air."[36] Then, like the layering of a palimpsest, or indeed a kind of surgical grafting procedure, he randomly interrupted the music and sound with fragments of written texts read aloud:

> Where I cut in of course the music or static and later the words were wiped off the tape creating new juxtapositions. I cut in sections from *Some of Your Blood* by Theodore Sturgeon—A high school magazine called *Excelsior* edited by Alan Berger—*Horde* Magazine edited by Johnny Byrne, Lee Harwood, Roger Jones & Miles, No. 1, December, 1964—pieces of Pete Brown, Michel Couturier, L. M. Herrickson, George Dowden, Spike Hawkins, Lee Harwood, Miles, Neil Oram—*The Day Jesse James Was Killed* by Carl W. Breihan (April 3, 1881)—and some texts of my own...[37]

This remarkably detailed and heteroclite list contains only one "prestige" author (Sturgeon), the rest of these names having significance for us mainly because Burroughs employed their texts in this historic composition. Indeed, by stating that radio static is the "most interesting sound on the air," Burroughs already advocates a radical overturning of the primacy of the author and the supposed sacredness of the act of premeditated creation. Still, we glimpse a number of Burroughs' major interests expressing themselves through the choice of these texts: teenage life; Jesse James and Old West outlawism; science fiction, etc. This is, of course, how intertextuality works: the writer defines his personality not strictly through original utterance but through his demonstrated affinity for what has already been said. The aura of creation comes from the act of appropriation itself. Intertextuality is something like the look of love.

Here, the experiential text serves to directly mimic the enacting or performing of daily life itself. It is what we already read, already know, already think about. Indeed, here, the cut-up process does tap explicitly into universal, latent powers of the unconscious. In a 1976 lecture at Naropa, Burroughs questions the true "randomness" of one fragment being "cut in" to another:

> Now how random is random? We know so much that we do not consciously know that we know, that perhaps the cut-in was not random. The operator on some level knew just where he was cutting in.... So cut-ups put you in touch with what you know and do not know that you know.[38]

The unconscious mind contains all possibilities, everything known and unknown by the self; therefore, it is already a site of transformations, or juxtapositions. Burroughs specifies that we all know exactly (in the unconscious) what we were doing ten years ago to the day,[39] but what is most significant about this, from a creative standpoint, is that in the unconscious mind, in spite of all appearances to the contrary, nothing is left to chance: neither the tiny daily details of life, nor the largest and most abstract components of identity, voice, style. Like traces of repressed gay desire, perhaps, it is all already inside oneself, waiting only to be acknowledged.

In intertextuality, or experiential textuality, then, self-knowledge and taste (both functions of knowing whom one is and what one favors) are stressed as the basis of art. It is somehow innate, preordained not only in the realm of the unconscious, but in the body itself, the reflexes and involuntary systems. Not coincidentally, self-knowledge and taste are also things cultivated by homosexuals, as attributes which develop from an awareness of being different from, and outside of, straight culture, and also as tools for further delineating one's difference from straight culture. Thus, we can view the strategy of intertextuality as an updating of camp strategies: as in camp, the identification of a loved object (whom others might revile) is still a central way of turning stigmatization inside-out, and of reversing the customary subservience of the margins to the mainstream. Now, however, there is active involvement with the loved object rather than rapt, passive appreciation or fan-worship, as well as the willingness to violently cut into, cut up, the loved object rather than preserve it in plastic or under glass.

A far more blatant example of how queer intertextuality functions can be seen in *Gefangen* (*Locked Up*, 2004), a gay German prison drama/love story which re-stages tributes and even entire scenes from such diverse films as Jean Genet's *Un Chant d'Amour* (1950), Rainer Werner Fassbinder's *Querelle* (1982), and Todd Haynes' *Poison* (1991); even the rape scene from *American History X* (1999) is "quoted" with its queerness more deliberately heightened. The entirety of *Locked Up* seems to be saying, "Here is what I have seen, and here is what it meant." Of course, *Locked Up* is not a particularly "great" film by conventional standards, but that is part of what makes its sincerity and its imitative qualities somehow poignant.

What becomes most intriguing in this process is the question of whether or not the artificiality speaks authentically, in some ways, to actual lived experience. Is the lead character, Dennis (Marcel Schlutt), standing and smiling exactly like Brad Davis in *Querelle* because *Locked Up* requires this embodied intertextuality, or because a gay young German might well have learned how to carry himself from watching *Querelle*? Do the macho bullies taunt an effeminate inmate (David Parstein) the way they do because they "got the idea" from *Poison* (available on DVD throughout Europe but not in the U.S.)?

In a normative context, it might seem fatuous to insist that culture could have such a direct and necessary impact on actual lives. After all, we have largely moved beyond the thinking that watching violent films, for instance, can make someone commit crimes; and this is true, culture does not place anything in someone that is not already there. But in the construction of queer identity, when it comes to matters of self-expression, it is still just as common for gay men to model themselves on images of gayness rather than on other (gay) people. *Being* gay is never a choice, but coming out and living as a gay person is still a near-endless series of sometimes painful, sometimes joyous decisions, if only because the identity must be announced and enacted in some fashion; it's not the automatic default position. Moreover, as *Locked Up*'s prison setting makes clear, this construction of identity is a vital process of overcoming literal (and perceived) restrictions upon one's thoughts, emotions and behaviors.

Intertextuality jumpstarts the creative mind, frees it from its shackles. In this way, Burroughs avoided, as he pungently says, "sitting on my ass waiting for my 'very own words.'"[40] We could say that the cut-up is a kind of scientific method meant to revivify an author's own voice through mutilated and mutated fragments of other authors' statements. ("Experiential" and "scientific" are nearly synonymous.)

This is also very similar to the advice on the secret of writing which the famous novelist Forrester (Sean Connery) imparts to the gifted student Jamal in Van Sant's *Finding Forrester*. Forrester sits at the typewriter and starts punching keys in a mindless, improvisatory manner (the soundtrack turns be-bop) in order to begin a virtuosic flow of words. Beyond this, Forrester recommends retyping a page or two of something that someone else has already written, until one lapses into the rhythm of one's own thoughts and words: "Sometimes the simple rhythm of typing gets us from page one to page two. When you begin to feel your own words, start typing them." The fact that these thoughts and words are triggered, or unconsciously shaped, by an existing text is not troubling in and of itself, since all expression will always bear the stamp of unconscious processes that stem from *somewhere*.

Barthes would call this technique of re-typing (not to mention Burroughs' cut-ups and also any auteur's various direct appropriations) a "trouble saving device," "an economy signal"[41] in which a given author merges with the entire history of language, of expression. One avoids the pointless deception of a delusional originality (also the loneliness of bearing solitary witness) and instead promotes an aggressive intertextuality. Barthes believed that this characterized even writing that purported to be wholly original, since elements of language, or what we call "common usage," are shared cultural standards whether we admit this to ourselves or not. The assumption shared by both Burroughs and semiotic deconstructionists like Barthes is that there is no such thing as original writing, only a pool of socially standardized expressions which is dipped into, or rechannelled, or subverted, to serve the purposes of (new) writers.

Moreover, all of the texts Burroughs refers to are part of a vast network of recorded *heterosexual* history. Cutting it up makes a space for queer desire to enter into play. In this sense, intertextuality does not only mask (the way camp, for example, rather broadly denied valid human emotions, or substituted fake-heterosexual scenarios for real but "unspeakable" gay ones); rather, it is a mask which both conceals and reveals the real human face behind it. It makes raids on mainstream culture in the name of marginalized queer identity. It augments the identity of the artist as being this *and* that, rather than reducing it to only one thing, to something which may be judged as "less than" or woefully compromised. Like the right of gays to legally marry, anti-canonical and anti-hierarchical intertextuality places gays on the same level as straights, as they already are experientially if not in terms of general ideological conceptions.

The mask creates an equivalence with the appropriated text through the act of borrowing. Although Burroughs suggested that simple journalistic texts (a newspaper page, for instance) could provide raw material for a literary cut-up as easily as anything else, he often worked with the grand prose of some of his favorite authors, Hemingway for one. There is an implied satisfaction in placing canonical texts at the service of queer desire. Burroughs: "Subsequently we cut up the Bible, Shakespeare, Rimbaud, our own writing, anything in sight."[42] There is something particularly subversive in the way Burroughs moves, in this single list-sentence, from holy writ to "anything in sight" (the nameless, the omnivorous, the compulsive, the unordained): everything becomes fodder for intertextual experimentation, an available program which Marianne DeKoven describes as "actively democratic, egalitarian, and participatory."[43]

All of this is to say that intertextuality, or cut-ups (these terms will be used nearly interchangeably throughout this book, especially in the next three chapters), create fertile ground for new and formerly marginalized sensibilities to take root within established disciplinary fields.

Van Sant: Types of Intertextuality

Van Sant is greatly influenced by Burroughsian cut-ups. He has pointed to this influence many times, not least when he recorded *The Elvis of Letters* (1985), a CD in which he edited, tape-looped and distorted Burroughs' reading voice into a kind of *musique concrète*, backed by Van Sant's own minimalist rock. A genuine attempt to apply cut-up techniques to Burroughs' own texts, texts that may have already begun their aesthetic lives *as* cut-ups, *The Elvis of Letters* creates a kind of infinite regress of intertextuality. And even if this CD is ultimately a fan's work, doing little to illuminate Burroughs' legacy, it nonetheless celebrates, in a shorthand way, some of Burroughs' main preoccupations in the form of mantras like "word is virus" and "hipster bebop junkie." (It is also a lot of fun to listen to.)

We will examine three types of intertextuality in the films of Gus Van Sant. In some cases, these intertextualities occur within Van Sant's own body of work, while in others they reflect intertextual relations with texts by other authors. The first, considered in Chapter 2, examines recurring visual motifs, specifically cloudscapes and Pietàs. We will call this *visual intertextuality*.

The second, discussed in Chapter 3, revolves specifically around *Psycho* as a film that engages one other text in a profound dialogue, the original *Psycho* (1960). We will call this *quotational intertextuality*. This kind of intertextuality is also known as "appropriation," and often has political ramifications when practiced upon a canonical text.

Third, we will look at the theme of father-son relationships, whose ubiquity in Van Sant's films creates what we will call *thematic intertextuality* among the films themselves. This is the subject of Chapter 4.

These categories are more provisional and descriptive than prescriptive, since they contain overlapping elements. Visual intertextuality can also be elucidated thematically. Quotational intertextuality often announces itself through a shared visual language. Thematic intertextuality recombines all the different kinds of intertextuality into a complex pattern which is both recognizable and changing, thereby both concealing and revealing its own textual sources.

2. Cloudscapes and Pietàs: Visual Intertextuality

Let's begin our examination of intertextual connections with the visual motif of cloudscapes occurring in a number of Gus Van Sant's films, often in time-lapse cinematography. These panoramic shots of the sky, where storm clouds scurry ominously, seem to quote or at least relate to each other, thereby becoming identifiable as a consistent visual-intertextual element — those are "Van Sant skies," "Van Sant clouds."[1] And yet, although all the cloudscapes resonate with each other across the films themselves, their meanings, or their narrative uses, can be different: the same intertextual cue that links up visually leads in different directions thematically.

In Van Sant's early films, clouds are metaphorical, and subjectively mirror the viewpoint of the main character. Befitting tragic heroes, the clouds possess both loftiness (nobility) and changeability (passivity). There is a long history of clouds used to express internal states in cinema, going back to one of the first horror films, D. W. Griffith's adaptation of Poe, *The Avenging Conscience* (1913). There, the clouds act in concert with the hero's own conscience, as troubling celestial presences — however diaphanous — which seem to watch or bear down from above: "a background for angels (the white clouds) and demons (the dark clouds)."[2] The fact that they are so high above the world, and so ungraspable, makes them alien and judgmental: clouds "look down on us." In this sense, it isn't difficult to see them as Griffith's attempt to reinvest the sky with the classic Christian meaning of "heaven" and "God's abode." Griffith's cloudscapes are distinctly allegorical.

Van Sant turns the clouds away from the religious-allegorical and toward the natural-secular, even as he turns Griffith's Victorian morality toward a more modern humanism. Yet the clouds, by their very nature as representations of the world-above and the ungraspable, remain within the realm of mind, of conscience, of reflection. They continue to pass over, and in passing over, pass judgment over the foibles of man. They are also external expressions of internal states of being (as is also true in *The Avenging Conscience*). In *Mala*

Noche, there are two shots of clouds pouring across the sky — actually seeming to march directly toward the viewer as if they were billowing out of a fog machine aimed at the camera. These shots mark the passage of time after the first night that Walt spends hanging out with Johnny and Pepper (and having sex with Pepper), and the next time he happens to see the two boys. Their relationship is casual, although Walt is in love with Johnny, so his meetings with them are always serendipitous, random but meaningful. In fact, the boys now and then return to the neighborhood store where Walt works, usually trying to scam him out of money, but also offering their boisterous companionship.

Here, then, the clouds emblematize, among other things, the agonizing passing of time during a period of unrequited romantic longing. (Time-lapse clouds are also used to denote the passing of time — and the excruciating wait for the next fix, another kind of unrequited love, perhaps — throughout *Drugstore Cowboy*.) In *Mala Noche*, we are made to wonder when, if ever, Walt will see his beloved Johnny again? Walt wants to speed up the dead time between his sightings of the boys; thus, the clouds are made to move quickly. The clouds also represent this love's complexity, the turbulent mixed feelings on both sides, including Walt's quixotic hope that Johnny will change his sexual orientation for him. The clouds possess simultaneously a sense of constancy (they keep arising, billowing, enlarging endlessly, from some eternal source) and a sense of drift (they lose form quickly, slip away). Although most of *Mala Noche* is relentlessly materialist (it is one of the most specific records of what poverty really looks like in the U.S.), Van Sant goes to the cloudy sky when he wants to suggest the semi-transcendentalist nature of Walt's romantic love.

In *My Own Private Idaho*, Van Sant's cloud symbolism becomes even more complex, and also more of a constant leitmotif running throughout the film. Shots of dark, streaky clouds moving quickly across the sky accompany all of the moments when the main character, Mike, lapses into his comatose, narcoleptic slumbers. In the opening scene, set on an anonymous road in Idaho, we see this "change" come over Mike for the first time, without much explanation, and the effect is rather frightening. Indeed, Van Sant brings in imagery from horror films — including the stormy, fast-moving clouds — as if to suggest the kind of metamorphoses that occur in werewolf films, where nature symbolism, usually the full moon, is intercut with a man's transformation into a werewolf. This turns out to be a false lead, however; and for a few moments the viewer's expectations are temporarily at odds with the film's true meaning and intention. This has to do with Van Sant's complicated narrative layering, where the flow of events is broken down, almost cubistically at times, into moments that can only be understood from within Mike's subjectivity; we lack all the knowledge or data about Mike to be able to understand everything about him all at once, not until the film has established a behavioral pattern in relation to Mike's narcoleptic attacks (and troubled past history).

Thus, the first attack, and the time-lapse cloudscapes which accompany it, push against and test the limits of our identification; like a Rorschach test of sorts, it becomes a clue to our own powers of empathy (and how we will experience much of the rest of the film) whether we are primarily afraid *of* Mike, or *for* him, during this initial incident. The attack begins with an outburst of aggression on Mike's part: he chases a rabbit into the brush, shouting, "Where do you think you're running now? We're stuck here together, you shit!" We do not know yet that he is actually speaking, in his mind, to his faithless ex-lover, Scott. Then we see the clouds rumbling, and a close-up of Mike's hand trembling at his side, then his face twitching, his eyes rolling back. But just when we think his aggression (the outburst, the profanity, the shouting) might be the prelude to his transformation into some kind of assaultive monster, what happens next is a surprising deflation: he drops straight down onto his duffel-bag in the middle of the road, and falls asleep. Although set up to play as a somewhat scary object of fear, he instead becomes a vulnerable object of pathos and compassion.

In fact, the narcolepsy functions as a total undermining or negation of Mike's selfhood and also his masculine identity. As the pattern develops, we see that it is frequently during moments when he must defend himself or perform sexually as a man that Mike becomes instantly paralyzed by sleep, taken out of the action of the film in a foretaste of ultimate defeat and death. The trigger for Mike's narcoleptic attacks is almost always the fact that he finds himself in an uncomfortable confrontation, where he must become aggressive with someone — later, he will pass out when telling the creepy Hans (Udo Kier) to stop following him, yelling, "Why don't you go home? Go the fuck home!" — or, again, where sex is expected from him. The violence underlying these exchanges shuts down his system, bringing on collapse and unconsciousness. The visual cue for the attacks is the fast-moving cloudscape — partly a visualization of the metaphorical "storms" within Mike's spirit, as in Griffith's *The Avenging Conscience*, where guilt manifests itself as clouds, but also partly a token of that "big sky country" from Mike's Idaho childhood.

But there is yet another layer to the pattern. After the narcoleptic attack that occurs while chasing the rabbit on the road, we see Mike (as he dreams himself) sleeping on his mother's lap as she gently strokes his hair and murmurs, "I know you're sorry, I know." And indeed, Mike's thoughts of his mother are truly the deepest trigger behind these attacks. When he notices an older woman on the street who resembles the mother in his dream, or when an older female (Grace Zabriskie) attempts to have sex with him, his eyes roll back in his head and the same subjective vision of fast-moving clouds occurs (even when Mike is indoors).

When we find out, much later, that Mike was abandoned by his mother at an early age (as a baby he was placed in an institution to keep him safe from her) and that his father is actually his older brother (well played by James Russo as a seedy, hard-drinking, slightly older version of Mike and his hustler pals), we see that Mike's guilt is an inverse of buried rage. Rather than being able to blame his mother, he has internalized her as a lost ideal and taken on the onus of abandonment as his own fault — the basis of his crippling tendency to self-sabotage. Like a classic hysterical symptom stemming from repressed knowledge, the narcolepsy is Mike's body speaking for, and physically manifesting, the conflicts which paralyze his psyche.

The clouds in *My Own Private Idaho* signal the maternal, and perhaps the guilt of not really loving the maternal; therefore, they are literally the revenge of "Mother Nature" on Mike's scattered, helpless activities as he tries to live his damaged life, unable to escape its central rage and concomitant guilt. The shapeless, unindividuated clouds have the power to unhinge Mike, and their discontinuity has the power to interrupt his (our) narrative, and make it discontinuous as well. This relates to Barthes' theory, in *Writing Degree Zero*, that in its discontinuity modern writing is "full of terror," and that this discontinuity derives from a vision of nature itself that is no longer harmonious and whole. Modern writing (we can expand this to include the language of modern cinema) "relates man not to other men but to the most inhuman images in Nature: heaven, hell, holiness, childhood, madness, pure matter, etc."[3]

Van Sant's cloudscapes contain these vicissitudes of Nature. They are not populated with human figures, nor even rooted to the earthly realm, except obliquely, in their effect on Mike. The cloudscapes seem to transform Mike's earthly existence into more and more of an unstable dream, and at the same time, they reify his sense of imprisonment, his conflicted place on earth, pulling him ever closer to the ground in sudden losses of balance: he slumps, sprawls and, laughing hysterically, crawls on his stomach near broken glass. Again, these mad, inhuman vicissitudes (up, down; low, high; dark, light; windy, still) relate to a situation of constant turmoil in which nothing can be stable, everything is pell-mell, formless and, as Barthes says, "piecemeal." To paraphrase Barthes (he is not speaking here of clouds specifically), the clouds are *landmarks of the unfulfilled*, partly because they do not stay in place long enough to qualify as successful landmarks, and partly because their tumultuous changing bespeaks the very restlessness of unfulfillment.[4]

However, Barthes' theory of discontinuous nature is ultimately more pessimistic than what we see in Van Sant's films. Barthes says that "nobody reduces [vestiges of modern nature] to the manifestation of a mental behaviour, or of an intention, or some evidence of tenderness...."[5] Modern writing, according to Barthes, has surrendered the field of communication to meaningless discontinuity, no longer aspiring to the "immediately social" and "persuasive continuum" of classical form.[6] But for Van Sant, there is an attempt — if only by filming the clouds and editing them into an overarching and meaningful narrative framework — to link these ragged edges of the natural world back to the human emotions and thoughts whose referents they are: the longing that Walt feels for Johnny (a billowing emotion, too large for the time and space which tries to contain it); the frustrated longing that Mike feels toward his absent mother (as an eternally recurring cycle of memory, awareness, and subsequent physiological shutting-down).

Van Sant makes his cloud-poetry resonate with human emotions, while Barthes is unwilling to acknowledge that such "poetry" *can* ever be human, at least by classical standards, because it is, he says, "a *climate*" rather than a language. Barthes uses the oddly contradictory adjectives, "uniform and indecisive," to describe this climate.[7] And yet, the idea of a (visual) poetry as a climate further explicates the meteorological metaphors in Van Sant's films. And not only because feelings and circumstances can be intense and contradictory, a conditional state of flux best defined in terms of weather, as the fateful downpour in *Psycho* reminds us, or as Alex notes in *Elephant* when he quotes *Macbeth* in the middle of the massacre: "So fair and foul a day I have not seen." But, even more than this, because the societal realm is itself the truly unstable one. Both Walt and Mike are veritable children of the clouds, displaced here on earth, where they limp along like the albatross in Baudelaire's famous poem, a king in exile once he is deprived of his majestic flight.[8] Walt and Mike are in a similar exile, stemming from the fact that their impossible romantic love — much like the modern language which Barthes characterizes precisely as an in-between thing, simultaneously in thrall to a scattered, fragmentary Nature *and* a futile attempt to somehow "fix" this Nature in time and space[9] — is a language not commonly spoken in the world, or rather, not immediately answerable by the objects (straight men) to whom that love attaches. Such love lacks the communal-social aspect of the unity and conformity of classical language,[10] and of heterosexual standardization, and thus falls into alienation.

Cloudscapes are not the only example of visual intertextuality in Van Sant's early films — grungy variations on the Pietà are another. The Pietà, the image of the dead Christ being cradled by Mary, is a religious icon which has transcended religion itself and become, in many ways, a universal image of

2. Cloudscaptes and Pietàs: Visual Intertextuality

In *Good Will Hunting* (1997), the troubled Will (Matt Damon) finds solace and redemption in the arms of Skylar (Minnie Driver). Van Sant borrows, here as elsewhere in his films, the classical composition of the Pietà, in which Mary holds the martyred Christ. Although retaining some of the form of traditional iconography, Van Sant often reconfigures the genders, so that the comforting male-female embrace, shown here, becomes male-male in *Mala Noche* (1987) and *My Own Private Idaho* (1991).

succor and mourning. It was a staple of classical painting. Modern compositions appropriated from, or based on, the Pietà occur in all four of Van Sant's first features, and are particularly numerous in *My Own Private Idaho*.

Van Sant's Pietàs are interesting in that they sometimes reconfigure the standard gender assignments of classical Pietàs (mother as comforter/mourner, son as sacrifice), resetting the image in contexts which become infused with the sexual energies of both heterosexuality and homosexuality. In *Mala Noche*, for example, when Pepper is shot by the police, the angry, grief-stricken Walt kneels beside his body and clasps him in his hands. He looks up as if to condemn the virtually faceless authority of the cops who have killed the immigrant youth. Here, we see the subversive potentiality of a Pietà with two male lovers, in which the venerating love of the survivor is no less sacred for being homoerotic, nor the death of the young man any less a kind of martyrdom.

In *Even Cowgirls Get the Blues*, there is a moment quite similar to the death of Pepper in *Mala Noche*; when Bonanza Jellybean is shot from her horse, her lover Sissy Hankshaw (Uma Thurman) bends down to her body and looks up, again, as if to condemn the authority responsible for her death (the state troopers). Yet, earlier in the same film, there is a scene in the lobby of the Countess' New York highrise, where Sissy meets Julian (Keanu Reeves), who is in love with her and collapses under a violent asthma attack due to the pressure of meeting her face to face; the unconscious Julian is dragged from the lobby out to the sidewalk by some of his companions. Unlike classical Pietàs, this rough carting-about of Julian (Van Sant intercuts a shot of Julian's legs kicking and thrashing against the pavement) belies the idea that the cradling of an inert, helpless body is always an act of tenderness and compassion; instead, we sense something almost sinister and malign, as if Julian were being left to languish and even die, and as if his companions were merely disposing of him rather than trying to come to his aid. (In fact Julian is taken by taxi to a ritzy condo where he recovers after a shot of adrenalin.)

The Pietà-compositions in *Drugstore Cowboy* involve the two couples in the film, Bob and Diane (Kelly Lynch), and Rick (James LeGros) and Nadine (Heather Graham). All four are junkies, "crucified" by their habit and by the drug-enforcement police bent on hunting them down. During the scene in which Bob and Diane warn Rick and Nadine of the jinxes that result from dogs and from hats on beds, we see Bob leaning into Diane's bosom, and Rick virtually curled up in Nadine's lap. However, unlike the death scenes in *Mala Noche* and *Even Cowgirls Get the Blues*, the sense of angst, here, is more inflated than real; the junkies are self-obsessed and self-sensitive, viewing themselves narcissistically as tragic heroes trapped in endless cycles of superstitious bad luck and persecution. Of course, bad things have a way of happening to junkies, recalling Nietzsche's aphorism, "Terrible experiences pose the riddle whether the person who has them is not terrible."[11] The junkies create their own "bad luck," so to speak, and their obsession with jinxes is revealed as a structure which they attempt to impose upon the random and constant ill effects of their addiction, giving them the illusion that they can manage and stave off the always impending disasters while continuing their drug use unabated. The problem is not with them or the drugs themselves, but instead with the occurrence of little dogs in their lives, or hats on beds. This lack of self-knowledge means that the comfort depicted in the film's pseudo–Pietàs becomes as inflated and fake as the tragic, "woe-is-me" posturing which the physical proximity is meant to console.

We see that real tragedy, when it does occur in *Drugstore Cowboy*, cannot be easily slotted into familiar, easy, culturally conditioned visual patterns like Pietàs; nor can it be shared in the Pietà-like cradling of bodies. Nadine, the friendliest and least hooked of all four, and the one providing succor to Rick throughout the film, is (with dark irony) the one who overdoses and dies. There is nothing inflated and grandiose about the presence of actual death. Indeed, real death exposes the Pietàs, along with the junkies' needy self-pity, as phony and incommensurate, and aesthetically the film's stylings simultaneously become more abstruse and alienated. Like a glass-eyed doll, Nadine's corpse is laid out in the fluffy, snow-like insulation of a motel-room crawlspace; later, Bob zips her into a dry-cleaner's garment bag and buries her in the woods alone, to the dissonant background music of what sounds like a zither and an accordion; and when Bob himself is ultimately shot and driven off in an ambulance, he, too, must face the nearness of death alone, a livid, sweating death mask strapped to a gurney, passing through alternating light and shadow, and without anyone's arms around him. (This motif becomes central to *Restless*, in which Enoch's general obsession with death is finally clarified and exorcised by falling in love with and saying goodbye to the terminally ill Annabel.)

The Pietàs in *My Own Private Idaho* all revolve around Mike as the sacrificial son figure. In one (a dream), he is cradled by his mother, and looks, at this moment, more peaceful and beatific than anywhere else in the film. In the others, he is held by his best friend and love-object, Scott. In one shot, he sleeps on Scott's lap at a fountain in Portland. Later, he is carried, also sleeping, in Scott's arms. But again, in a way that is similar to *Drugstore Cowboy* albeit more tender, these comforts are fleeting and largely figurative in contrast to Mike's need, which is genuine and fathomless; the succor which he receives in these various Pietà-compositions is, sadly, incommensurate with that need. In the end, when Mike is picked up, comatose, on a highway and placed in a car, it is by a passing stranger whose intentions seem ominous. Again, Van Sant seems to say that when death comes it is always faced alone — and the secondhand cultural meaning of the Pietà, to universalize suffering and mourning, and to ameliorate loss, collapses in the face of stark reality.

Indeed, like the cloudscapes, these Pietàs tap into what we might call "cultural emotions." They are invested with the solemnity and significance of the original Pietà itself, even as they play with the possible permutations of who the Christ figure can be (immigrant, junky, hustler) and who the succoring figure can be (a lover, gay or straight). In this sense, Van Sant's Pietàs subvert the narrow idea that comfort is *only* a function of Christian iconography. As we see in the work of such diverse directors as Buñuel and Fellini, Pasolini and Peckinpah, so we also see in Van Sant: "the divine" applies more to people from the lowest rungs of the social order than the highest, and even forms of love considered abject and taboo must be held sacred because they are already sacred to those who feel and experience them. Especially when it comes to the visual art of cinema, spirituality lies within the realm of immanence and earthly feeling, rather than within the (unvisualizable) realm of "transcendence."

When time-lapse cloudscapes reappear in Van Sant's later work, specifically the opening credit sequences of *Elephant* and *Paranoid Park*, they seem to take on a different meaning. For one thing, they are no longer embedded within the narrative, as poetic metaphors for specific actions within the film. Instead, they seem to take place outside the diegesis, although they could be seen as commentaries on, even radical encapsulations of, the entire narrative, in that they highlight the fleetingness of time and the shifting, anti-linear nature of circumstance. *Elephant*'s sequence is dominated by a streetlamp, the one fixed element in the time-lapse, surrounded by indistinct off-camera voices, changing light (the streetlamp comes on as the twilight darkens into night), and moving clouds. *Paranoid Park* opens with a cityscape of Portland featuring Burnside Bridge, seemingly over a twenty-four hour period while traffic flows back and forth across the bridge and the light changes from day to a night-time glittering with city lights.

A few things come to mind when watching these sequences. First, these cloudscapes are more attached to the world-below than the airy ones in Van Sant's early films. They are united to the earth by human voices and the streetlamp in *Elephant*, and by Burnside Bridge and the Portland skyline in *Paranoid Park*. Thus, rather than isolating a metonymy for pure, even rarefied feeling within a baseless patch of air and sky — Barthes' "indecisive" climate — they marry the drift of clouds with the ostensibly grounded network of urban and suburban spaces. As such, they represent an even greater turn toward secular humanism: no God is watching over us, only a streetlamp, placed there by electrification and city planning. Only civilization can police, condemn or improve civilization — a bad bet in *Elephant*, where civilization breaks down completely, but more hopeful, perhaps, in *Paranoid Park*, where remorse follows crime and the hero may receive a second chance. Likewise, a bridge like the Burnside is itself an emblem of humanism, one of the most awe-inspiring examples of human ingenuity, a wonder of science, engineering and the determination to link the world and improve it. As the poet Hart Crane knew, writing about Brooklyn Bridge, such a mammoth connecting structure "lends a myth to God"[12] — humanity's triumph overshadows the claims of a God.

Second, there is a strong sense that these sequences telescope an entire twenty-four period, say — given the change of light in both from daylight to darkness — into a matter of minutes. Thus, they become a kind of shorthand for the unity of time and place in ancient Greek tragedy. Van Sant makes a conscious link between the modern era and the classical past; furthermore, these classical unities are largely upheld by the films, both of which, apart from a few flashbacks and time-shifts (more complex and numerous in *Paranoid Park*), take place on single days: *Elephant* on the day of a school shooting, and *Paranoid Park* on the day when the beleaguered Alex writes and then burns his lengthy confession in an act of personal exorcism. The use of blocks of "real time" in both films only serves to reinforce the idea that we are watching a unified unfolding of events (albeit open to memory and other instances of layered time).

In addition to evoking the dramatic unity of ancient tragedies, these time-lapse skyscapes essentially replace the role of the tragic chorus, who usually introduced the main action, characters and themes of the drama to follow. The chorus was the play's overt link to society, presenting a collective viewpoint through which the audience could identify with the play. The chorus asked the same questions about fate and justice which the audience was expected to ask and perhaps answer. *Elephant* and *Paranoid Park*, then, are modern tragedies without a chorus, and finally without judgment per se. Audience identification is left to itself to decide how to interpret the action and with whom to identify. More than this, the social nature of art—what Barthes noted in the certainties of classical rhetoric, its ostensible ability to speak for all of society in an immediately comprehensible language[13]—is jettisoned in favor of the modern and discontinuous, where viewpoints come and go accidentally, cut into each other, and largely end in stalemates, vortices of inaction.

To the extent that these sequences are self-contained, they also function, in a way that perhaps could be called "*cinema* degree zero," as near-quotations within the films. They are non-specific quotations, and suggest a kind of filmmaking technique (time-lapse cinematography) which we recognize from common usage. They function like the obligatory elements of painting or writing which are pure technique, and which serve to create background — but to a certain extent, that sense of *being all-background* is precisely the point. Obligatory displays of technique, as we know from Barthes in *Writing Degree Zero*, always signify that the artist is participating in something communal or universal: "'Poetic,' in the days of classicism, never evokes any particular domain, any particular depth of feeling, any special coherence, or separate universe, but only an individual handling of a verbal technique, that of 'expressing oneself' according to rules more artistic, therefore more sociable, than those of conversation, in other terms, the technique of projecting out an inner thought, springing fully armed from the Mind, a speech which is made more socially acceptable by virtue of the very conspicuousness of its conventions."[14] The fact that time-lapse photography *always* evokes feelings of time, change and mortality only serves to strengthen its efficacy as technique and as a trigger of communal feelings.

This is not to say that the sequences have no meaning beyond themselves. In fact, with their concentration on single phallic architectures (streetlamp, bridge), they are reminiscent of Warhol's experimental film *Empire* (1964), as

Stephen Koch describes it, "eight hours of the Empire State Building and the majestic passage of day and night."[15] *Empire* was the opposite of time-lapse, it was real time; the light changes naturally, barely perceptibly. Koch writes: "The sun moves through the sky. At dusk, the floodlights illuminating the upper thirty floors come on. (The spectator must be attentive; the climactic moment is brief and easy to miss.)"[16] Is time-lapse the impatience of real time, and is its rewarded attention, therefore, less genuine? The idea in *Empire* was to turn the building into a kind of readymade star: "Warhol himself famously declared ... 'The Empire State Building is a star ... an eight-hour hard on'"[17]; but more than that, *Empire* is also clearly a kind of valentine to Warhol's adoptive home of New York City, which at that time was also the "empire" of the gay underground cinema which Warhol (and others) represented.

In beginning *Elephant* and *Paranoid Park* with what I would call mini-tributes to *Empire*, but setting them deliberately in Portland, Van Sant may be performing a double critique of history. On one hand, he may be suggesting that the empire (as in center) of experimental filmmaking has moved from New York to Portland (at least for him). In another, larger sense, Van Sant may also be suggesting that the idea of American empire itself is shifting, away from the coastal megalopolises and into the heartland of rural and suburban America. This corresponds with Van Sant's vision of a cinema that revolves around the experience of marginalized groups, particularly adolescents. Indeed, we might think of *My Own Private Idaho*, in part, as a re-envisioning of *Midnight Cowboy* (1969), in which "Joe Buck" chooses to remain in the Midwest and do his hustling there as if it was New York; and of course, he finds, wherever he goes, the same urgent, offbeat desires and the same willingness to pay for that temporary refuge which "perfect flesh" affords.

When he becomes desperate, Bob in *Drugstore Cowboy* (both novel and film), prays, "God, Sun, Devil, whoever you are up there," revealing the roots of modern religious belief and superstition in ancient pagan worship of the sun and sky, a worship born from incomprehension, terror and awe. Indeed, it is not hard to imagine that the earliest conceptions of a powerful, life-giving and life-destroying God came from ancient man's bewildered relation to the sky, and his yearning for its remote, desolate purity.

Cameras — from the camera obscura to the digital — have mediated between man's desire to see directly into the sun, and his inability to do so without harm to the naked eye. How many literally went blind trying to satisfy an understandable curiosity about the felt, blazing presence above and all around them, that primal source unavailable to direct sight, and how many superstitions about the cosmos did this torment give rise to? Photography and cinema have come to seem like new religions in our time, because of the way in which they have allowed man to trap light in a flat, harmless surface, something one can gaze at and hold in one's hands; put otherwise, to finally see and grasp the infinite, the ineffable, the divine. The metaphysics of the camera, like all other kinds, is concerned with crossing the borders of visibility and invisibility. Since the sun "could only be indirectly re-presented to a human eye," camera technology "was a defense against the madness and unreason of dazzlement."[18]

Not that Van Sant seeks to destroy ineffability and mystery with his camera; he is a pioneer of the mystique of plain images (somewhat like Bresson, and with a similar propensity to select non-actors with evocative looks or surfaces and simply film them "being"). In all of this, again, we can see the importance of the sky- and cloudscapes, and the factual, rather than allegorical, way in which they are presented by Van Sant. Why further bedazzle what is already sufficiently dazzling?

At the same time, the sky, that ultimate barrier to man's sight and movement, remains panoramic, chilling and awe-inspiring in Van Sant's films — what we also feel in the deep hyperspace of Kubrick's *2001: A Space Odyssey* (1968) but in a more natural, less artificially constructed way. And the enigma of the sky, in turn, obliquely responds to, and amplifies, the mystery of Van Sant's offbeat characters, who have no solid ground to stand on, and who (sometimes fatally) try to see too deeply into the burning center of life itself, the place where light is strongest but also most volatile and annihilating.

3. Schizo-ing *Psycho*: Quotational Intertextuality

Freud says that the only happy men are those whose boyhood dreams are realized. The danger is to walk through life without seeing anything. — Burroughs[1]

And of course you can kidnap someone else's characters and put them in a different set. The whole gamut of painting, writing, music, film, is yours to use. — Burroughs[2]

The insignificance of the origin increases with the full knowledge of the original ... [T]he nearest reality, that which is around us and inside of us, little by little starts to display colour and beauty and enigma and a wealth of meaning — things which earlier men never dreamed of. — Friedrich Nietzsche[3]

But why should I be original? Why can't I be non-original? — Andy Warhol[4]

The story goes (it plays like clever fiction, but it's true) that in 1953 the young Robert Rauschenberg showed up at Willem de Kooning's studio with an odd request. Rauschenberg wanted the older, established painter, whose work he admired and emulated, to give him a pencil drawing. He told de Kooning that he wanted to erase the drawing and sign his own name to it. This landmark episode in the history of the New York art world was also an important moment in the evolution of conceptual art. Conceptual art is a gesture of redefining what a work of art can be; it does not have to be utilitarian or aesthetically pleasing or especially original. It simply has to have the boldness to exist.

Or to barely exist, as Rauschenberg's *Erased de Kooning* ended up "a ghostly monochromatic work without imagery."[5] De Kooning's worthy biographers describe the moment as an Oedipal exchange of power between a spiritual father and son: "He told Rauschenberg: 'I know what you're doing.' ... De Kooning recognized that Rauschenberg's request was a deep if disturbing compliment: the son loves the father whom he must kill. And so, he returned the compliment.... Finally, he selected an important, fleshy drawing for sacrifice — a dense mixed-media image"[6] that took Rauschenberg more than two months to erase sufficiently.

I would suggest, however, that a strictly Oedipal reading of this scene is one which misses the crucial forging of an intertextual relationship between the artists, both of whom were needed for the concept to work, and both of whom understood this. However, "de Kooning became angry when the younger artist publicly exhibited *Erased de Kooning*. De Kooning believed the [Oedipal] murder should have remained private, a personal affair between artists, rather than splashed before the public. He was from an older generation."[7]

As with any work of conceptual art, the triumph for Rauschenberg was that he had thought to do it in the first place, and also that he had been able to finesse the unique opportunity to do it. In being able to erase and sign his name to a more famous artist's work, Rauschenberg, "like a boy with his hand eternally caught in the cookie jar,"[8] had pulled off a social coup *en famille* more than an aesthetic one. He had laid claim to a certain place at a certain table; he had succeeded in getting art itself to make room for him.

Psycho, Van Sant's reworking of the Sir Alfred Hitchcock classic, has been one of his most disparaged and neglected films, usually dismissed with either a simple "Why — what's the point?" or with nearly rabid outrage that *anyone* would touch something so sacrosanct, ostensibly a sacred text of cinema. Indeed, the original *Psycho* is one of the handful of movie experiences that has left an indelible mark on our collective imagination. (Although I hope no one is still refraining from taking showers.) And yet, as perhaps the most famous mainstream film ever made about schizophrenia, doesn't *Psycho*, of all films, cry out for a kind of schizo-ing, a doubling, an intertextual "evil twin?" Doesn't Hitchcock's exhibitionistic display of scopophilia cry out for another to witness it, as if in an infinite regress? Finally, doesn't Hitchcock's systematic deconstruction of the fetish object (maternal body, knife, stuffed bird, money, etc.) intersect with the aesthetic project of deconstructing what Burroughs called "the fetish of originality ... the sterile and assertive ego that imprisons as it creates"?[9]

Van Sant's film needs to be considered not as rote remake but as one of the most significant examples of his intertextual approach to filmmaking. Nearly all of Hitchcock's original *Psycho* is "quoted" in Van Sant's version with no attempt to disguise or edit these quotations. Thus, it is an extreme example of Barthes' "writing degree zero" applied to filmmaking: originality is bypassed as a meaningless fetish; Van Sant expresses his own aesthetic will precisely through his appropriation of Hitchcock's aesthetic will, making *Psy-*

cho an example of quotational intertextuality, or appropriation. However, as with all intertextuality, this quoting is significant in itself, and is not devoid of Van Sant's own artistic personality.

We see this in certain places where the seams of appropriation are made to show through, in the form of changes or comments which Van Sant makes to the original material. For example, in a viscerally literal way, the slashing of Norman Bates' carving knife[10] allows Van Sant the opportunity to "cut up" the recreation of Hitchcock's text with inserted shots of hallucinated, collective-unconscious imagery during the murder scenes. Van Sant leaves open the question of whether this imagery (a bull in mist, a masked nude, a time-lapse cloudscape like the ones discussed in the previous chapter) is being "seen" by Norman as he kills or by the victim as she or he is killed, or if it is the filmmaker's interpolated descriptive commentary upon the act of murder itself. (Inserts of fast-moving clouds are later used during the murder scene in *Gerry*.) In any event, these hallucinations cut up the original and make new textual readings possible. Also, Norman's final monologue, in his cell, is a brilliant aural cut-up of the original text, here delivered both by Norman's and the mother's voice (in fact a group of several voices was overdubbed in choral fashion[11]), echoing, interrupting and foreclosing upon each other's statements. Meanwhile, whole set-ups, décors, and indeed, most of the dialogue have been retained — "folded in" so as to create the basis of rapport between the texts.

Not that the two films ever present simplistic or identical mirrors of each other, even when Van Sant's quoting appears to be more or less seamless. Although most of the same shots, edits, and dialogue are repeated, it is not so much a question of duplication as of parallelism. When considering both *Psychos* in tandem (and they are best watched that way), it is useful not only to consider intertextuality theory, but also the theory of parallel universes. Events, situations, dialogue — all are familiar. Yet all are slightly or considerably different as well, as if a single original tweaking gave rise to an entirely different evolutionary path which subsequently changed everything.

The actors, for one thing, are living presences who do not so much mimic the original performances but recreate them, often in very distinctive and inspired ways. One might liken it to two different football teams running the same plays. Likewise, everything in Van Sant's *Psycho* is automatically different because it is a color film where Hitchcock's was black and white. His decision to use color instead of Hitchcock's classically noirish black-and-white was an enormous aesthetic risk; but the decision ended up being perfect for the film Van Sant wanted to make. We live in a color world, a world of spectrums, and I don't mean this to sound as superficial as it might seem; the world is no less savage, tragic and strange for being a world of spectrums. *Psycho* was always a tale of poisoned family ties, of normal appearances harboring twisted, disturbed meanings, and indeed, in Van Sant's *Psycho* many of the film's psychological elements are given a greater and more consistent sense of nuance precisely *because* they exist within a recognizable spectrum. As a culture, we are already far beyond Serial Killing 101, so to speak, and since cinephiles already know the plot (the mother is a stuffed corpse; Norman commits the murders dressed like her, etc.), Van Sant is free to explore the characters' motivations while letting the story unfold, rather than waiting to tie everything together, as Hitchcock did, with the court psychiatrist's final analysis: a rather long-winded, textbook-like speech which Van Sant reduces to bare bones of hushed fascination.

Among other things, the use of color allows Van Sant to reflect the characters' states of mind through a symphonic riffing on different shades of green, one of the film's main palettes (the entire red spectrum. from crimson to pink, and various off-whites are also used significantly).[12] In a film whose plot is doubly motivated, for Marion (Anne Heche) by greed and money, and for Norman (Vince Vaughn) by extremely morbid jealousy (the jealousy which we are told is the ruling passion behind all his murders), green is the perfect color to express their colliding trajectories as co-protagonists. The opening credits (preserving Saul Bass's stylish design) are in black and Day-Glo green. Marion wears a green bra and slip in the scene where she packs to abscond with the money; the highway patrolman who stops her on the road wears a green uniform; her drive from Phoenix out to Fairvale, California, is pervaded by increasing amounts of trees, shrubs and grass along the highway. At the used car lot, she trades in her car for a light green one.

By the time she arrives at the Bates Motel, Marion has entered a kind of green hell. The tones have become more lurid, warning signals: the neon Vacancy and Office signs glow chartreuse. Norman wears a forest-green corduroy jacket over a light green shirt. Marion's motel room features green drapes and a green bedspread, and a vibrant emerald robe is the first thing she unpacks from her suitcase. The interior of Norman's office, where she talks with him over sandwiches and milk, is predominantly green, and during Norman's angriest moments, the green décor behind his medium close-ups becomes an unfocused, nearly abstract space; meanwhile, in her medium close-ups, Marion is hemmed-in between a green loveseat and a green phone. Moments later, when Norman spies on Marion through his peep-hole, she strips down to her green bra, then puts on the emerald robe. There are numerous other green details strewn throughout the film, last and not least the green blanket offered to Norman in his cell as the world's final comfort. If it originally begins as expressing greed, on one hand, and jealousy, on the other, the color green comes to occupy several different stages of meaning, suggesting decomposition — the hatband worn by the detective Arbogast (William H. Macy) is the pale green of certain kinds of mold — as well as, notably, a color coding for homosexuals "passing" in straight society. Norman, accepting the blanket in the high, polite, feminine voice of his mother, causes the police officer to do a double take: green is, finally, the devastating, terrifying color of the closet and what might lie (moldering) inside it.

According to Van Sant, one of the main differences between the original and his version is the moralistic baggage surrounding Marion's murder: in the original, she is killed as "a punishment for having stolen the money," a 19th century "deus ex machina" which we as audiences no longer trust.[13] Nor, for that matter, do most people today need to be enlightened about the difference between a transvestite/transsexual and a mother-fixated killer like Bates. Again, one of Van Sant's biggest textual changes to the script is the climactic (or anticlimactic) speech by the court psychiatrist, Dr. Simon (played by Robert Forster in the remake), who, in Hitchcock's original, seems to have stepped out of Ed Wood's *Glen or Glenda?* (1952) to give a few stentorian notes from Kraft-Ebbing. Indeed, no one in the 1998 film is quite so naïve.

Thus, we must first confront the archetype of the Bad Girl (or Fallen Woman) who, even in 1960, had one high heel planted in the 19th century. Narrative has always thrived on the conflicts inherent in socially proscribed/prescribed relationality. In fact, it is time that we stop considering narrative, as brought to fruition within the 19th century novel, *strictly* in Marxist-materialist terms (narrative as material accumulation, as imperialist colonization, etc.) and view it in terms of the way society enforced the institutions of heterosexual marriage and family. The impulse to tell stories about how people come together, love, find happiness or tragedy, existed for centuries prior to, outside of, and even now beyond the high era of industrial-capitalist production. What motivated the novel in its epic-saga form was less the replication of rampant materialism so much as the tensions that resulted in a society where even the most private relationships were conditioned and controlled by the social order. In eras when people could not easily walk away from bad marriages, or when adult children had to obey their parents in all decisions, narrative thrived on teasing out the resulting conflicts, the stigma and shame. Many of the greatest novelists — Hardy, Flaubert, Tolstoy, Fontane, Wharton, James, etc.— wrote about bad marriages that could not be ended; about love affairs with people who were socially inappropriate, and therefore doomed to fail and bring ruin.

The subsequent decline of narrative, and the search for alternatives to old-fashioned, linear narrative forms, are, therefore, sociopolitical phenomena, inextricably tied to the individual freedom that people have today, relative to olden times, to lead alternative lives. Today, we tend to see relationality much differently: people walk away from committed relationships and marriages every day; they also defy their parents' judgments, or become involved with people whom their "social sets" might frown upon. The laws have not only been rewritten but completely overturned — and in terms of personal romantic and erotic freedom, this is a very good thing. It has been a confounding thing for art, however, since fiction has been, ever since the early 20th century, thrown back on the solipsism of the free but restless individual, and the "atomized" society. The stream-of-consciousness and existential novelists, for example, hardly concerned with issues of social morality per se, focused instead on psychoanalytic revelations, jumbled time and abstruse private associations; while Beckett and the workers of the Nouveau Roman presented externalized metaphors for solitude, paralysis and decay. Again, we see that relationality, more than material plenitude, drives narrative, and just as discursive freedom replaced social conventions, so it has replaced conventional narrative in the aesthetic realm.

But loneliness is often an unintended side-effect of freedom. Thus, intertextuality serves the purpose (among others) of doing "the work of culture, a culture that has become scattered, fragmented, dispersed in the invisible archives of many languages, but one that is seeking to gain wholeness, unity, and logic."[14] The intertext attempts to fuse imposed cultural separations, to make the incoherent cohere, and if we do not recognize "the work of culture" immediately in the formal violence with which intertextuality often presents itself, this is only because we must "cut" further and further, juggle the pieces in our hands, before we can begin to take their measure, and start piecing them back together.

So the cut-up enables the writer Burroughs to rework or manipulate a prior text. This intertextuality with texts of the past defines narrative as an anachronistic art; it is only possible in reference to the past. Entry points into present and future begin by tweaking a textual past, shifting it until it yields a different meaning — like those evolutionary tweaks that comprise the progress of life within the (parallel) universe. One can manipulate the past until one no longer exists, or one's existence is a diaphanously floating fact, rather than an arduous labor. In *Psycho*, for example, the past is locked in an ongoing dynamic of changing the present and future, based on identity problems and deceptions that must be followed through once undertaken, mainly the reification of Norman's childhood world within his adult one, but also, in other, more specific ways: Marion struggles with going back to Phoenix, the scene of her crime; Norman has committed other murders in the past and covered them up; no one is buried in Mrs. Bates' plot, etc. This leads, strangely enough, not to a point where storytelling is rendered impossible by discontinuous identities, but instead to a kind of ongoing nirvana of narrative, in which identity is finally meaningless but the story itself, as a master narrative, precludes anyone from stepping outside it (death comes to some characters long before the tangled story is unraveled). Like intertextuality itself, everything refers backwards to a previous point of identification which has not yet ended, and whose efficacy, like the adoption of an alias, or an alibi, can go on and on, "covering for" the present. It is like an author's creations taking on a life of their own, and preempting any need on his part to maneuver them. Burroughs writes: "Here we are in texts already written. Where [the writer] doesn't need to write anymore."[15] And elsewhere he invokes the "recurrent writer's dream" of channeling perfect and prewritten words by

> picking up a book and starting to read. I can never bring back more than a few sentences; still, I know the book itself will hover over the typewriter as I copy the words already written there.[16]

Like a successful alias/alibi, intertextuality *protects* someone from the demands of identity.

To create anything new is to experience doubt, to have one's self thrown into question; there is paradise in drawing on a universal, unconscious reservoir of meanings that seem to have always already existed, and which are not, therefore, conditioned by an impossible or distorted or false relationality. Relationality is redeemed, intertextually, even as it is seemingly sundered by the same intertextual (cutting-up) process. In this sense, the original *Psycho* already speaks to the growing postwar realization that narrative had become anachronistic due to changing rules of relationality. On one hand, it is centered around perhaps the ultimate fate of arbitrary modern relationality: falling prey to a serial killer. However, as if in order to ameliorate such extremity, it surrounds the killings themselves with relationships that express a sort of impossible nostalgia for bygone relationality, impossible even in the 1960 original: Marion's boyfriend Sam and sister Lila take comfort in each other as they search for Marion; the detective Arbogast is helpful and kind, etc. Nonetheless, even the original atypically frustrates the logic of happy endings: Abogast, too, is killed, and although we have seen Sam and Lila pose as husband and wife in their search for Marion, there is no easy hope that they will come together as a couple. In fact, by the end of the film, Norman's shocking "coupling" with his mother has entirely foreclosed upon our natural feelings toward *any* kind of marriage. *Psycho* makes one root for staying single.

Psycho showed how sexual mores were beginning to change in the postwar years; but only just. For the first audiences who watched *Psycho* in 1960, they must have been watching to see who the "psycho" in the title was — and indeed, everyone behaves strangely, impulsively, suggestively. It could have been Marion herself, since there was ostensible stigma in her affair with a divorced man still economically tied to his ex-wife, her willingness to meet in hotels on her lunch break. Only mid-way through the film does Norman emerge as the true aberration because he stops all narrative and relationality cold in its tracks; he and his mother truly stand outside relational logic — the insane ones, terrifying but also oddly touching in the way they are so thoroughly excluded from the world (and must therefore hack their way back in).

Van Sant's version preserves Norman as a tragic-romantic figure who preempts narrative logic. But in 1998, we are less convinced by the logic of Marion's shame: why shouldn't she date a divorced man, or have sex out of wedlock — or in a hotel on her lunch, for that matter? The theft of the money, which arises from guilty sexual passion in the original, and functions as a would-be shortcut to marriage and respectability, becomes almost a separate issue in the remake, proof of an even deeper kinkiness in Marion.

Marion, a quintessential "Fifties Woman" in her subjugation of her own ego to the needs of men, does not have to be, for us, a Fallen Woman, or rather, not the 19th century kind, for whom sex in itself signifies moral failing. However, her sacrificial nature remains to be explained; thus, she must become something more like Submissive Woman, whose tendency is to seek out unattainable, unavailable men, or even get herself into situations where she is being used. In the original, Sam (played by John Gavin) strove heroically to demonstrate that he was a good man in spite of the fact that he was sleeping with Marion sans commitment. In Van Sant's *Psycho*, Sam (Viggo Mortensen) is less stalwart, less concerned with proving his virtuous intentions: he may be struggling financially, he may want to be rid of his ex-wife, but he might also, in the sense that we have come to think of as endemic to scenarios of affairs and the "other woman," be leading Marion on. The specter of the ex serves to keep the current relationship from falling into too strict a commitment; psychologically, this is a more penetrating understanding of Sam.

Marion attempts to set ground rules with Sam: "We can see each other. But *respectably*." In other words, no more nooners in cheap hotels. In the original, Janet Leigh as Marion speaks this line forcefully, whereas Anne Heche rushes through it, giggling lasciviously, as if baiting her lover to trample on yet another attempt of hers to state her relationship needs. And indeed, barely missing a beat, Van Sant's Sam more or less deflects Marion's spoken and unspoken misgivings. A key Marion line in the original is her response to Sam: "You make respectability sound so ... disrespectful." Leigh puts a full pause before the final adjective, as if flustered anger were forcing her to search for the right word, and, with eyebrow raised, cheekbones set, eyes flashing in Leigh's inimitable way, she takes the conversation further away from sexual flirtatiousness and more toward a kind of accusatory soul-searching. Above all, she rejects being made to feel like a bad girl. Heche, almost by total contrast, speaks the words ironically, with downcast eyes, as if it were a kind of inside understanding which the couple shares; she gives Sam opportunities to disrespect her because it turns them both on. Also, she does not face Sam but looks at their double reflection in a mirror, which distances their eye contact even as it frames them in a complicit two-shot; then, Marion's rote protest rendered and summarily shut down, Sam, fully nude, walks away to raise the blinds of the hotel room window, his nakedness on open display to disarm the guilt that Marion has tried to make him feel. He makes an appeal to her on the basis of the unconquerable lust which he understands her to have for him. Again, Marion's submissive side, in Van Sant's film, is aroused by the way Sam deliberately *makes* her feel like a bad girl.

In the largest sense, permitting Sam and Marion to be more of a modern (and kinky) couple, Van Sant unscrambles some of the Manichaeism — almost Medieval in its logic — whereby the Fallen Woman, repentant too late, gets snatched away by punitive, violent death in the 1960 *Psycho*. Marion met

In *Psycho* (1998), Sam (Viggo Mortensen) puts the squeeze on Marion (Anne Heche) in a jail-like hotel room. One of the main ways that Van Sant and actress Heche opened up the original *Psycho* (1960) was in modernizing the character of Marion Crane, transforming her from a baffled "Fallen Woman" to a markedly more knowing "Kinky Woman," thereby able to take more agency in her own self-destructive, "naughty" behaviors.

Bates in the original as the Fallen Woman meeting her grisly fate. In the 1998 film, it's a more complex movement: Heche's Marion, more easily suggestible, extends herself to Bates as if he, too — henpecked by his mother — were somehow a kindred spirit to herself and Sam, henpecked by the ex-wife. Leigh's Marion is convinced by her supper talk with Norman that it is crazy to act impulsively for love, and that sexual pleasure (which she euphemizes as her "private island") is most likely not worth it; whereas Heche's more bewildered Marion is almost dismissed by Norman with a sense that she has not quite gotten what she hoped for from the encounter. By the end of the supper scene in the original, we are uncomfortably aware — as the characters also are — that Marion and Norman are from two different planets; in fact, for once, Marion is normal! By the end of the same scene in Van Sant's film, we see, disturbingly, how Marion could have all too easily fallen in love with this Norman, had she shared his lonely rural childhood, perhaps.

Marion bravely and compassionately invites Norman's attention, here, although of course, she does not see the danger in him, or at least does not see it as life-threatening. The 1998 Marion has not been sheltered from angry men. Bates' more extreme rage in Van Sant's handling of the supper conversation does not faze Heche's Marion: she seems to recognize it, not as the original Marion does (as a rude warning, a crossing of lines), but rather as a kind of generic seduction, an abusive male energy that feels familiar even as it displaces her confidence and selfhood. In some ways, Van Sant (if only because of current sexual forthrightness) improves upon the way the original draws a relentless net of probing, narcissistic male attention around Marion — all drawing to a literal point in Norman's carving knife.

In fact, Van Sant does something more to valorize Marion and remove the onus from her as a sexual being who somehow "invites" her slaughter: he heightens the second murder, that of Arbogast, and creates more of an equivalency between the two killings. Van Sant does this, in one way, through the cutting-in of hallucinated apocalyptic imagery during both killings. But he also prepares Arbogast's murder in the earlier scene where the detective interrogates Norman, catching Norman in a lie and arousing Norman's suspicions. In the original *Psycho*, this interrogation scene is taken at a more rapid clip, with the staccato, interruptive dialogue-rhythms of classic noir. Van Sant, on the other hand, lingers over the dialogue, as well as holding reaction shots longer. From the moment where Arbogast pulls up to the motel to the fade-out on Norman alone again as Arbogast drives away, Van Sant's version is nearly a full minute longer than Hitchcock's. Hitchcock's lighting is also more muted, the entire scene is lit more starkly in the original, while Van Sant suffuses it with a strong glow that inflames both Norman's and Arbogast's faces, and renders their staring-match eye-contact all the more intense. Arbogast's

The interrogation scene between Arbogast (William H. Macy) and Norman (Vince Vaughn) compares well to the original. A stronger emotional tension is established, partly in Vaughn's taller and more solid physical presence, but mainly in the fact that Macy is kindly and searching, attempting to genuinely reach Norman. This emotional intimacy, like the more pointedly sexual one with Marion, triggers Norman's murder of Arbogast in a way that creates a greater and more psychologically penetrating equivalency between Norman's female and male victims.

wide eyes seem especially exposed and protuberant in this light, vulnerable; likewise, Norman's puffy, pouting lips are highlighted — his lips sputter out transparent lies which Arbogast's kindly but wary eyes drink in, knowing them to be lies. Arbogast is generally more kind and even deferential toward Norman in Van Sant's film, unlike the more streetwise performance which Martin Balsam gives in the original, where Arbogast seems more to be toying with Bates. In Van Sant's film there is a sincere attempt on Arbogast's part to reach Norman emotionally, an attempt which quickly stirs Norman to commit another murder. The conversation between Norman and Arbogast is one of the best directed scenes in all of Van Sant's work — and in the palpable tension between the men, close to the mesmerizing confrontation when Gunnar Björnstrand fails to reach Max von Sydow in Ingmar Bergman's *Nattvardsgästerna* (*Winter Light*, 1963).

The result of this tension is that, when Bates kills Arbogast in the Van Sant version, it is not just someone being "gotten out of the way" according to film noir convention: it is very nearly as intimate and sexualized a murder as Marion's killing was. Just as Marion's bare abdomen (the part which aroused Norman when he peeped at her) must be slashed, so, in this scene, it is Arbogast's eyes which have aroused Norman's emotions and must be slashed. This eye-slashing was in the original, but did not seem to mean as much, beyond being grisly and perhaps an oblique "punishment" to Arbogast for snooping or looking where Norman did not want him to; in the Van Sant version, this punishment is brought out as a further expression of Norman's projection of his own guilt, as highlighted previously in the exchange of guilty and suspicious stares between the two men during the interrogation.

As Norman, Vince Vaughn has the unenviable task of tackling another actor's signature role. Anthony Perkins was scrawny where Vaughn is beefy; Perkins was effeminate and nervous where Vaughn often seems on the verge of slipping off to some frat party. Perkins chewed the inside of his mouth like a man seemingly turning himself inside-out right in front of us. But Vaughn is deliberately less of a "gay stereotype" (the overtly neurotic Mama's Boy) than Perkins was. In 1960, what gave audiences the creeps was precisely a gay-seeming man so attached to his own dead mother that she foreclosed upon any possible sexual relations he could have with women: the homophobic stereotype itself was imbricated in the film's horror. What Van Sant wanted to correct about Bates seems to have been this flagrant homophobic element. Vaughn's Bates is a little boy unable to grow up emotionally, but in an overgrown adult body — this is the creepiness of his performance, the mismatching of childlike faces and words with outwardly adult appearance. As Sebastian Stoppe writes, this changes the dynamic between Norman and Sam, for instance; in the original, the scene where they chat over the check-in desk in motel office is more like casual "small talk," whereas in Van Sant's film, Norman is never not menacing. Norman "*bleibt auch hier, vor allem durch seine starke Gestik, die dominantere Person.*" [Norman "remains, even here, mostly through his muscular physicality, the dominant figure."][17]

Likewise, the sexuality of Vaughn's Bates is not hidden or repressed: he is able to masturbate, for instance, while watching Marion getting undressed through the peephole. This was something that Perkins' Bates could never have done, mainly because of 1960 censorship laws; but those laws fed into the presentation of Bates as so castrated, so latently gay, that he could not even become erect for a female much less bring himself to climax over one. Van Sant wants to redirect the terror that Vaughn inspires — as violator, as killer — away from homosexuality and toward heterosexuality, factually the more typical orientation for serial killers.

At the same time, as if to suggest that heterosexuals can be even kinkier than gays, Van Sant extends Norman's drag moment when he attacks Lila in the fruit cellar. Stoppe has noted that Van Sant holds the shot of Norman in drag, with knife raised, and even highlights it with a "vertigo effect," a forward zoom that makes the background seem to rapidly recede behind Bates.[18] Indeed, in the original, the moment of exposure — when Norman's wig slips off after Sam grabs him from behind — is traumatic enough to paralyze him almost instantly with guilt; he allows himself to be almost instantly subdued. However, the fight scene in Van Sant's version is altogether longer and, as Stoppe says, "more brutal."[19]

Also toward this end of emphasizing Norman as a disturbed straight rather than a closeted gay, Vaughn is more directly angry than Perkins, who tended to swallow all his negative feelings. The supper scene in the back office is perhaps the best evidence of this, where Vaughn seems about to fly into rage and kill Marion right there over the milk and sandwiches, under the glass eyes of the stuffed birds of prey. Perkins, in the original, became more intense, too, but with more of a sneer, a catty sarcasm in his voice than the potentially explosive rage which Vaughn brings to the scene. This more direct anger reminds me of Vince Bruce, the antihero played by Warren Beatty in another 60s classic about schizophrenia, Robert Rossen's *Lilith* (1964). Beatty's shy smile, his seething stares, his military build, his outbursts of physical temper — all are referenced by Vaughn in direct contradiction of the more familiar Perkins characterization of Norman Bates. Also in *Lilith*, Bruce becomes a schizophrenic and a killer as a result of sexual attachment to his mother; and Rossen's film, more ambitious than Hitchcock's, links schizophrenia and insanity to a social order besieged by prejudice and war. As a psychiatrist character explains in *Lilith*:

> I often compare [schizophrenics] to fine crystal which has been shattered by the shock of some intolerable revelation. I often have the feeling when I talk with them that they have seen too much with too fine an instrument. They have been close to some extreme, some absolute, and been blasted by it — that they have been destroyed, one might say, by their own excellence. Regarded in this way, they are the heroes of the universe, its finest products and its noblest casualties.

Subversively, during this final sentence, Rossen isolates a medium close-up of Bruce, as war veteran, and an unnamed African American orderly. At that time, schizophrenia as a diagnosis was often attached to black people, particularly ones who protested racist and segregationist policies. Indeed, what this speech implies is not only the redemption of blacks and veterans from the abusive application of judgmental psychiatric labels, but the implied treatment of schizophrenics themselves as an oppressed class, in general a more enlightened, progressive view of mental illness. Taken on its own merits *Lilith* is, in some ways, even more disturbing than *Psycho* because it replaces overt bloodletting with psychic malevolence and a subjective fantasmatic which disorients the viewer by placing him or her within the viewpoint of an actual schizophrenic.

Julianne Moore gives a bravura performance as Lila, a role that in the original was a largely thankless, even mousy one. Moore takes the character in the complete opposition direction, turning her into a tough, pseudo-lesbian figure. Claiming that there was literally nothing in the role, Moore said she decided to make her "aggressive."[20] Anne Heche has confirmed that Moore chose to play Lila as a lesbian:

> Well, she [Moore] said she was playing a lesbian, and ... probably if you weren't gay, you probably wouldn't be able to pick up on that, but ... the subtleties of what she was doing related specifically to the lesbian audience ... the way that she's walking and her "tough girl," it's a very stereotypical gay woman, with the keys on the belt and you would never say, "I like women," but that need to be angry immediately ... which is a great choice for a female especially....[21]

Moore's aggressiveness makes her tenacious and sisterly defense of Marion more comprehensible, as well as all those moments where she out-braves Sam in their covert investigation of the Bates Motel. "I can handle a sick old woman," for instance, is a line which Vera Miles delivers in the original in a state nearly beside herself. "*Can* she?" we can't help thinking, convinced she's too overwrought, too much of a wallflower, to handle anything. The same line is spat out by Moore as she jerks her arm from Sam's would-be paternalistic grip. In the scene where Lila explores Mrs. Bates' room and is startled to suddenly see her own reflection in a mirror, Van Sant tones down Lila's panic. Sebastian Stoppe writes about how Hitchcock doubles the reaction shot of Lila turning, cringing and gasping in fear, cutting in a quick side-angle shot before settling on a head-on close-up,[22] as if the camera itself was attacking Lila, the effect being to increase her fragility and panic; whereas Van Sant pares the entire reaction down to a cut from the glimpsed reflection to a coolly distant medium shot of Lila placing her hand over her mouth to stifle her fear, reacting but at the same time dealing with the reaction, and remaining under control.

During the final showdown with Bates, while Sam is still struggling to pin him on the floor, Lila strides over and kicks Norman in the face. Appropriately, a woman delivers the "maternal" comeuppance and disavowal missing from the original, where the mother's corpse can only laugh and grimace spitefully at her son's downfall. Here, it is a real female presence who literally brings Norman down. Moore's Lila is also much more repulsed, in a post-feminist way but also in a way that suggests personal trauma, by finding the sex magazine in Norman's bedroom, and also by the court psychiatrist's testimony that Norman was "aroused" by her sister. Vera Miles blushed and flashed consternation; Moore looks as if she's about to throw up *and* slug someone.

This newfound independence, even toughness, for Lila suggests that both she and Marion are products of a dysfunctional household, with markedly opposed results in how their personalities turned out. From a psychological standpoint, this is probably not uncommon: in households where the children are abused, one sibling (Lila) could develop a caretaker role toward the other; while the other (Marion) reenacts the abuse through promiscuity and self-destructive behaviors. Sam does not begin to fully understand his lover Marion until he comes into contact with her defensive, angry sister. It is one of Van Sant's triumphs that he gives us a shadow glimpse of motivation, linking several main characters together, where the original did not.

Incidentally, there is a more localized and no less significant update which Van Sant makes to the original: Norman Bates' (and Mrs. Bates') favorite record, the LP which Lila finds when she is investigating his/her bed room. In the original, of course, it is Beethoven's *Eroica* symphony, written in tribute to Napoleon, and therefore bringing in issues of the artist's identification with imperialism, conquest, power. In Van Sant's film, it is a country record, "The World Needs a Melody," a duet between Georges Jones and Tammy Wynette. Jones and Wynette were two of the most conservative, establishment-identified figures in Nashville; they liked to call themselves "The President and His First Lady." They often assumed, in their songs, an omniscient, judgmental viewpoint: "God's Gonna Getcha For That" is one of their most pungent and resonant titles. If Bates identifies with the artistic project of imposing one's will upon the world, then the song choice is a perfect one. The world may indeed "need" melody — but which melody, and how will it be imposed? In the effacements of authorship which intertextuality always brings out, such questions become particularly salient, since the record as artifact also exposes the strange distortions by which we can say we often fail to know how a work of popular art is made, or rather, who actually produces it. The folklore from which it arises? The artists who conceived and sang it? The corporate technology which recorded and distributed it? Or the fan who, by selecting it as a consumer choice, makes it signify some meaning beyond itself? When a work of art is a capitalist commodity, it can be entirely proper to say that it is created as much by the purchasing power and decision-making of the fan as by the artist. Intertextuality, by exposing part of the act of creation as an act of fanship, of selection and incorporation, likewise exposes this chain of exchange values under capitalism. *Psycho* itself, Van Sant seems to imply, is owned and created as much by its myriad fans as by the entity "Sir Alfred Hitchcock." Intertextuality here strikes a significant blow against the tendency of auteurism to disguise the fate of artworks as inevitably commodified objects. As cinematographer Christopher Doyle has said: "[Van Sant's *Psycho*] out–Warhols Warhol."[23]

Another kind of labor is presented in Van Sant's extension of the original's final shot, in which Marion's car is dragged from the swamp. In Van Sant's ending, the car is not pulled out easily; the tow truck's chains get stuck and the police investigators must untangle them. This moment of getting jammed and then unstuck reifies the film's entire movement of the repressed returning to conscious life. Van Sant's recreation of a crime scene investigation provides a certain closure, a restoration of order, while also highlighting the behind-the-scenes labor that goes into police work. The policemen comb the brush, fanning out to search for evidence. It is a scene of palpable and coherent action taking over from the disturbed world of chaos that has dominated the film. "Guys, it's done! It's clear here!" one of the cops says, as if to render official how the social order has closed up over the raw wound of Norman Bates and his graveyard-swamp. But the image is held long after the police cruisers have driven away down the road, showing, in condensed form, how the passage of time can move to make even such a scene of horror idyllic and nearly unspoiled again. The sun-dappled mountains, the sagebrush, the blue swamp water: it's all like some picture postcard which a vacationer in California might send home to relatives, not realizing there were once murdered bodies buried here. In fact, the policemen are played by the film crew, props people and best boys,[24] making explicit, in front of the camera, the activity of "preparing a set" which usually goes on before the camera rolls, and which we commonly "forget" has taken place (repress) whenever we watch a finished film.

Ultimately, Van Sant's *Psycho* bears an intriguing relationship to the commodity as articulated by Matthew Tinckom in relation to gay cinema in his book *Working Like a Homosexual*. If we think of the original *Psycho* precisely as a commodity, an archetypal Hollywood film, then what does it mean to have this commodity refashioned and rebranded "by no less than the proper name of a [gay] director."[25] Tweaking Tinckom a bit, Hitchcock's *Psycho* is closer to a mass-produced commodity since the desire of the director (apart from scaring people) was an unknown quantity, or rather generically heterosexual by default. Yet his film was an excavation of numerous "perversions" and has always attracted a huge cult following among gays, for whom Norman Bates, in his delirious mother-fixation, has been at least partly recognizable— albeit someone who cannot be claimed as a hero. (Intriguingly, later sequels to the original *Psycho*, starring and even directed by Perkins while he was dying of AIDS, reinvented Bates precisely as a heroic persona and defender of women.) The nature of rebranding is to insinuate that currents of queer desire always already run through and animate tokens of pop culture and commodity culture, whether this has been strictly acknowledged a priori or not. Like Kenneth Anger's close-ups of comic strip frames, something more or less benign and default-heterosexual from the great supermarket of pop culture is being reclaimed as a specific locus of queer desire.

As endless reifications, commodities have no future: they repeat an eternal past, and wait only to be used up. Intertexuality can give the commodity-form a future by questioning the uses to which it has always been placed; by rescuing it, so to speak, from its own maker's intentions. It is not coincidental that one of Van Sant's earliest films, from 1978, was a short parody commercial for something called Psycho Shampoo ("It takes care of dandruff ... and then some!") that appropriated the shower scene from Hitchcock.[26] Both *Psycho* (as a specific commodity) and shampoo (as a generic one) are given new uses by being brought into unlikely conjunction with each other, in the production of a new text (a parody film). In any event, the satire questions what exactly we are "buying" when we watch. Death as entertainment? The anxiety that even if we should get killed we must be sure to purchase spotlessly clean scalps beforehand? Put otherwise: radical art never entirely denies the hypnotic appeal of the commodity, it only inverts it (through Dadaism, stasis, disorder, abstraction), or else positions itself in a relation of mimicry vis-à-vis the commodity in question. As in a family of origin, one returns to certain primal texts, deconstructing them only to claim our own place within the chain. Again, this is equally true for the fan, whose entire aesthetic life might be thought of as an ongoing series of intertexts, as it is for the consciously or unconsciously intertextual artist. And the queer may have special insight into how much the family-text must be deconstructed before it can admit something inherently *unheimlich*. Is there a bigger fan of family than Norman Bates, or a bigger cutter-up of those who remind him that the boundaries of family must be continuously reconstructed, redefined as possessing an inside and outside — i.e., those who prompt in him, as it were, a sense of alien, alienated intertextuality?

We might well come back to re-ask the question with which we began this chapter, "What's the point?" Only now we think we might have some answers. One is that pointlessness, or anti-utilitarianism, might be the point in and of itself, as an ultimate attack on the demands placed upon any commodity form. Whether beautiful or ugly, effective or ineffective, original or imitative, a commodity must perform a necessary function or it ceases to have value. If the function of a horror thriller is to frighten the audience with suspense, and with things which it has never seen before, then Van Sant's *Psycho* more or less blatantly and consciously fails as a commodity.

And Norman Bates fails, too, of course — as the proprietor of a hotel where no one ever sleeps in the beds. But what appeared mainly as gnawing anxiety and guilt in the original Bates, emerges as the spectacle of a happy Bates, a happy maniac, in Van Sant's version. He is Freud's "only happy man," his boyhood dreams — antisocial, pre–Oedipal, desublimated — fully realized. This is in keeping with Van Sant's career-long fascination with the desublimating powers of crime, its antidote to the oblivious, hypocritical wish (as in the ironic end titles of *My Own Private Idaho*) to "have a nice day." After Vaughn's Bates kills Marion, he goes back to his mother's house and sits in the kitchen, playing with a red apple; he will soon explode at the reminder of blood, but for this quiet moment he is allowed to seem more contented than Perkins' Bates. Likewise, his boyhood room, seemingly preserved at a prepubescent age, feels homier and cozier in Van Sant's film than it did in Hitchcock's. And finally, the close-up of Bates grinning at the end, having merged for all time with his mother, feels more genuine and all the more creepy for the way it conveys a real sense of relief, perhaps, or even achievement. Polar opposite to Marion, killed in her anal (her license plate begins with the letters ANL), fussy, self-sabotaging search for a private island, this Norman Bates really is successful in his mission — as gruesome as it is. He needs no validation: his life's work (becoming his mother) is truly what he loves.

There is interest, here, in how film itself — not only rough-hewn, experimental films, but lavish mainstream ones — can evade commodity status, by sacrificing utilitarianism to a *mise-en-abîme* of endless reification, where it does not matter that we know what will happen next because there is no claim to new, original product. It can be, in short, a "happy cinema," openly realizing its dreams, untroubled by any potential negative consequences. Van Sant has said, in one of his most Warholian statements:

> What would happen in you literally followed in the footsteps of any film? ... You can do every film, remake *Fargo*, which was only two years ago, and what would *that* be like, if we followed every single line? Would it be *Fargo* or would it be something different?[27]

We recognize Warhol's delight in the categorical, the blanket statement, in that loaded word "every" ("You can do every film...") as if the act of distinction itself was oppressive; as if all things, even canonical works, must be placed on the same level until they begin to give under the pressure of viewpoints and desires heretofore excluded. We also recognize Warhol in the strange anti-utilitarianism of the project: why should every film be remade? As an act of love? As an act of hate, or more specifically protest against an older film's more conservative, tradition-bound qualities? As a routine, mechanical process that simply puts people to work in one or another artistic capacity? As a kind of diachronic "happening," revealing inadvertent vagaries of history and time? To interfere with the "prerecording" of the universe, as Burroughs might say[28] — cutting into the textual past to let the future leak out? It is the future (again, a very Warholian time frame; Andy was always trying either to predict the future or bring it directly into existence) which beckons in Van Sant's assertion, ever mindful of the next generation: that, finally, nothing should be allowed to exist for the past that cannot simultaneously exist for the present as well, and for the time to come.

4. "Where's Dad?" Thematic Intertextuality

In a sense all Americans are orphans because they have rejected the culture and society from which they came; fleeing from Europe or Asia, they have destroyed their own fathers in order to become "new men, masterless men." — Nicholas Garnham[1]

I can never get names straight. Why? Because I have no name. And the arbiters of destiny decided that I would not be allowed to profit from an assumed name. My last bequest from the Burroughs estate was $10,000. And very welcome at the time. — Burroughs[2]

Assumed Names: Naming Assumptions

Intertextuality always has something to do with re-encountering, remaking, or redefining a primal relationship to the familiar — a work of kinship or family. The reverse is also true: even when they are not especially fraught with conflicts, father and son relationships, for example, can be thought of as living intertextualities. The father begets the son as a "copy" of himself. The son in turn edits the father, either enhancing or expunging those traces of the father which he recognizes in himself. Often, the son's defiant act of obliterating the father-within only serves to bring him closer to whatever ruthlessness or selfishness he is trying to disown. Shakespeare's *Henry IV* is all about this, as Van Sant knew when he appropriated lengthy passages from it into the screenplay of *My Own Private Idaho*. Dethroning the father-king means, among other things, that the son can no longer define himself as the eternally youthful, irresponsible rebel-prince: he must find a place for himself in the world that will most likely resemble the erstwhile father's. Fathers and sons are intertexts, even, or especially, where they seem to most diverge. And intertextuality, as we know through all sorts of authors, from Kierkegaard to Kafka, from Harold Bloom to David Grossman, becomes a way of dramatizing, externalizing and working through the father-son relationship. The kind of stories we tell, and the language we use, are inculcations of paternal authority—again, whether we celebrate this or attempt to "cut into" and rearrange the ties of meaning.

We can read, then, the violence of experimental texts as violence against paternal authority in the same way that primitive tribes cut up and ingested the bodies of their vanquished prey (both animal and human). The idea was to absorb the strength and authority invested in the prey, which belonged now to the warriors who had killed it. One of the features of Burroughs' cut-ups is that it performs this kind of cannibalistic ritual on what we might call a father text, or the original text which the cut-up literally bisects and breaks down, both to unleash and circumvent—and lay claim to—its all-powerful, primordial authority. Burroughs often cut up pages of Rimbaud, who could qualify as an aesthetic forefather of Burroughs' radical, queer, aggressive sensibility. A son must sometimes quarrel with and cut up a father even if he is in agreement with that father, in order to liberate those lines of direct, physical communication which time itself has otherwise rendered impossible. More to the point, gay men reproduce through works of art. Only through cut-ups could Burroughs—shall we say—have intercourse with Rimbaud and bear his child; homoerotic intercourse which is so often distantly (and not so distantly) related to the structural love of father and son: as replication, commentary, substitute, improvement.

Burroughs became an early aesthetic father-figure for Gus Van Sant. "I was always interested in his style and his theories," Van Sant has stated.[3] Openly gay, slyly and fiercely intelligent, Burroughs, as we have already suggested, helped point the way toward a gay art that was free from the problematic and frequently self-hating blandishments of camp. Burroughs also broke, for the most part, with his own family, who had been a model of Midwestern conservative values. In the quote above, the author goes so far as to call "Burroughs" "an assumed name," or what we might think of as a kind of criminal alias. Here, the guilt is all on the side of the paternal forebears. What were they hiding from? According to the hypocritical standards of society, they made money through ostensibly legal work. Burroughs' grandfather invented the adding machine and founded the Burroughs Company. It is the heir, William, who chooses to live a life that makes manifest the criminality he perceived behind the family's legacy of capitalist oppression. In this case, having "an assumed name" may mean "what others assume the name to stand for."

Words of Advice: The Discipline of DE

In *My Education*, Burroughs reports a dream about his father:

Talking with Paul Getty III and my father in Italy. We are in a parked car by something that looks like Central Park. I am talking in a sophisticated, knowing way about drugs and such, and wonder if Dad will be upset, but it's time he learned about the birds and the bees, I guess.[4]

The blurring of well-known locales — Rome and Central Park — suggests the conjunction of the familiar and the uncanny, here, common enough to dreams but especially intriguing here. The architectural hybrid conjured by a space that subsumes both Rome and Central Park suggests sheer awkwardness and dislocation, which becomes immediately realized in the double room which Burroughs occupies, in this dream, vis-à-vis his father. First, he reminds himself that he is speaking out of turn, possibly scandalizing his father in front of a wealthy friend of the family, and therefore overstepping a son's bounds (it is unclear how old Burroughs is in this dream: ageless perhaps, as we often are in our dreams). Second, and by contrast, he makes the decision, for his father, that it's time to get all of this out in the open; intriguingly, he likens illicit drug knowledge to what we commonly designate as a euphemism for sexual knowledge, "the birds and the bees." Thus, there are even deeper levels of guilt and reticence which the drug talk both embodies and conceals. The dream reveals that drugs were perhaps Burroughs' way of feeling like, or becoming, a man, specifically the heir to his forefathers' legacy of scientific and business knowledge. Later, in keeping with this tendency to become, in dreams, his father's peer or equal, or even someone who can control his father — a father to his own father, as it were — Burroughs describes a dream of embracing "Dad there in a light-brown suit" in a train station[5]: another warmly casual dream which, moreover, stresses physical affection between father and son overcoming the distance of alienated or generic architectural space (a train station).

Overall, there is something offhanded, even charming, about the way seemingly agonizing Oedipal obstacles are hurdled easily, in both of the above dreams. Like dreams of flying, they seem to stem from, and satisfy, a primal psychological yearning or need. This perhaps speaks more to how deeply the conflict *might have run* (in the sense that the dreams are compensations), and it is not difficult to understand how father and son conflicts would have been exacerbated for Burroughs' more homophobic generation.

For his first short film, Gus Van Sant chose to adapt a text by Burroughs, *The Discipline of DE*, which partly takes the form of fatherly advice to a son-like reader. This advice involves doing everything easy ("DE" stands for "Do Easy," which of course has an oblique sexual connotation) so that the "kid" being addressed will not stumble and hurt himself in the course of his daily activities. The Zen-like training of changing one's entire life begins with concentrating on performing every task at hand with a minimum of effort and motion, which eventually becomes second nature and requires no concentration at all. What is ironic is how the advice moves from mindless daily chores and uneventful homey settings to distinctly momentous and dangerous tasks, such as piloting a spaceship. Indeed, the film culminates with the enactment of an old west shootout in a saloon, in which the DE trainee must either kill or be killed.

It is worth examining some elements of the intertextuality between Burroughs' story and Van Sant's film adaptation of it, also called *The Discipline of DE* (1978). The story is about ways of remaining in the present moment of action so as not to lapse into haunted memories and regrets. But plain, mechanical efficiency cannot be an end in itself. It omits too much of the free will that composes life, and which can lead someone into painful feelings — unless, of course, the point is to reduce the importance of even losses and regrets.

As if to symbolize "losses and regrets," Van Sant begins his film with an image of the proverbial spilled milk, an overturned glass with its thick white contents running down over a stovetop. A mess, in other words, but not unbeautiful in its messiness. DE ostensibly will show us how not to "cry over" that spilled milk — by not spilling it in the first place. The Burroughs story begins with a poetic interlude about the author imagining himself back in the St. Louis of his early boyhood, which "looks completely unfamiliar as if seen through someone else's eyes."[6] This latter phrase may have been taken by Van Sant as an invitation, extended from one author to another, to re-envision the text through his own eyes. We might also assume that something is passed on, via the text, from Burroughs to Van Sant, in the same way that the most significant element shared by both story and film is the idea of passing on knowledge or wisdom between older father-figures — the Colonel who invents DE, and also Wyatt Earp (both played by Frank Birney in Van Sant's film) — and a son-figure — also known as the student or the kid, as well as the novice gunfighter whom Earp advises (all played by David Worden).

Van Sant picks up Burroughs' narrative with the Colonel, a parody of the rote establishment of character and location in 19th century fiction (in fact Van Sant uses an old-fashioned establishing shot of the exterior of the Colonel's Victorian-style cottage): "Colonel Sutton-Smith, 65, retired not uncomfortably on a supplementary private income ... flat in Bury Street St James ... cottage in Wales ... could not resign himself to the discovery of Roman coins under the grounds of his cottage interesting theory the Colonel has about those coins over two sherries never a third no matter how nakedly his guest may leer at the adamant decanter."[7] Van Sant uses this verbatim as voiceover narration (by Ken Shapiro): Burroughs' collage writing cuts into the placid, old-fashioned description with the disconnected, or rather misconnected phrase, "interesting theory," which, by seemingly interrupting or cutting directly into the sentence flow, prepares the audience for the way in which the discipline of DE itself will occur to the Colonel out of the blue. DE, likewise, interrupts the normal flow of actions and behaviors with the mental reminder to streamline each and every one for maximal efficiency.

During the course of trying to complete his memoirs (significantly, Van Sant highlights a revolver and a small toy horse among the objects on the Colonel's desk, thereby seeding in the viewer's mind the physical evidence that will "pay off" later in the western shoot-out), we learn that "The Colonel decides to make his own time." He writes down a new calendar, whose (ten) months are named after train cars in which he lived for the first eighteen years of his life; this makes the Colonel one of Burroughs' "wild boys," with a feral upbringing hopping trains, but one who has survived to the ripe old age of retirement — therefore, seemingly, a potential father figure to new wild boys. (As Bob will be in *My Own Private Idaho*.) The problem of making one's own time takes on a larger existential dimension, somewhat unique to filmmaking, which, in the largest sense, is itself a way of literally creating blocks of time, since finished lengths of films freeze periods of time for all eternity, and can then be re-experienced by viewers as chunks of guided or, indeed, directed time.

But the Colonel's reverie only serves the purpose of jolting him "back to THE NOW,"[8] emphasized in Burroughs' written text and in Van Sant's voiceover. It is the present that matters most, he decides "to bring his time into present time,"[9] and so begins what becomes a year-long practice of the emerging discipline of "Do Easy," how to stand, sit, walk, clean the house, etc., all with the greatest of ease. "Do easy" is not a frantic search for industrial efficiency, but a unique congruity of timing with the most relaxed, even gentle of movements: being coming into oneness with itself. Many of the tasks involve elimination of garbage and waste, which, in DE, become game-like exercises in how to instantly forget the past: the Colonel tosses empty cigarette packs over his shoulder and right into the wastebasket like the "miracle of the Zen master who hits a target in the dark...."[10] Van Sant changes this to "as a Zen master can hit the target with his arrow in the dark." The abstract "miracle" is omitted, and the visualizable element, "his arrow," brought out. The arrow itself is significant, since, as with the image of the gun on the Colonel's desk, Van Sant adds notes of phallic mastery throughout his film.

At bottom, it is use of the phallus which the father teaches the son. One of the pieces of advice from Burroughs' story which Van Sant translates into visual imagery involves pulling up a zipper smoothly rather than tugging at it, and it is a close-up of the zipper on the crotch of the DE student's corduroy pants. "Every object you touch," the film narrator says while the student is cradling his zipper in his hand, "is alive with your life and your will." But even though Van Sant interprets *The Discipline of DE* as a passing on of specifically fatherly or phallic knowledge, we are free to read undertones of homosexuality into this induction: the threats which DE helps resolve arise partly from the kid being inherently "different" — out of step or out of time — with the world around him. The Colonel and the kid are both, to put it bluntly, queer in a straight world, and with his greater years of experience the Colonel will show the kid how to survive this sense of difference without letting it trip him up, thereby ensuring longevity to otherwise impulsive youth.

The film highlights those moments of paranoia, in the story, which suggest that DE is a response to an almost psychotic tendency to see the world as massing against oneself even through inanimate objects and random events: "You may experience a strange feeling, as if the objects are alive and hostile, trying to twist out of your fingers, jump out at you and stub your toe and trip you." Paranoia is the link between queer father and son. Likewise, Van Sant dramatizes Burroughs' line about how one should pick things up "like an old cop making a soft arrest" by showing a gay-looking policeman with sad, wide, tired eyes creeping up on a fussy-looking Colonel in a print jacket and placing his hand on the Colonel's shoulder. This would seem to evoke vintage vice squad raids and arrests against homosexuals (as Van Sant will show again in the newsreel-footage prologue to *Milk*).

Above all, the gay father-guru's advice to the gay son is not to fight with himself about what he really wants, to let what is natural to oneself *come out* from within, and to not let himself be held back by his own and others' negative energies. This comes to mind in the shots where the student is striding proudly and purposefully down a street, "picking his way through slower walkers." Van Sant understands the stakes to be higher than simply not stubbing one's toe as one crosses the living room, or not dropping a cup as one reaches for it. In fact, the stakes are those of high classical drama: the boy finally becoming a man, and the ultimate triumph of life over death. This is why Van Sant chooses to end the film with Burroughs' evocation of a classic shoot-out in an old west saloon. The film has been moving toward bringing the father figure and the son figure together, and now they are: the same actor who plays the Colonel plays Wyatt Earp, and the student appears (now in cowboy hat and vest over his plaid shirt) as a young, would-be gunfighter who may be scared and inexperienced but nonetheless refuses to run from the challenge of "Two Gun McGee." The same revolver that was highlighted as one of the objects on the Colonel's desk early in the film is in the hands of the kid, who stares at it intently and rubs it reverently. It is the gun itself, symbol of the phallus and phallic knowledge, which the kid does not wish to disappoint; he wants to be worthy of holding the gun — an obvious extension of that zipper he was learning to work only a few scenes earlier.

But how easy *is* easy? There is, naturally, a massive irony in making any kind of film that promotes the idea of "doing things easy," since even a short film is extremely complicated to accomplish, from a technical and logistical angle. "I've told people who have just started to make a film that the one thing you might experience is this feeling that everybody is conspiring against you," Van Sant has said, "because you're not necessarily able to tell what's real and what's not. There are all of these messages that you get from third parties that say, 'You can't get that location. You can't shoot at Yankee Stadium.' ... And it's too hard for you personally to take care of it because there are too many things going on at the same time. It's almost like torture."[11]

However, the idea might be to make it *look* easy, precisely when it is most complicated. For example, there are shots in *The Discipline of DE* in which freshly washed dishes seem to stack themselves, and cleaned silverware flies into the compartments of a drawer seemingly unaided by human hands. These special effects have a charmingly rough-hewn, even antiquated feel — reminiscent of the stop-action techniques used in silent films, such as Benjamin Christensen's *Häxan* (*Witchcraft Through the Ages*, 1921), in which magic coins amass and form themselves into playful shapes on a table — but even these effects, hardly state of the art for 1978, still required painstaking technical manipulation, as Van Sant describes the process behind *The Discipline of DE* as "Super-8 transferred to video, then manipulated on video and converted back to 35 mm...."[12]

But even the arduous difficulties of making any kind of film pale beside certain violent, irrevocable human acts, such as the climactic shootout, when the kid ends up killing Two Gun McGee. Here, the kid's anxious, terrified expression (still holding the shaking gun) speaks volumes about how this extreme act of taking a life — however "easily" accomplished from the aspect of conserving energy, of offhandedness, etc. — will not be easy at all to live with. The recognition of a young person having to live with the consequences of an (accidental) homicide becomes the painful theme of *Paranoid Park*, a later Van Sant film (to be considered further on in this chapter, and elsewhere in this book) in which fatherly advice is nowhere to be found, and is in fact revealed as both an illusion and a psychological luxury that must often be dispensed when as a boy is forced into adult responsibility.

So there is actually nothing "easy" about "Do Easy," the older teacher wants to help the young man, perhaps, more than he actually can. The inability to help or save someone whom one loves returns to haunt nearly all of Van Sant's cinema: Walt loses Pepper and Johnny; Bob and Mike are cut off by Scott; Sissy Hankshaw is left alone with her memories and relics of Jellybean Bonanza; in *Elephant*, John (John McFarland) tries to warn people against going into the besieged school; *Restless* revolves around a young woman with terminal illness. These inevitable losses and failures are a kind of valorization of the way people are vulnerable to fate, and the fact that we can sometimes only get so far in life, no matter how good or loving we might be.

And yet, to attain the father's level of power one must "act like" the father: the gun in one's hand must come to feel natural. Patiently, and quickly — put otherwise, in perfect time. We return to Burroughs' dream from *My Education*—"it's time the old man learned about the birds and the bees"—and we recognize that all declaration of present time is, to one degree or another, a form of redeeming or reclaiming the past (even the pre–Oedipal and Oedipal past before one's own life properly commences) from those who would manipulate it by keeping one in a constant state of helplessly reliving one's own overshadowed, watched-over past. All marking of present time is an act of revolution, an act of dethroning the father-king within us. Obsession with time is equal to obsession with one's father; non-linear, bent time, or the outstretching vistas of cinematic real time, in which everything is foreshortened to have the same emphasis, are ways of overruling a sense of time being controlled by patrilineal traditions and conventions. The present moment is de-contextualized in order to deny its preordained place in a genetic chain of reproductions that casts oneself always as a later, more dependent link.

Thus, to teach one's own father "about the birds and the bees" is to assume responsibility from one's own life, to engender one's own life—this same syndrome occurs to comic effect but with distinctly Freudian overtones in *Back to the Future* (1985)—just as figuring out *The Discipline of DE*'s final, koan-like line, "How fast can you take your time, kid?" is the kid's ultimate induction into (gay) manhood, but not without attendant doubts, regrets and traumas. Like someone coming out of the closet, one might feel damned if one does and damned if one doesn't, so to speak; but in any event, it is "time" that one is either losing, or gaining, mastery over.

Finally, "time takes time," no matter how much we want to find a shortcut. We find this phenomenon operating in the experience of coming out of the closet — still difficult for many gay or bi men to do, particularly in front of their parents, the ones who made us in their own (heterosexual) image. For some gay people, this still feels like an act of betrayal, and requires a courage to individuate which they do not necessarily possess. (And some parents are still intolerant and non-understanding.) It is not necessarily even a function of age or life experience; some people delay coming out even long after they have learned to individuate in every other way. The need to be guided by wise fatherly advice, in cases like this, is tortured by the fact that the problem in question (being gay) must be kept from one's father. This is why, in the gay community, gay men have often been coached to come out, and learn how to be gay men, from figures of what I would call "fatherness," as distinct from fatherhood.[13] We find this fatherness in *The Discipline of DE*, notably between Wyatt Earp and the young gunfighter (though it surely also exists, meta-aesthetically, between Burroughs and Van Sant).

I don't want to use the word "fatherliness," since this is already freighted with the classic image of the father himself, connoting someone older, genial, perhaps bearded and smoking a pipe; while *fatherness* is a kind of masculine and authoritative responsibility taken over by, or invested in, a man who could be any age or demeanor. Fatherhood implies literal paternity, it is random and may or may not be imbued with feelings of warmth, care and parental responsibility. Anyone with working equipment can become a father. Fatherness, however, is a choice that two men make to enter into a relationship in which one of the men will advise, love and nurture the other like a son. Fatherhood, like the fact of paternity itself, is immutable, legalistic, cut and dried, even where the relationship is not upheld; whereas fatherness is labile, subject to personal choosing or interpretation — again, even when the relationship is not upheld. Put otherwise, both fatherhood and fatherness can go unrequited, by either the father or the son. (This is the tragic element which fathers and sons, or any two men in a makeshift father-son relationship, often share.)

Therefore, the attempt to replicate family bonds among non-family is a difficult, mixed and volatile project, when even actual families have difficulty sometimes upholding their responsibilities to each other, or loving each other selflessly. What is most complex about "fatherness" in a homosexual context is that it sometimes works on one level but not on another. For instance, there is a scene in *Milk* in which Harvey instructs his staff that they must all come out to everyone they know, to set an example and let straight people know that they "already know one of us." Dick (Joseph Cross) ruefully admits that, in that case, he must call his father; the tension is palpable as Harvey hands him a phone. It is an insoluble problem: Harvey is right in an ideological sense, but so is Dick, in a personal one. Pushed into a painful confrontation with his father (whose love he presumably loses when he makes the admission of his gayness to him), Dick seems to never fully forgive Harvey for forcing his hand — instead, he helplessly displaces his love/hate of his authoritarian father onto the (in this case) "authoritarian" Harvey. Both Pabich's father and Milk, after all, are older men who think they know what is best for Dick.

Dick becomes a kernel of bad karma in *Milk* — Van Sant isolates a shot of Dick looking perturbed in an audience where Milk is speaking — and this complicates (among other things) the already extremely complex assassination scene, in which Van Sant composes a wide angle shot of Milk's assassin, Dan White (Josh Brolin), stalking past Pabich down a corridor of the municipal building. As the camera tracks in front of White, Pabich remains visible in the background, following the angry, deranged-looking gunman with his eyes but doing nothing to stop him. It is as if a portion of White's homophobia is invested with the angry growing pains of Milk's own followers, a kind of helpless retribution for the kind of would-be paternal authority which Milk has somewhat recklessly assumed in lieu of their rejecting families.

Fatherhood Versus Fatherness

Let's examine these ideas more closely. First of all, the theme of father-son relationships has been acknowledged by Van Sant as an important element of his films. "All the stories that I have done so far," he said in a 1993 interview, "have had some sort of family metaphor." This family-passion would continue beyond 1993, so that what remains Van Sant's most commercial and probably overall least personal film, *Good Will Hunting*, comes alive when dealing with Will's traumatic abuse by his violent father, or the bitchy jockeying for position among the "brothers" of the extended Irish-American clan, while all but fizzling in the unlikely anti-chemistry between Will and his assertive but bewildered girlfriend Skylar (Minnie Driver), or the burdening of the shrink-character (Robin Williams) under the weight of so many stock-humanist speeches. Humanity and family are best revealed, in Van Sant's work, through aching images of obsessively fixated, visceral need: the knife scars on Will's torso, or the sublime scene in which Will, after solving a difficult math proof on a blackboard in a college hallway, inches warily away from the father-figure Professor Lambeau (Stellan Skarsgaard) whose sudden attention both intrigues and intimidates the damaged boy.

This basic, primally human need for family — either one born into or one reassembled from surrogates and peers — forms the elusive basis of *My Own Private Idaho*, in which we see that homosexual fatherness is a kind of substitute, displacement, imitation, or improvement upon heterosexual fatherhood. "It's more about family," actor Keanu Reeves said while the film was in production. "I call it 'Where's Dad?'"[14] The need for a father runs throughout the film like the interstate highway where people find themselves stuck, stranded, again and again, searching for a benevolent guiding force which simply isn't there.

Reeves plays Scott Favor, a character based on Prince Hal from Shakespeare's *Henry IV*. Hal has two fathers, the King (his real one) and Falstaff (a kind of Über-beggar, clownish and hedonistic). Scott's father is the Mayor of Portland, a wealthy businessman (Tom Troupe), but he considers the man who truly raised him to be Bob Pigeon (William Richert), a veteran street hobo and lover of boys who has mentored generations in the various arts of theft, drugs and prostitution. Scott says he loves Bob more than his parents, and elsewhere calls him, in an over-the-top Ginsbergian moment, "great psychedelic Papa!"

In the shooting script, which has been published in book form, Van Sant wrote these lines for Scott to say, to explain what he is doing on the streets: "Actually, I'm on the street to settle a bet with my goddamned stone-faced old man. I've decided to live away from home for three years. To prove a point. That I can live on my own. And to appreciate the value of a dollar."[15] These lines suggest that we should not romanticize Scott's outrageous, druggy, oversexed slumming too much: his time on the street is actually a tutelage in the survival of the fittest, which turns out to be better training for the business empire he intends to inherit from his father than life as a pampered rich man's son. Scott already knows that when he turns twenty-one the party will be over; or rather: the urchin street party will be over, while a different party, of limitless wealth and power, will just be beginning.

For his part, Scott's father the Mayor is sickened by his son's bad reputation as "an effeminate boy." When the Mayor spits out these words (in a staff meeting where he is bemoaning Scott's waywardness), Van Sant cuts to Scott driving a motorcycle with Mike riding on the back: this juxtaposition is seemingly meant to question the word "effeminate" as a subjective, rather than objective, judgment. In the world he moves in, or perhaps any world, Scott is actually quite tough. Mike, who looks up to Scott and loves him, has these lines in the shooting script: "The first time I met Scott, I had a feeling he was a sort of comic book hero. He was always saying the right thing at the moment, and standing up for me when there was no reason to.... Strong and soft at the same time.... Scott's the only kid that I had ever met that had a swimming pool."[16]

This is how fatherness works between Mike and Scott: Scott is the same age as Mike, yet he outranks him. Scott is above Mike, although still a "kid." Therefore, he is "strong and soft at the same time." Both Scott and Mike are street hustlers; but Scott possesses (as Hal does in Shakespeare's plays) aristocratic advantages of good breeding. These advantages appear to be both internal (he always says the right things, he stands up for the weak) and external (he has a swimming pool), and the logic of Mike's love-struck speech is such that it makes one wonder how far the internal and the external derive from each other. Is Scott a "hero or a saint" *because* he comes from money, or do his privileged confidence and charisma help in his attainment of worldly successes? *My Own Private Idaho*, for all its subversive insider knowledge of street life, leaves this as a provocative open question: intriguingly, Van Sant is much less forthcoming about rich folk than he is about street people, and although his street characters always possess a certain charm which his rich characters pointedly lack, they are also uniquely unfit for survival, nor are they especially noble or brave.

Then again, neither is Scott's father, depicted not only as a narrow-minded, judgmental bureaucrat but a physical weakling as well: he is paralyzed and wheelchair-bound. Thus, all of his power comes from the artificial attributes of having money, a prestige title, and hired flunkies to do his bidding. Nonetheless, or rather because of all these artificial attributes, Scott is placed in a relation of anxiety at needing to measure up to his father's power:

> I almost get sick thinking that I am a son to him. You know you have to be as good as him to keep up. You have to be able to lift as big a weight. You have to be able to throw that weight as far. I'll make as much money, I'll be as heartless. Then go underground.

Both father and son state that they physically make each other sick, the visceral reaction of two people who are closer than they would like to admit, perhaps, and whose expectations of each other are identical to their own self-expectations (letting each other down is equal to letting themselves down).

Scott concludes the above speech by saying: "My dad doesn't know that I'm just a kid. He thinks I'm a threat." These last two lines, while poignant, ring somewhat disingenuously from Scott, since we know, from *Mala Noche* and *My Own Private Idaho* as well as *To Die For* and other Van Sant films, the distinct power which "a kid" can have. A kid is, finally, capable of possessing that quality of masculine authority, of fatherness (sometimes at the point of gun), which can turn even an older man into an abject, pleading child.

But not all kids have this power, or at least not equally. Mike, for instance, is deprived of it, because his damaged upbringing has left him with little sense of self. He can barely take care of himself, much less provide a father's strength and support to anyone else. He adores Scott's masculinity, and essentially turns Scott into a father figure. But Mike himself is no one's father, there is no one "weaker" in the chain of relations in *My Own Private Idaho* (except perhaps the submissive masochist Hans); the elusive state of fatherness never attaches to Mike. But Mike has a different symbolic purpose. In a number of Pietà-like compositions — some with Mike dreaming of being cradled on his mother's lap, others with him being held or literally carried by Scott — Mike is always the Christ-figure, the ultimate sacrificial son. Likewise, all of his johns are old enough to be his father; some, his grandfather. Just as he is more passive, helpless and adoring than Scott, so he cannot take refuge in the idea that he could ameliorate his own feelings of "weakness" by becoming, or substituting for, someone else's father; nor does he even know, exactly, who his own father is (beyond surmising that it is most likely his older brother), so he has no model to emulate or rebel against.

One might think, fathers being what they can be in the world of this film, that Mike might be better off not having one. However, the absence of family seems to be what locks him into the role of son; rather than a liberation, the fact that he has no father (or mother) to answer to becomes an unfulfilled longing in Mike, since filial emotions do not vanish for lack of a legitimate object to attach themselves to, but instead build up inside him until they overflow (in his bouts of narcolepsy). In some ways, when it comes to fathers and sons, the "grass is always greener." In the shooting script, again, there is an exchange between Mike and Scott in which Mike envies Scott for having a dad, however reprehensible his dad might be. In a friendly way, he takes Scott to task for not visiting his father, but Scott explains to Mike that, if anything, he envies Mike for not being burdened with having a father he cannot love.[17] Although this conversation did not make it into the finished film, it speaks to one great question posed by *My Own Private Idaho*: is it better to be tied down to a real family, with all its human flaws and failings, or to poeticize the need for family (and fathers) into a mythology which is then free to attach itself to anyone in a pattern of potent if doomed substitution? The encounters between Mike and his older male clients reify the absence of a real father in his life, and after Mike loses Scott, he seems increasingly loath to engage sexually with these men — as if the real emotional need behind the sex had been revealed to him and he could no longer pretend to function without it. The problem with the investment of fatherness that Mike places in Scott is that Scott feels no real responsibility to uphold it: Scott demonstrates this when he falls in love with Carmella (Chiara Caselli) and abandons both the father-like Bob and the son-like Mike. Again, substitute fathers are *chosen*, sometimes like real fathers, in an act of love that can go unrequited.

Van Sant has indicated that father-son relationships are a great theme of his work (I consider them in this chapter as an example of thematic intertextuality within his films), and that even *Mala Noche*'s relationship between Walt and Pepper, for instance, although it begins erotically, becomes "more like a father-son relationship."[18] This is certainly true, to the extent that Walt helps Pepper, getting him cough medicine when Pepper has the flu, offering him support, etc. If we consider this as an example of Van Sant's theme of fatherness, we see how male roles become more labile in a homosexual context. Walt only begins to nurture Pepper as a way of displacing (and perhaps redeeming) his still-intense romantic feelings for Johnny, who has, at this point, left town. Unlike Johnny, Pepper has given himself to Walt sexually, but only in an aggressive dominant role (Pepper is gender-essentialist and macho in bed), while Walt submits more or less passively to this domination.

In this sense, the younger man becomes the authoritarian father vis-à-vis an infantilized older man, and this scenario also obtains between Walt and Johnny, who teases and hits at Walt and orders him around. "Infantilized" is not too extreme a word, for the sexual power differential seems to reverse their respective ages. Indeed, Walt seems to regress to an even more child-like status than the teenagers. There is a fantasy scene in which Walt goes to the desultory welfare hotel where the boys live at midnight; he emerges from a smoke-filled hallway and crawls on his stomach across the boys' floor to lie at their feet "like a dog." The boys howl at him mockingly. "And after an hour or so, when no one knows what to do anymore," we hear Walt musing on the voiceover, "I get up and leave.... How many gringos have responded that dramatically to him [Johnny] ever?" The older man's fantasy of abject submission, crawling at the adolescents' feet, overturns all traditional, hidebound laws of patriarchal (and for that matter, racial) authority. Fatherness, then, when it is displaced onto markedly younger men, always contains within it a sadomasochistic element of self-negation, a state of erasing one's (adult) purview in order to create a total abnegation of one's symbolic patriarchal "rights." But because the need for masculine love is so powerful and extreme, so such an extreme sacrifice upholds patriarchy even as it subverts it through the blatant age difference, "giving it away" to teens who may or may not have "earned" the right to be patriarchs. We might say that, in turning away from older males to younger ones for domination, the sacrifice is seeking to know that the idea of the father is always already there, inescapable, and something that even the young know and master instinctively. We might call this syndrome "the innocent oppressor." The sacrifice absorbs the abuse as part of his own shame at not having mastered what would seem to come so easily to other, even younger males.

However, this is only true in an abstract, rather than experiential, sense. Indeed, there is also an adrenaline and a risky self-exposure in the hotel room scene that the sacrificial gesture of regressive submission from older toward younger males is, more than anything, transgressive and invested with a certain sacred element. They are a rite of passage which must be shared, not among peers who reach and pass through the same stages of development in uniform, but among people of widely differing ages, who will or lull themselves into a condition of comparability.

I am not using the idea of "regression" in any kind of psychoanalytically precise sense, and not along the lines of the syndrome which Freud identifies specifically as related to narcissism and megalomania, in which the "infantile" becomes a kind of hostile or threatening phenomenon. Freud writes: "We are entitled to suppose that megalomania is intrinsically infantile and that in later development it is sacrificed to society...."[19] I mean something essentially opposite to this, in which the male in regression may indeed give vent to antisocial, infantile yearnings, but these yearnings revolve around becoming weaker, more powerless and helpless — a grown man becoming precisely like a dependent child in the presence of an adolescent, in order to invest the adolescent with "fatherness." This thrill, potentially fatal in numerous cases, means that, in "dishonoring" the status of fatherhood/fatherness, the older male secretly longs for the younger one to uphold and avenge patriarchy, rather than accept the gift of submission benevolently, for this would mean that the dynamic no longer contained any father at all, which would be insupportable for the submissive figure. This logic, again, is largely unconscious, and therefore beyond the scope of what is literally transpiring; furthermore, it does not reflect an actual subculture of sadomasochistic sex (where everything is organized, often in advance, and therefore unspontaneous) so much as an eruption of pure and uncontrolled emotion originating from gay men internalizing the homophobia of straight society and idealizing the masculine strength of the younger, more father-like partner.

Age Reversal and Regression

Similar situations occur in other Van Sant films, where age and conventional authority get reversed, older male characters regress, and younger males violently and nervously take charge. In *To Die For*, Suzanne (Nicole Kidman) manipulates Jimmy (Joacquin Phoenix), her stoner high-school student, by having a sexual affair with him; her plan all along is to induce Jimmy to shoot her husband Larry Maretto (Matt Dillon). This exchange of power is allowed for by the noirish plot (*To Die For* was based on real-crime events). In the murder scene, Larry ends up on his knees before his teenaged assassins, pleading for his life. This is less fancifully masochistic than the scene in *Mala Noche* where Walt crawls at the Mexican boys' feet. At the same time, perhaps because Maretto represents more of a phallic threat to Jimmy (partly based on lies that Suzanne has told him, about Maretto beating her), he must be killed for Jimmy to usurp his position of "fatherness" and masculine authority. Nonetheless, we note that in *To Die For* it is a female figure, Suzanne, who controls fatherhood and fatherness: she will not give Larry a child, and she uses sex to build up Jimmy's ego until he is capable of taking a life. In the heterosexual world which is grimly lampooned in *To Die For*, men hurt and punish each other in the name of woman.

The heterosexuality in *Mala Noche* is far less threatening, perhaps because Walt's more complete submissiveness and overt self-neutering in relation to the boys seems to absorb any potential ego-damage to them and their macho heterosexual identities, and therefore protects Walt from reprisal. Although we should stress that the scene of Walt crawling at their feet is a fantasy, and anyway the boys do "beat up" on Walt, mostly playfully. Therefore, weakness does leave a man open to abuse, but perhaps not always the kind of vicious abuse that strength, or the perception of strength, seems to court.

4. "Where's Dad?" Thematic Intertextuality 95

A number of Van Sant's films feature a scenario in which there is a power exchange and a concomitant "age regression" between an older man and one or more younger ones. In *To Die For* (1995), Larry Moretto (Matt Dillon) ends up on his knees begging for his life from the teenage assassins (Casey Affleck, center, and Joacquin Phoenix, right) whom Moretto's wife has bribed to do her dirty work, using the inducements of sex and money. Younger males nervously assume responsibility for removing the "phallic threat" that is perceived to be represented in an older male.

This might be the origin of the intriguing line which Van Sant added to his adaptation of James Fogle's novel *Drugstore Cowboy*: "There's nothing more life-affirming than getting the shit kicked out of you ... so I relaxed and gave in to the notion that for the very first time in my life I knew exactly what was going to happen next." We hear Bob say this in voiceover while he is being beaten and stomped by the younger addicts who have come to rob him. In an earlier scene, he called the younger generation of addicts "the TV babies" because they show no basic respect for others ("They've been watching people killing and fucking each other on the boob tube for so long, it's all they know, hell, they think it's legal, they think it's the right thing to do."). I interpret Bob's "masochism" and acceptance of being beaten as being in keeping with the way masculinity expresses itself in these and other Van Sant films, as the need to regress to a dependent state vis-à-vis some powerful father-figure — this need is even felt by Bob as a heterosexual (and perhaps even helps explain his dependency on heroin, something that keeps "kicking his ass" on a daily basis). Inside the "tough guy" is a masochist who hopes the world will push back against him, redeeming him through pain and expiating his own transgressions.

Violence, then, in Van Sant's films, can be cathartic when it occurs around an age reversal and an investment of the father's powers (at their most destructive, punitive and whimsical) in a younger male. In a key scene from *Elephant*, one of the school shooters, Eric has cornered the principal, Mr. Luce (Matt Malloy), and is sadistically baiting him, kicking him when he is curled up on the floor, as if trying to repay him for years of oppression. Eric relishes the power he now holds over an authority figure (a symbolic father) who once held power over him. Here, we do see that masculine weakness serves to elicit greater abuse: by cowering, terrified, on the floor, the principal only eggs on Eric's sadism. Eric lets the principal go, but as the dithering, simpering older man starts to run away, Eric takes dead aim and shoots him in the back.

Something about the primal enactment of the son's murder of a father seems to have become integral (and overt rather than latent) within Van Sant's cinema around 1993. It takes on the ethos of a distinctly political act precisely because of the age reversal involved. Narratively speaking, these killings are not equivalent: we feel that Maretto is a true victim and does not deserve to die, while the principal's undignified panic strikes a blackly comic note. But in general the ethos here is reminiscent of Diane Wakoski's poem, "The Bouquet," in which an adult man is thrown from his bike by a child who jams the spokes with his foot. A housewife comes out of her house and thinks about mopping up the puddle of blood on the pavement, but she stops, as if recognizing that the uncanny, even strangely historic nature of this suburban allegory must not be effaced: a grown man made to look ridiculous, and indeed, made to bleed, in public no less, by his own child.[20] (The bicyclist in this poem evidently needed the discipline of DE.)

Returning to *Mala Noche*, where there is also a racial as well as an age difference, we see the games between Walt and Johnny veer toward the subversive, and the sadomasochistic, because Walt has handed paternal authority over to someone who is essentially a child, and who also has had enough negative life experiences to mistrust and want to get even with "gringos." (Early in the film, the boys tell Walt about a friend of theirs who was beaten and nearly killed by white cops.) The thrill of this seems to sustain Walt's powerful romantic connection to Johnny, and Johnny himself takes up this bait. Walt acknowledges, in a strategic moment but perhaps the only possible overstatement which Van Sant permits, the symbiotic exorcism of racist demonology that transpires between him and Johnny: at one point in voiceover he says, "A gringo like me has an easy life, a privileged life, and just because I see someone attractive like Johnny doesn't mean I should be able to have him, to buy him...." The sentiment is correct, but leaden and dry within the film's otherwise hypnotic poetry.

Therefore, Walt can allow his sexual longing for Johnny to go unfulfilled, since he doesn't want to push himself on the kid, and Johnny can determine the means by which he "fucks" Walt. Instead of Walt's body, he drives Walt's car, fast, recklessly, out of control, battering it against the metal guard rail along a highway. He fucks Walt's property, his possessions, his status, rather than him personally. It is canny that white U.S. manhood is symbolized by car-ownership, although Walt's car is, of course, a clunker; Walt does not represent white privilege so much as the willingness of a (gay) white male to jettison white privilege in the presence of the Mexican boys' "superior manhood." But of course, even though he represents the lowest economic order of white society, Walt does possess more than the migrants, and not only his car: a steady job, food (in one scene he cooks for the boys), alcohol (in another scene he is able to go to his local bar and get drunk over Johnny), as well as access to pen and paper with which to be a writer (even writing poetry requires materials that must be purchased, banally enough, at some store). Thus, for Johnny, battering Walt's car as an idle game is both an overtly political act and a covertly sexual one. Unable to admit that he is turned on by the act of masochistically letting Johnny damage his car, Walt becomes stern and takes back the keys; Johnny, like a kind of sit-in protest, hunkers by the roadside refusing to get back into the car unless he can drive again. And soon enough, he *is* driving again, playing yet another humiliating game with Walt where he pretends to strand him by driving off without him.

Love creates a situation in which have-nots (like Johnny and Pepper) can briefly feel what it is like to "have" something like a car. But Walt resists sadomasochistic regression even as he courts it. Fear comes up and forces him back into a role where he attempts to lecture the boys didactically, as if being their passive friend and sometime sexual plaything could be redeemed only if they also consent to accept him as their Socratic teacher. Although sometimes willing to divest himself of respect as a distinctly sexual thrill, he also feels the basic human ego-pain and ego-fear of losing respect. What can happen from these small revolutionary acts, and how far will Walt have to go as a sacrifice to the cause of enhancing Mexican selfhood? In any event, the rapture of each moment largely precludes thinking of it as a game with an outcome, or a progression with a vanishing point. At the same time, the scene where Pepper penetrates Walt roughly is treated much more like rape in Curtis' book, where he writes: "I wouldn't let him try to fuck me again. I'd fight him."[21] When Walt feels too violated, he sometimes wants to take his ego and selfhood back, at the Mexican boys' expense. Van Sant brings out some of these mixed feelings, but focuses more on Walt's gay pride at having been deflowered at last by an attractive stud. (Walt has lost his anal virginity, at a rather late age, to Pepper.) There are brief misgivings on the soundtrack ("and the more I think about, the more I know I asked for a reckless evening") but the image track tells a different story: it shows Walt swaggering down 6th Street, enjoying a cigarette and smiling at people he meets, seemingly at harmonious one with himself.

Nonetheless, when the magic wears off, he becomes a stern, lecturing father-figure again, reading to Johnny and Pepper a newspaper story about a 21-year-old migrant who stabbed a 53-year-old man to death when the older man made sexual advances to him. "Don't you see how sad that is?" Walt asks, leadingly. "This guy's really boring," Johnny says to Pepper in Spanish, and the boys walk away. The boys' blasé reaction seems to certify that Walt's fears of them are imaginary and unfounded; but although this reaction induces us to scoff somewhat at Walt's momentary fears, we do not judge him either, recognizing that in many ways, he is in over his head with these boys, just as they are in over their heads in the cold, money-centered, racist U.S.

It is only later, after Johnny leaves town, that Walt sublimates his still-intense romantic and sexual longing for him into caring for Pepper, who has pneumonia. "I want to be your friend, your amigo. I'll help you any way I can." Walt is learning the value of being a guiding figure in the younger man's life. However, *Mala Noche*'s complexity allows for Walt and Pepper to find sexual contact with each other again — as if passing fairly rapidly through various stages of trust in which Pepper was first a body "bought" by Walt; then a vengeful body; then autonomous enough to be able to deny Walt sexually and still receive his friendship; and finally, a true intimate. Yet, Walt's car, again, becomes the proxy for unresolved sexual anger and machismo, when Walt is teaching Pepper how to drive (a typical father-son ritual) and Pepper crashes it into a phone pole. "You drive like you fuck!" Walt succinctly observes, all at once making the sublimations and substitutions definitively overt.

"We're just not compatible," Walt decides, watching Pepper with a girl and feeling doomed always to be slotted into the unfulfilled and submissive role. Then, in the very next scene, he rationalizes his desire for the boys all over again, saying it's not their fault if they lack sexual imagination and suffer from macho-essentialist ideas. Almost as if he created or willed these Mexican boys into existence (the ultimate creative act of a father), Walt cannot avoid thinking of them as aspects of himself, of his desire, feeling closest to them in those moments where he is able to surrender to them in an abject masochism which denies that these are basically lost and frightened boys.

Parenting Skills

Regression and age reversal occur in *Elephant* between an actual father (Timothy Bottoms), reduced to an infantilized state of unreliability and helplessness by alcoholism, and his teenage son, John, who finds himself having to take over in certain situations and parent his drunken father. In the film's opening scene, the father drives John to school in the morning: he is already drunk, weaving all over the street, clipping a parked car and taking off the rearview mirror, nearly running down a bicyclist, and finally driving up on the sidewalk. John gets out of the car and says, "Mom's gonna kill you. What are you doing? I'm driving. Get out of the car, Dad." This showdown seems to be one which John has played out before: he seems weary, frustrated, bemused and frightened all at once, but he holds firm in standing up to his father, taking the keys. Reluctantly, the father gets out of the driver's seat and John quickly gets in. The father ironically orders him to put on his seat belt, then slurs, "What's the big deal?"

Bottoms is an inspired choice of actor, evoking his own early performance as the curly-haired, unlucky kid from *The Last Picture Show* (1971). That movie opened with Bottoms' "Sonny" character having some auto trouble as well. That sweet kid's name suggested that he was never quite meant to grow up, and with Mr. McFarland losing control of his car, it's as if *he* never grew up, either, just grew into a miserable rut of perpetual disappointment, curly hair like a fuzzy halo going gray at the tips. There was a lot of driving in *Last Picture Show*, in fact, with cars and trucks prominently featured as the movable entry points of high-school kids into (sexual) adulthood, even if the kids often seemed to be driving around in circles, and were "free" only to the extent that hardly anyone ever bothered to pay any attention to them. *The Last Picture Show* depicted the underside of the prosperous postwar American Dream, where hopes for the future were already turning backward toward a nostalgia that was both idealized and tawdry: Sonny ends up with a middle-aged lover (Cloris Leachman), the young retarded boy (Sam Bottoms) is struck and killed by a truck, the town falls into disrepair after the death of its patriarch (Ben Johnson), etc. These vanishing points of the American future emerge fully blown in the carnage of *Elephant*, even as the keys are symbolically handed over to the next generation when, again reluctantly, Mr. McFarland eventually climbs into the passenger side, and John starts the car, driving smoothly and well. But the son driving "instead of" the father occurs, here, not as part of a natural order of progress, much less out of some kind of love between older and younger generations, but only because the father's crippling impairment forces John to grow up more quickly and cynically than he should.

The incident has made John late for school; as a result he gets in trouble

100 Part One : Experiential Texts

It takes the sobering tragedy of the school massacre in *Elephant* (2002) to bring about some appropriate parenting in the dysfunctional father-son relationship between Mr. McFarland (Timothy Bottoms, right) and his son John (John McFarland). John has been forced to parent his alcoholic father, but this gesture of comfort — the father placing his hand on his son's back — feels the beginning of a possible reversal back to "normalcy."

with the principal and ends up in detention. Oddly, the principal, although nominally a father-like symbol of authority, is a prissy, avuncular figure. He nearly leers at John in his office, and we return to this odd moment when Eric, one of the teen gunmen, assaults him later in the film. It is yet another way that the violence of the shooters seems to emerge from the secret thoughts of the school system itself, and from its broken code (like the violated honor code in *The Wild Bunch*). We might think of the school, ideally, as sheltering and protecting the students, but the energy inside the school is already awry, already amok with perversity.

Sexual Energy

Through Van Sant's thematic intertextuality, we have become primed to look for traces of homoeroticism in nearly all relations of "fatherness," especially ones which fail spectacularly. When Walt tries to reach out to Pepper as an "amigo," the younger man pulls away warily at first, suspecting sexual interest behind Walt's kindness. Sexual energy deludes or mystifies the bonds of "fatherness" at their most would-be nurturing, which could explain why sex sometimes seems to have a double edge in Van Sant's films. Graham Fuller has called the sex in Van Sant's early films "cold, commercial, elliptically framed," and even where this might seem to be a slight overemphasis — I would argue that there is real heat in *Mala Noche*— Fuller's words apply, even for the later films, in spite of a real breaking-through to a new and welcome level of tenderness in *Milk*. Sex is often more puzzling than revelatory; it is stylized, ritualized, and we often see it as if through the viewpoint of those who are excluded from it, as when Sissy Hankshaw runs from the sight of Howard (Crispin Glover) and Marie (Sean Young) copulating like animals in *Even Cowgirls Get the Blues*. In *My Own Private Idaho*, both gay and straight sex is rendered through frozen poses, as if the actors were stripped manikins, as if sex were artificial and somehow outside the normal continuity of living.

Van Sant's use of held, manikin-like poses turns out to have had an influence over current gay cinema. In *Anonymous* (2004) Todd Verow turns the same conceit into a kind of party game, where Verow controls the action of an orgy by saying either "Green light" or "Red light" at random intervals; at a red light, everyone has to freeze in place, no matter how awkward the position; continuing to move on a red light disqualifies you. The idea that sex would like to be untrammeled but is often subject to unforeseen interruptions, distractions or inertias has both a light-hearted and a grim side. Everett Lewis plays with frozen sexual posing, but in a markedly more narcissistic and onanistic way, in *Lucky Bastard* (2009), when Denny (Dale Dymkoski) takes Polaroids of himself in a dim room, and Lewis freezeframes each shot for a couple of seconds in time to the flash of the camera. Denny has AIDS; thus, his intention to stop time for just a moment is a poignant one. The tension of tautened muscles holding a pose adds to the streamlined sensuality of the naked body even as it undercuts the narcissism invested in bodily worship; we see strain there, effort. Indeed, Van Sant seems to suggest that we tend to remember sex less as a frenzied rush or smooth flow of activity but instead in a series of stunned, heightened moments. Put otherwise, we remember it as Apollonian (poised and formal) even when the reality is more Dionysian (heaving and sweat). Sex and photography are also linked in some of Van Sant's films: one of the sexiest scenes in *Milk* involves Harvey taking snapshots of his lover Scott (James Franco).

Double Identities

In *Elephant*, John's burden is largely secret; there is a brother, Paul, whom he calls to ask to come and pick up the father ("Dad's drunk again"), otherwise he does not share his father's alcoholism with anyone outside of his family. John is not allowed to be a kid in the usual sense. His already acute feeling of responsibility for others becomes impossibly magnified when he becomes the first one to spot Alex and Eric approaching the school, dressed in military gear and carrying heavy bags. "Get the fuck out and don't come back," Alex warns John, "some heavy shit's goin' down." With Cassandra-like foreboding of the impending massacre, John rushes around looking for his father, who has wandered off from their parked car. (John kept the car keys as a precaution.) Meanwhile, John warns random people not to go into the school. He tells one older man: "Sir! Don't go in there! Trust me!" It is as if his wish to save his troubled father gets displaced onto saving strangers; however, no one does trust him, perhaps because, as a kid, authoritative fatherness does not come naturally to him, nor does accepting him as an authority come naturally to adults. The age reversal we have come to expect only "works" within the dysfunctionality of John's family, as a symptom of the dysfunction itself.

We are reminded of *Mala Noche*, in which people are shown to have different meanings depending on where they are and who they are with: the Mexican boys are powerless peons in U.S. society, except with Walt, who treats them like gold; Walt himself is little more than a hobo, his clothes tattered and ripped, his living situation distinctly down and out, still he has a socioeconomic edge over the Mexican boys. Furthermore, Walt is treated as a distinguished poet among his literary friends, a hard-drinking purveyor of romantic sob stories among his gay friends, and an enigma, half loved, half mocked, by the Mexicans. Similarly, both *Drugstore Cowboy* and *My Own Private Idaho* turn upon the ability of some of the characters to conceal a part-time membership in the criminal underworld. Whereas *Psycho*'s Norman Bates is yet another example of a split or divided identity. (Van Sant may have read references to "gay passing" or "gaydar" in all of these scenarios where the real truth about someone is partly or wholly concealed.)

John in *Elephant* is a quintessential Van Sant character for the way we see him adopting different adaptive tendencies depending on his circumstantial needs. (We see this also in Will Hunting.) Having the role of father/savior/protector forced upon him, he fails at the task, but in the film's final moments, reunited with his father, there seems to be some possibility that this father-son relationship will improve, and the roles will go back to normal. As a crowd gathers outside a burning wing of the school, the father seems sobered by the sight of dark smoke pouring from the roof, and tries to comfort John, who has lost friends in the shooting. "Where'd you go?" John asks, a sign that, in spite of his father's problems, John has missed him and is concerned for his well-being. "I just — I'm sorry," the father offers, rubbing John's arm. (This is similar to the arm-rubbing which Walt in *Mala Noche* attempts to use, at one point, to comfort Pepper, but Pepper pulls away from the stroking, sensing Walt's sexual interest; in the game of fatherness, heterosexuality often demands that it be exclusively straight men who console each other, with the irony being that straight men are not often driven to console each other that much, whether emotionally or physically.) In Van Sant's elliptical, terse dialogue, so many implicit, underlying needs and regrets are expressed in this brief exchange. Fatherness, an inappropriate fit for the beleaguered kid John, migrates back to the father, becoming actual fatherhood again.

By contrast, *Elephant*'s heterosexual couple, Nathan (Nathan Tyson) and Carrie (Carrie Finklea), seem to make no apologies for being immature; we learn that she beats up other girls who flirt with Nathan. More significantly, when she hints to him that she might be pregnant, he leans in close to her and says everything will be all right. We expect to hear him say that everything will be all right because he will help her or because they will make a decision together, but instead he finishes his sentence by saying that everything will be all right because they and their friends can "go fourbying" after school and have "a blast." ("Fourbying" is slang for driving a 4 × 4 truck through people's lawns and gardens, demolishing them; needless to say, it is considered vandalism and reckless endangerment. "You remember what happened last time,"

Nathan (Nathan Tyson) and Carrie (Carrie Finklea) are the popular couple in *Elephant* (2002), and the only young people in the film who really get to enjoy "being kids." Their irresponsibility about committing acts of vandalism, throwing jealous tantrums, and possibly getting pregnant has a sort of ironic, poignant innocence when brutally interrupted, here, by the first gunfire of the school shooters.

Carrie reminds Nathan reprovingly.) Nathan wears a red Lifeguard sweatshirt and is physically strong, but he is clearly not ready to take on the responsibilities of fatherhood (or even fatherness, for that matter). In another scene, he is shown as being one of the bullies who pick on Alex, pelting him with wads of wet paper that stick in his hair and on his clothes, making it look (according to the bullies' sadistic sense of humor) as if Alex is covered with semen.

If they weren't so young, Nathan and Carrie's conversation might seem like brittle, self-absorbed posturing, or dark parody. And yet, in spite of their out-of-control sides, Nathan and Carrie, in contrast with the kind of inappropriate adult responsibilities forced upon John by his alcoholic father, and certainly compared with the psychotic plans of the shooters, seem to be one of the few emblems, in *Elephant*, of "kids just being kids" — suddenly interrupted in their dreamy imitation of life when the first shots ring out inside the school.

At the same time, "staying a kid" into one's adulthood can also be a sign of having been parented badly. The character of Will in *Good Will Hunting* (scripted by Damon and Ben Affleck, who won a Best Screenplay Oscar) is extremely de-unified, similar to the kind of rebels that Jack Nicholson played in the early 70s. Will is filled with contradictions. Superficially, the plot suggests that his greatest contradiction is that he is a janitor at a college while possessing a mind brilliant enough to solve mathematical proofs that elude even the professors. The scene in which this is revealed is, again, a tense and perfectly rendered moment of near-showdown in which Professor Lambeau catches Will working the tutorial proof on the hall blackboard and at first assumes that he is committing some act of vandalism. As the professor moves closer down the hallway, Will skulks away, afraid of the attention, yet also lingering at the end of the hall for a moment, looking back at Lambeau with an abashed but curious look. The father-figure's judgment and anger have briefly paralyzed and hypnotized Will, an indication of the traumas he suffered from his own abusive father, traumas which the rest of the film will excavate.

Will likes to party with his buddies, a motley group of neighborhood tough guys who, if this were a Scorsese movie, would probably be called "mooks." He does not shrink from showing off his intellect if it means putting a snobbish college student in his place in a bar; but for Will, these intellectual displays (like his fist-fighting prowess) must be exercised inappropriately — not in a classroom where they would earn him real credit, but in situations where they bring something more immediate in his shifting, hardscrabble attempts to survive. Will's vast knowledge (he reads in secret) does not serve to reduce but to increase the chip on his shoulder. He is immature and childish, but at the same time somewhat grim: an unhappy child with an adult's capacity to do harm.

The shadow of the long-gone father is cast over all of Will's movements and choices. Just as Will rejects potentially helpful father-figures like the teacher, so he keeps alive, through brutal and self-destructive means if necessary, the father who had hurt and nearly killed him. Too much is at stake for Will to learn to convert the hard feelings of fatherhood into the serene and life-affirming sublimations of fatherness. By chaining himself to his father, he is able to go on hating and blaming him for the dead end that his life has become. He cannot help himself to achieve real success because this would mean finally forgiving the father, finally saying, as it were, "In spite of you, in spite of everything, I turned out all right." Stubborn and pugnacious, Will would rather remain messed up, alone, violent, in and out of jail, and mopping the floors of overprivileged students less intelligent than he is — rather than let the father off the hook, and let him go.

Fatherhood and Fatherness in Sokurov's Father and Son

We find similar themes of heterosexual fatherhood and fatherness in *Otets i sin* (*Father and Son*, 2003), directed by Aleksandr Sokurov, whose work Van Sant deeply admires. Because of his strong and affectionate relationship with his father Andrei (Andrei Shchetinin), the adolescent Aleksei (Aleksei Neymyshev) is a well-adjusted young man. He is even able to enact fatherness toward his less fortunate peers: standing up to Sasha (Aleksandr Razbash), whose lack of a father has left him angry and restless, and comforting Fyodor (Fyodor Lavrov), who lost his father to war and has become a nervous wreck. Having a father, a good one, is exalted to such a degree in *Father and Son* that when Sasha does break out of his shell it is finally to ask if he can move into the apartment that Aleksei and Andrei share and "be with you guys." Also, in a scene where Aleksei and Fyodor ride a trolley, Fyodor lingers by the older driver, watching him drive the car with admiring fascination: an unstated longing for fatherness. Although Aleksei's father (symbolically) dies of tuberculosis at the end of the film, Sokurov shows that the love he has invested in Aleksei will enable the son to survive this and other hardships of life. As in Van Sant's *My Own Private Idaho*, *Elephant*, *Paranoid Park* and *Milk*, having a good father is unlikely but a distinct advantage, while having a bad father or no father at all is a nearly insurmountable stumbling block; although *Elephant* suggests that a son can find inner strength in parenting an irresponsible parent (John and his alcoholic father), this exchange is, of course, far from ideal.

Sokurov may, in fact, have felt Van Sant's influence when making *Father and Son*, which begins with a disorienting scene in which Aleksei's father is comforting his son from a nightmare. "It's over, it's over," are the first words of the film, spoken by the father, and suggesting that the film, which has only just begun, will take place within a strange kind of bending, or bubbling, of exceptionalized time. The two men are in bed and nearly naked, and we do not know yet that they are father and son. Sokurov films them through a distorting wide-angle lens, and with such tight close-ups of isolated male body parts touching and moving against each other (arms, shoulders, etc.) that it is reminiscent of the sex scene between Walt and Pepper in *Mala Noche*, where the sex is made to seem intense and explosive (also somehow incomplete) by being compressed in a series of tight close-ups rather than shown in full. Suddenly, in extreme close-up, a mouth opens like a black, debriding wound. This silent scream is like an orgasm. Finally, in medium two-shot, Aleksei lies in his father's arms, in a tender rapture that is nearly post-coital.

The homoeroticism between father and son extends beyond this startling initial scene: at another moment, Aleksei seems to leadingly remind his father of his father's love for Tchaikovsky (seemingly always a code name for gay feelings), then rapturously describes the parts of his father's muscular body as he sketches him. Even allowing for a greater emotionality in Russian culture than American, Sokurov's deliberate conflation of father-son physical affection and the homoerotic seems to suggest how rare, and how (in some ways) taboo, father-son love really is. In *Father and Son*, the father allows his body, his love, to become a site on which the confused and nervous emotions of the son can be exorcised and worked through, rather than the more typical, homophobic scenario in which male bodies must not be too affectionate with each other, but instead must be kept apart except in physical acts of competitive rough-housing, and in which the expression of the son's curiosity or admiration for his father's body must either be sublimated or punished. Put otherwise: homophobic fathers raise homophobic, alienated, hateful and self-hating sons, while an un-homophobic father, in Sokurov's vision, is always prepared to comfort his son and to let his son be himself; thus, he can raise a son who is neither hysterically homophobic himself, like the brazen, cocky Sasha, nor "hung up" on unexpressed and unfulfilled wishes for male affection and love, like the weak Fyodor. The extreme affection shown in *Father and Son* only serves to demonstrate that most men do not share such intimacy within the father-son relationship. Thus, the more common lack of it gives rise to psychological weaknesses and dislocated needs.

Blake's Dad's Last D Chord

This is because, what the father cannot do, the son often cannot do either. The father's failure erects a psychological block. In his novel *Pink*

(1997), Van Sant has the hapless rock-star character Blake relate the following story:

> He said, "When I was five, my father taught me how to play the guitar.... Yeah, I wish I could play better now, but then, with Dad around, I had a lot of confidence. Anyway, one day we went out to the river, a place north of Stubtown, a river that he often went to, and we played music together. The bank of the river was made of round shiny stones that could skip across the water. And the water was deep right there. Dad stood up with his guitar, and because he had a little wine to drink, he fell over the slippery round stones, that were loose, and he went into the water with his guitar. But the messed-up thing was, he could play the guitar like a top, but he had never taken the time to learn how to swim. And I had never learned either, so I stood on the bank and watched him go under the deep and muddy water ... still playing a D chord. I remember the chord. And to this day, I cannot play in the key of D."22

A father must know how to do everything, or the son, like a Xerox copy, will contain the same smudges and blanks, the same unfinished business. At the same time, the father who does know everything — and thereby cuts off the son's chances of self-discovery — is equally problematic, directly rather than indirectly destructive of his son. In the case of Blake's Dad, the father's fatal weakness even serves in some didactic and perhaps superstitious way to protect Blake by traumatizing him into a sense of limits. Do not play that D chord. Do not go near water. The neglected, abandoned son finds ways of transforming even the father's self-centered obliviousness into words of advice, into proof that the father *meant* to protect him all along.

Too Many Dads: Paranoid Park

The crisis of fatherhood/fatherness reaches its critical mass in *Paranoid Park*, whose hero Alex is a teenage boy trying to grow up without the constant presence of a father, but surrounded on all sides by various father surrogates and substitutes. Alex's father (Jay "Smay" Williamson) has left Alex's mother (Grace Carter) to live with his gay lover, Uncle Tommy (Christopher Doyle). In an early scene, Alex is at Uncle Tommy's beach house and pointedly moves from the living room to his own private room to avoid being around his new step-dad. Neither the father nor Uncle Tommy is particularly developed as a character, so the film doesn't seem to be presenting Alex's discomfort as a homophobic response so much as general discomfort at having his family uprooted during the already vulnerable time of adolescence.

Alex's great passion is for skateboarding; but although he carries a board and is known as a skater by the Portland community he inhabits, we do not see him skating much. When he goes to the infamous skate park, nicknamed

Paranoid Park, with his buddy Jarod (Jake Miller), Alex sits on his board watching everyone else's moves. Alex has expressed trepidation about Paranoid: "I don't think I'm ready." A similar unreadiness seems to pervade his dating life; he is putting off having sex with his girlfriend Jennifer (Taylor Momsen) based on the logic that if he takes her virginity things will get "all serious" between them.

One night when Jarod has a date, Alex goes to the park alone. This uncharacteristic risk jars his routine out of its stasis. Right away he suffers some hazing from an older youth, Scratch (Scott Green), who asks him, "Your Mom know you're here? Is she hot? You should bring her by." This vaguely Oedipalizing conversation, in which Scratch usurps the father's usual prerogative of sexual interest in the mother, is treated as casual and good-natured, but it primes Scratch to become a figure of fatherness for Alex.

The need for male approval pushes the shy Alex beyond his own comfort zone, into danger. Scratch convinces Alex to drink with him and jump trains. Scratch leads the adventure, dispensing wisdom and advice about how to jump a train safely and undetected. Yet, classically, the best laid plans go awry. At the train yard, they are spotted on a passing train by an old security guard (John "Mike" Burrowes), who chases them and whacks Alex with his nightstick. Alex strikes the guard with his skateboard, knocking him backwards, and in a freak accident, the guard stumbles into the path of an oncoming train.

Alex flees the scene, throwing his board off Burnside Bridge into the Willamette River when he notices blood on it. However, his board is later found and matched to the guard's blood, making all local skaters potential suspects. Now, accusatory father figures begin to multiply like pod people in *Invasion of the Body Snatchers* (1956). The evening news anchorman, Ken Boddie (played by himself), seems to look directly from the TV screen at Alex with a quizzical, penetrating look. Detective Lu (Dan Liu) takes a special interest in interrogating Alex when Alex's alibi can't be corroborated. One of the ways the detective tries to win Alex's trust is to adopt a father-like demeanor, saying he understands if Alex lied to his mother about where he was going when he went out that night: "Probably that old trick ... I used to do that." Alex has invented nothing when it comes to teenage trickery, there is nothing new; the detective did it all before him. In a flashback to before the killing, we even see Alex's learning-disabled younger brother assuming a paternal role toward Alex, pointing at him and admonishing: "And follow the rules of the road, Mister!"

But what of Alex's real Dad? The night of the killing, Alex thinks first of turning to him for help. "My Dad. That was the person to talk to," Alex says in voiceover. "I could already feel the relief of telling him." But when he tries to call Uncle Tommy's beach house (it's always referred to this way, as if the father has gone away on some kind of endless summer vacation), he gets a staticky answering service. Alex's devastation is palpable.

Because of the strained relation with his father, the film implies, Alex is at a disadvantage in life. He often exchanges significant looks with potential father-figures: his best friend Jarod, Scratch, Detective Lu. Often Van Sant uses slow motion to highlight these exchanged looks as if they contained an eternity of questioning, longing and withheld information. In one playful scene, Alex and Jennifer try on clothes at a boutique, and Alex comes out of the dressing room swimming in an enormous three-piece suit. "I think that's your sexiest look yet," Jennifer giggles, waving her hand and rolling her eyes. Again, as with his expressed unreadiness, Alex does not comfortably fit in an adult male world. One of the ways in which we see this is that he seems baffled by the kind of adult rituals which his friends dismiss out of hand. His peers, all of whom have been questioned at some point by Detective Lu, sit around in a hot tub and criticize the detective as another clueless adult: "He doesn't know anything, he's just acting like he does.... Adults do stuff for money, no other reason." Alex, of course, has more to hide than they do, and he is stuck with his guilty knowledge, unable to bluff it away, unable to get it off his chest.

Outside the very symmetrical hallways of his school and perhaps when he is driving, Alex literally has no real path, no forward-moving track; hence, the meandering, back and forth timework of the film, and also those shots of the grassy beach where wilderness is steadily encroaching. (A bench for tourists surrounded by tall grass is disorientingly filmed so that it almost appears half-buried in sand.) There are also shots of Alex staring into space, cowering in a shower, or caught blinking in rapid changes of light. Late in the film, in flashback, we see the grisly image that has been haunting Alex: it isn't only that the security guard died when Alex accidentally knocked him into the path of the oncoming train; the train cut the old man's body in half, with his dying torso crawling insect-like toward Alex, looking up at him in bewildered agony, as if pleading for help from the boy.

This image — easily the single most powerful in the film, and an astounding poetic crystallization of the painful father-problems Alex has already been having — joins with other images in Van Sant's films in which a certain sado-masochistic atmosphere pervades the father and son dynamic. We are reminded, most directly, of Walt in *Mala Noche*, crawling submissively at the feet of the Mexican boys; in that scene (a fantasy), Walt was able to regress to an infantilized state so as to transfer his automatic authority (as an older man, as a gringo) to the boys, who relished Walt's submission. We are also reminded of the scene in *My Own Private Idaho* in which Scott Favor, wearing

The grisly image that has been haunting Alex (Gabe Nevins) in *Paranoid Park* is an astoundingly powerful crystallization of the father-son themes of power, painful love and difficult forgiveness in this film and others by Van Sant. The viscerally bisected body of the guard/father-figure also returns us to the Burroughsian technique of "cut-ups," in which a primary, "father" text is physically scissored into pieces in order to beget new "son" texts.

leather and a dog collar like an S-M slave, crawls into his father's arms, causing his father to vomit.

In both of these scenes, the homoerotic inflections are intentional and bold. In *Paranoid Park,* the old man's death scene is not sexual so much as an extremely dramatic, even shamanistic exchange of power. The old man, a father-figure by definition in his guard uniform, is sacrificed so as to occasion the potential for change in the son-figure. The guard crawls helplessly at Alex's feet; Alex, disgusted, helpless, overwhelmed with dread, runs away. In many ways, Alex is incapable of transforming the guilt and fear which this accidental killing inspires; in fact, in scenes where Alex wanders the school hallways like a haggard-eyed zombie or when, near the end of the film, he is caught sleeping in science class, one senses that perhaps Alex died along with the security guard, and along with the symbolic loss of his father. (Like a reverse of Sokurov's *Father and Son*, in which the son's future aloneness and independence after the father's death is welcomed as the natural way of things.) Yet, again toward the end of *Paranoid Park*, there is a moment in which Alex attempts to at least open communication with his father, and although the conversation does not go particularly well, we feel as though there is a first attempt at forgiveness and acceptance on Alex's part, occasioned by the fact that, having witnessed the security guard's death, he now understands something of the flawed and necessarily selfish nature of adult life. But for Alex to no longer "hate his father's guts," as the slang expression goes, he has had to see the guts of the dying father-figure literally eviscerated and exposed.

In a way, then, we could say that the visceral bisecting of the father's body makes the father and son finally equal, thereby creating a potential basis for reconciliation. The son, always smaller, always lagging behind the father in age and power, in experience, cannot love what towers over him. The "father" must be turned inside out, cut in half, or indeed placed in a sexually submissive posture (as in *Mala Noche*) before he can be forgiven by the son for that natural dominance which is almost read, by the young, as merely a deceitful trick of time. Put otherwise: it isn't the fault of the young that they were born later, and must grow up in public, in front of people who have already (supposedly) made that evolutionary transition. The bisected father is also a kind of living text and point of intertextual origin, like Burroughs' cut-ups; it is through the image of the security guard that Alex begins to write his own narrative, i.e. discover his own voice, his own language, in the form of his confessional letter which is itself the plot and voiceover of Van Sant's film, as well as the text of the novel on which the film is based. This is much the same as the way Burroughs' cut-ups begin with a text whose sacrifice (with a pair of scissors) creates the basis for a new work of art.

5. *Finding Forrester*: Postmodern Skin, or, The End of *Whose* History?

> *What we [African-Americans] write is often considered not to be literature. We have to define what it is. That discussion is typically an academic discussion. So if we succumb to the discussion on the same terms, most of our writers are left out. Most of our writers don't get in that conversation ... I think the general context for us is the written word that does tell our stories.* —Dr. Michael Simanga, speaking at the 2012 National Black Writers' Conference[1]

Gianni Vattimo's influential and erudite book, *The End of Modernity*, places near the center of its thesis the question of subjectivity and history. History presupposes the solid positioning of definable subjectivities. But history itself has long since reached a point of decay, of exposure. Acknowledging Walter Benjamin, Vattimo writes that the "victors are the ones who control history, preserving in it only what fits the image of history that they have created in order to legitimate their own power."[2] Here, Vattimo comes close to asserting that history is an entity a priori, but one which is controlled and turned into a (false) image by the interests of the powerful. Thus, one would deduce that there is such a thing as a real or valid history, somewhere beneath all the corruption and distortion. In fact, history is identical with humanity, since human existence "occurs when it historicizes itself and when we historicize ourselves."[3] Theoretically, anyway, we would not recognize humanity apart from its historicity, and indeed, vice versa. This is the reason why, when minorities are denied access to the processes of historicization, it bears a direct impact on the societal perception of them as recognizable human beings. Likewise, if one can improve the lot of actual individuals by entitling them to a subject-position within the narrative of historicization, one can also recuperate history itself by expanding the human subjectivities on which historicity is based: the conquered as well as the conquerors.

This is not what Vattimo does, however. Rather, he interprets the undoing of history's master narrative as an undoing of human subjectivity in general, which then reinforces the impossibility of historicity in a sort of vicious circle. The timeline, tending toward absolute zero, is rigged like a spy's recorded communiqué set to autodestruct after being played through. Just as plural histories begin to emerge — finally telling the whole story in its multiple and mutually interdependent dialectics — the entire project of history gets sentenced to death, by Vattimo, who calls it "a last metaphysical illusion":

> If there is no unitary and privileged history, though, but only different histories or different levels and ways of reconstructing the past in the collective consciousness and imagination, then it is difficult to see to just what extent the dissolution of history — in the form of a dissemination of "histories" does not also constitute an end to history as such.[4]

It sounds as though, if no one is allowed to ultimately "win" at history (as if it were some kind of game), then we must all pick up our marbles and go home. But wait. Aside from the fact that we can and must attempt to imagine collective histories in which all notions of "privileged" viewpoints recede before the factual retelling of how things actually happened, how groups impacted each other, we might first be tempted to ask, right off the bat: *whose* history or histories are we talking about? Why must the word *histories* necessarily become subject to ironic scare-quotes?

The playing field, once leveled, seemingly turns into something other than a playing field, and the former winners, the former privileged viewpoints, the Eurocentrists in a word (although it does not always boil down so neatly to only them), declare it *terra prohibita*; pull up stakes and let the grass grow over. Needless to say, there is a politics at work here, as Marianne DeKoven reminds us: "The political has come to be lodged primarily in questions of subjectivity. The subject is no longer clearly demarcated or even putatively or potentially unified, but rather is fluid, permeable, fragmented, shifting, nomadic, nonessential, non-self-identical, hybrid, and no longer clearly separable from any 'other.'"[5]

Some, however, are more invested in the lost sense of wholeness than, well, "others" are. What postmodern fragmentation dramatizes is not so much the holistic viewpoint of the historic masters but rather the rupture and estrangement felt by those straight, white masters at the thought of having to identify with minorities, of having to place their subjectivities upon the same level as minorities. "Unity" and "privileged" — these almost nostalgic words of Vattimo's betoken a kind of unconscious partisanship; for finally, the privileged history, the master narrative of the masters, is the only one that philosophy trusts as being fully certified in "collective consciousness and imagination," even if it has been proven factually wrong or misleading. In the face of needing to revise the master narrative, to include what DeKoven calls "voices, often misheard or misinterpreted,"[6] it is the revisions which are taken to be distorting or misleading, at any rate unverifiable in a supposedly "unitary" way.

The move, then, to use Benjamin's point — that the record of history must become more reflective of both (or all) sides rather than merely that of the victorious — as a springboard to a complete obliteration of humanity/history and the introduction of a post-human/post-historical age strikes me as radically tendentious, although perhaps Vattimo saw his conclusions as following a different line of philosophic or semantic logic rather than addressing actual experiential needs. Here is where current philosophy might opt for a certain inventive sophistry, tinkering over the enormous legacy of systems and dialectics in order to strand it within a nearly apocalyptic dysfunctionality and irrelevance which arise from within the legacy's own terminology. Spurious or outmoded terminologies can be harder to uproot than the concepts or, dare I say, the human emotions which rise like a water-line behind them and sometimes trickle or come flooding out through the cracks.

"Narrative" is a case in point: once this stood for a certain absolute value, the formation of principles through a clear line of progression from A to B, in which B arises from A but is not necessarily foreseen. Now it stands for the imposition of spin, of personal interpretation — the means to a predetermined end, in which B exists prior to A, and A is simply one of the illusory threads that make B appear inevitable. Hence, in art, the use of non-linear narratives which usually flaunt the idea that B comes before A, and which reinforce, in a way that has become synonymous with postmodern relativism, the inability to trust *any* narrative.

Yet, there should be way — and in fact there are already examples of it — in which both linear and nonlinear narratives can tell all the histories within history, all the viewpoints and the ways in which these viewpoints relate to each other, alternately combating and reinforcing each other. We can no longer be innocent of narrative and its intentions to mislead or misrepresent, but this does not necessarily mean that we can not ever again use it to find a truth or a meaning that pre-modernism and modernism once searched for, as Jason did for the golden fleece. Some would argue that modernism found this truth, precisely at the moment where it recognized that history had to become histories, that viewpoints had to cede centralized privilege to a more accurate and decentralized sense of the way systems deform subjectivities and realities; some would argue that this truth was never found, or was found only briefly and proved ruinous. The label "postmodernism," which Susan Sontag and others rightly declared to be a tendentious attempt to pronounce the 60s over and done with (and therefore make the progressive politics of the 60s somehow irrelevant), is already beginning to reconnoiter that abandoned field of modernist inquiry to see what might have been prematurely left behind; an attempt to see beyond the "end," as in endgame or stalemate, which relativism has inadvertently summoned forth, and also to see in the tattered idea of humanity itself a golden fleece worth searching for again.

There is an obsessive (and perhaps millennial?) turn toward thoughts of "ends"—Vattimo's book, *The End of Modernity*, for example, is only one symptom of this turn, not its sole source. It is only within religious thought that we find the same sort of longing for lost transcendence expressing itself through a trumpeting of the belated or overdue end of immanence, put otherwise, the end of the world. I do not mean to "attack" Vattimo. I merely want to delineate what his argument presumes and takes for granted. Vattimo suggests that the postmodern would fall into line with modernity as a natural extension of "the idea of history with its two corollary notions of progress and overcoming"[7]; however, this is short-circuited by a radical instability of being, which can no longer be conclusive or holistic, and thus cannot become historicized. Postmodernism becomes "dissolution of the category of the new — in other words, ... an appearance of 'the end of history' ..."[8] Vattimo's only qualification is offered in a quick parenthetical aside, that it does not matter if the course of civilization progresses or regresses.[9]

It is true that Vattimo sometimes glosses over important caveats in parenthetical or passing asides. These asides are nearly a countertext within *The End of Modernity*, revealing the human limits of largely semantic logic. For there is no doubt, first of all, that the "dissolution of the new" and the subsequent radical instability of being are biased, and relevant only to what Vattimo calls, matter-of-factly and without much exploration, a "crisis of Eurocentrism."[10] The Eurocentric mind was grounded, foundational, made from what it took to be whole cloth. Even then, we know that it borrowed from foreign sources in a way that was usually unacknowledged. But it was not until the earthy twentieth century artists associated with Fauvism and Cubism (Matisse, Picasso, etc.) paid open homage to African art in their own work that the cat came out of the bag, so to speak, and could no longer be hidden. For the Fauvists and Cubists, African art enriched them and made their modernity possible; I have a difficult time viewing this as a crisis of anything. Yet, rather than framing this as a triumph of panculturalism, an instance of art reinventing itself through hybridization, and even potentially an overcoming of imperialist tendencies that denigrate the cultural work of indigenous peoples, postmodernist theory frames it precisely as a deficit, a "crisis" of Eurocentrism and, by extension, of total subjectivity.

Put otherwise, a crisis of Eurocentric and, I have been hesitating to put this bluntly, of specifically white energies is presumed and then universalized as if the white European's subjectivity was the only one that mattered. Again, I am not making any claims that Vattimo or any specific postmodern theorists are, objectively speaking, racist. I do not believe that they are. Vattimo's text barely refers to race; moreover, Vattimo did not invent the intellectual framework here. Some of the apocalypticism of postmodernism derives from a long pattern of philosophical progress as defined by "killing off one's father." In this sense, great intellectuals are expected to define their thought almost exclusively around revising the thought of the past — but not in the sense that revolutions evoke the past in order to demolish its worn-out shibboleths. Philosophy almost never wipes the slate clean; it circles change, but usually settles for intervention, a humbler enterprise which ensures that the same body of thought or dogma (the body of the father, so to speak) will continue to stretch out on either side, lending its gravity to those who attempt to address and re-dress it. As Dr. Lucius T. Outlaw states, philosophy is responsible at bottom for "production of protective, legitimating canopies"[11] which are used to contain and maintain the order of things:

> Hence the fetishization by philosophers of various traditions (but by no means all) of univocal, universal, change-impervious Truth and Goodness, Right or Justice, and of the tools ... by which these are supposedly acquired. Here, too, is the source of the efforts to achieve legitimization (as in Plato's Myth of Metals) that would give to philosophizing in certain forms and practiced by certain certified persons its authority and honorific status....[12]

For the traditional order, the gravity of the past, of history, is a currency that never loses value. And thus, it *should* matter whether the course of civilization progresses or regresses, since an improved "vocation of philosophizing" — and by extension, human intelligence and culture in general — would bring about, as Dr. Outlaw writes, the "raising to consciousness the conditions of life, historical practices, and blocked alternatives that, if pursued, might lead to life experienced as qualitatively — progressively — different."[13] And it should also matter whether those who have been denied a subject position in history can emerge upon the historic stage, speaking for themselves at last, not in further isolation but in fully heard concert with all of the other voices; or whether that stage will be torn out from under them before they get the chance — conveniently enough for the white Eurocentric position, inevitably the most destabilized by now having to share the same public spaces which it formerly controlled. Unable to deny the Other any longer, postmodernism goes on a last kamikaze mission, to show that humanity itself is expired, beside the point. Subjectivity is denigrated and rendered moot just when those who have formerly been the objects of power and control (women, people of color, gays) are beginning, for the first time, to gain their own public subjectivities.[14]

But all is not a gloomy dead end. In fact, Gus Van Sant's cinema fulfills Vattimo's briefly expressed hope that we could envision postmodernism (current times) "as a field of possibility and not simply as a hellish negation of all that is human."[15] It also fulfills my own hope for complex, multi-leveled, sometimes nonlinear narratives which redeem narrative itself from the bad faith that it has fallen into. We are beginning to see how his films already move beyond postmodernism, toward an attempt to reunite the ironic and the sincere, the aesthetical and the ethical, partly via the faces and voices and bodies of marginalized and downtrodden people. We could say that Van Sant accomplishes this renovation of postmodern meaninglessness not in spite of standard postmodernist techniques, such as collage, queering, intertextuality (all things which are normally used as intellectual fragmentation bombs), but through these same techniques. He marshals the repertoire of the full array of "dehumanized" aesthetic stances but to use them not to create new chaos but instead to restore a lost human dignity. He appropriates not to prove that everything is meaningless and relative, but to stand in solidarity with other artists and texts.

One of Van Sant's most important and accomplished films, beautifully directed and filled with rich detail,[16] *Finding Forrester* assaults head-on the assumption of post-historicity and post-humanity, and does this from a specifically racial perspective. It centers around the character of sixteen-year-old Jamal Wallace (played by Rob Brown, a newcomer discovered by Van Sant), growing up in the Bronx. There is a seeming contradiction, at least from the standpoint of sociological-racial "norms," at the heart of Jamal's life: like the other black teens in his circle, Jamal is athletic and masculine, prizing physical strength and courage as the ultimate sign of being a man; yet Jamal's secret passion is literature. He fakes disinterest in English class so he can fit in, but his scores on his essay tests tell a different story. Jamal can write, and brilliantly at that.

In the beginning of the film, it is as if Jamal believes these "halves" of himself can be kept apart indefinitely. But already he is learning that much of the larger world sees or wants to see him more holistically. In a plot point, Jamal is recruited by an Ivy League prep school who makes no bones about wanting him both for his precocious test scores and for what he could bring to the fortunes of their basketball team. "Basketball is where he gets his acceptance," his public-school teacher Ms. Joyce (April Grace) observes sweetly in a conference with Jamal's mother (Stephanie Berry); Jamal focuses on sports and does just enough in class to maintain a C-average, so as "not to stand out." Jamal's mother beams with pride to hear that her son is a talented writer, but acknowledges that Jamal himself only feels comfortable telling her about his basketball games. Classrooms, basketball courts are public spaces infected by pecking orders and social expectations. But in the privacy of writing, the urges to express himself and to reveal his writing skills overcome Jamal, as if he did not think that such moments would ever be detected or traced back to him. His sense of needing secrecy and privacy, here, is poignant in spite of, or perhaps because, they seek to conceal a special, wonderful gift as if it were something shameful. In fact, Jamal keeps trying to hide from his friends, his teacher, his mother, urging his beloved older brother Terrell (Busta Rhymes), "Don't say nothing about those test scores to anybody."

Terrell is willing to enable Jamal's camouflage. He himself once had hopes of pursuing a college athletic scholarship but has ended up making a living as a ticket-scalper, a fact which does not make him bitter, and which he seems to accept, almost too easily, as part of being a young African American. He jokes, in a reflexively homophobic but essentially good-natured way, that the prep school which recruits Jamal looks like "the funny-man school." Again, there is the sense that one cannot try too hard to be part of a white system, one cannot succeed too much where the others in one's family and social circles have not been able to. An African American man bears failure in U.S. society as a sort of badge of proud honor, so to speak: it means, among other things, that he has not betrayed blackness. "Blackness," naturally, as more than a skin color; blackness as a set of ideas, a set of internalized voices.

When Jamal meets William Forrester (played by Sean Connery, who also executive-produced the film), the older man defines the paradox for Jamal as the question of what Jamal wants to do with the rest of his life, a question less banal than it might seem, or less than it would be for anyone not stuck in Jamal's particular bind, to either play into racist expectations and lose out, or to spend his life fighting the same (academic, literary) systems that he hopes to conquer. In some ways we can think of this question as central to Van Sant himself, as a film director who has had to navigate a career that spans all the way from challenging, outspokenly gay works of avant-garde cinema to mainstream commercial productions. This is nothing to have to apologize for, all filmmakers must navigate such winding courses today and Van Sant has accomplished it smoothly and honorably. Clearly, however, there is the identification of the artist with his subject there, in how Jamal will learn to pick his battles, to seek out allies with whom to collaborate, to hold back when he must and to meet the world halfway whenever he can.

Van Sant sets up Jamal's paradox visually, near the beginning of the film, by panning slowly up a stack of clearly well-read paperbacks. It's an eclectic tower: lots of Mishima, Jules Verne, Chekhov, Kierkegaard, the Marquis de Sade, James Joyce, Ken Kesey, Ray Bradbury, Sam Shepard. Such far-ranging, sophisticated fare would be unusual for anyone who was merely a dabbler in literary and philosophical culture, but it is also marked by its predominantly white–Eurocentric nature. Then, Van Sant cuts to an extreme close-up of a brown body lying supine (this is Jamal) and begins an equally slow pan over Jamal's exposed, slumbering skin, as his mother's voice urges him to get up and get to school. Jamal's flesh is held in such tight close-up that it is distinguishable, at first, only by its dark tone, as well as its fineness, its muscular smoothness. When the camera reaches Jamal's face, his opened eye nearly fills the screen.

The mother is not presented as villainous or excessively domineering, although she is (here) a kind of internalized off-screen voice who "nags" and hectors her son; she has his best interests at heart, though, and she herself is in the middle of leaving to go to her job. Rather, the larger point is that she mediates culturally between the eclectic, Eurocentric library and the world's expectations for young Jamal, just as Jamal's black skin does too. For a young black man, to internalize his mother's voice is probably a sign of his belonging to the family-based and often matriarchal black community; at the very least, we feel it as a sign of the love between Jamal and his mother. But the books are a different set of voices, equally internalized for Jamal, as we see from how dog-eared they are. To internalize these voices — of Mishima, of de Sade, of Joyce, et al.— denotes membership in a community that is not, at a glance, culturally coded as African American (or even *typically* American at all, as a matter of fact).

What does this mean? To be sure, there is a human cultural and intellectual tradition which belongs to everyone and is open to anyone who wishes to participate in it, no matter who, no matter what. No one is denying this, Van Sant least of all; what he is doing is making us, as viewers, ask ourselves how startling we find it that Jamal might give equal consideration to the voice of his mother *and* the voice of de Sade, for example? *Is* it startling that these books in particular belong to a sixteen-year-old urban black? Probably, in an objective way; but what Van Sant does here, and throughout the film as he continues to riff on similar visions of Jamal in various contexts in which the teen seems both self-contained, "perfect," yet also clearly out of place with the life around him, is to show us how the paradox of the books might only appear to be a paradox because of our viewpoint — and also, in a more complicated way, how the seeming paradox, such as it is, might be even more difficult for Jamal to accept than for others, given that he feels the need to be a certain kind of young black man, strong for his mother, practical rather than imaginative, a person of action rather than (mere) dreams or contemplations, etc. Living in a Bronx housing project, can he literally *afford* this much imagination, no matter how much he might need it?

For all of these reasons, this eloquent first shot of Jamal is, quite literally, his "awakening," and the prelude to a series of events which compel him to begin to stop his rejecting of his paradoxes as contradictory and negative, and instead to learn to embrace them. Part of seeing through to his own internal reality comes with seeing into the world of Forrester, an eccentric recluse in Jamal's neighborhood who turns out to be an author. And not just any author, but *the* author, a widely lionized, vaguely Salingeresque type who produced the Great American Novel and then chose never to publish another work. This is a pattern often repeated in American literature: Harper Lee never followed *To Kill a Mockingbird*; Harold Brodkey was briefly resurrected in his final years on the strength of one legendary early novel; the great lyric poet Jack Gilbert took twenty years to come out with a second book after his Yale Series win, *Views of Jeopardy* (1962). Great glacial myths of nearly inhuman purity settle around such figures who allow their sibylline muteness to be interrupted by periodic utterance. Appointed oracles, they form an anti-history of literature within literature itself, one which presupposes writing as the ultimate antisocial, preemptive strike on cozy domesticated consistency. Such authors seem to take us hostage, but they are also seen, famously, as prisoners: of their own taste for solitude; of their own exorbitantly high standards.

Indeed, Van Sant attempts to bring together a certain kind of literary tradition with modern urban culture, on a risky but ultimately rewarding middle ground: that of criminal activity, or, in a larger sense, acts of rebellion and revolution. Ms. Joyce tries to beguile her disinterested English class into caring about "The Raven" by introducing it, juicily, as a poem that Poe wrote "while he was strung out on cocaine and obsessed with death." No denizen of exclusive ivory towers, the white canonical author is here appropriated, biographically, as "one of us": specifically, a modern urbanite. The students do perk up a little, making shy and rather solemn jokes, but it does not bring them any closer to Poe (or poetry). Even Jamal, at this point trying to preserve his tough-guy reserve among his friends, will not admit to knowing anything about "The Raven."

In a way, Ms. Joyce's approach is reductive and Jamal is shown as being correct not to respond. As Van Sant shows us in the film, these Bronx kids may be tough and book-shy, but they are not thugs. Jamal poignantly explains, later in the film, that what breaks his heart about his neighborhood is that the police won't even protect it "after dark." When we see Jamal walking at night down a street where a police cruiser steers clear of a parked car that has been set on fire, we see how indulgent it would seem to him for a white like Poe to become strung out on cocaine and obsessed with death. Why admire anyone, much less a white, who chooses to flirt with falling through the cracks of a conservative society that has no qualms about removing its protections from, or never extending them in the first place to, someone born in Jamal's socio-racial-economic situation?

5. Finding Forrester: *Postmodern Skin, or The End of* Whose *History?*

In *Finding Forrester* (2000), a neglected masterwork, it is a long shot that a meeting of minds, as well as profound friendship, would occur between reclusive novelist Forrester (Sean Connery) and the gifted writing student and urban teenager Jamal (Rob Brown).

Where Forrester succeeds in a way that the teacher does not is partly because he shows Jamal that his own brand of renegade creativity is a kind of assault against the unfairness of that staid conservative society, but also something inherently honorable. The film centers around the fact that he and Jamal must honor the promises they make to each other as friends. One can be tough without being unkind, "hard" without being hysterical. One might be forced into an outlaw position, but through insulted honor rather than a flirtation with decadence.

It is not only that Forrester's postwar novel, "Avalon Landing," questioned American victory and exceptionalism; it is that the edgy Forrester himself makes the links between artistic creativity and criminal violence increasingly tangible throughout the film. It is part of the local urban legend surrounding him that he once killed someone; that is why he has become a recluse in hiding. In the early scene where Jamal sneaks into Forrester's apartment on a dare, the first object he touches is a large kitchen knife placed upon a stack of books; these objects of dissection or disarticulation (knife) and of creative wholeness (books) are brought together in a way which unmistakably recalls Burroughs' cut-ups, and which also leaves one wondering to what extent they can trade functions. Is the knife an exalted tool of wisdom? Are the books stabbing weapons? In a later scene, Forrester hands Jamal back one of his essays while gesturing at him in mock threat with this same knife in his other hand. The knife reoccurs at the end of the film, when Jamal uses it to open the last letter (the last writing) sent to him by Forrester — throughout *Finding Forrester*, writing and the blade are inextricable.

The knowledge which Forrester imparts to Jamal, about both literature and "life," has this double edge of affirming the young man as someone worthy of attention, worthy of being taken seriously as a man, a thinker and a writer, and also of carving away the young man's innocence. Forrester means nothing malicious by this, and certainly nothing racist, but Jamal's position of vulnerability suggests that in every exchange between whites and blacks, blacks always lose something. Whether the whites are openly disdainful, like the prep school's Professor Crawford (F. Murray Abraham), or friendly, like Forrester, the whites can only helplessly deliver bad news to the black characters — that things will be hard and uphill if not completely impossible. We see this, in fact, in the early "dare scene," where Jamal is supposed to bring something back from Forrester's apartment to prove that he has snuck inside, but ends up being startled by Forrester's sudden presence and running away, leaving behind his book bag. This loss of the book bag is immediately noticed the next day by Jamal's eagle-eyed mother, who questions him about it; having to replace such an item can mean economic disaster in a low-income household. What is even more unacceptable to Jamal's mother is that when she asks him how he lost the book bag he tells her only, "I don't know." Such obliviousness is a luxury that blacks cannot afford.

Finding Forrester evokes age-old problems of visibility and invisibility in relation to minorities within the dominant society. It is not only that blacks are "invisible" to whites, but that this invisibility is imposed because of an all too unavoidable *visibility* which displeases and discomforts white people. Van Sant includes several brilliant, succinct scenes in which Jamal is made to stand out as the sole dark face surrounded by whites: the slow-motion shots, somewhat reminiscent of Bruce Weber, in which Jamal is framed as the darkest member of the prep-school basketball team as they run onto the court; likewise, the crowded subway in which he is the only black riding in a train full of middle-aged white businessmen, all turning away from him in a way that seems less polite than chilly and deliberately ignoring. What stands out too easily can also be easily targeted; anyway, it is whites who control this looking, as when the young black teens are aware of Forrester spying on their basketball games from his window. This is before Jamal has befriended him, and indeed, Forrester's local nickname among the kids is "The Window," even as they somewhat ruefully acknowledge that the view is one-way only: "You ever seen him?" one kid asks, and another says, "Nah, but he see us, man." After Jamal loses his book bag in Forrester's apartment, Forrester hangs it up in this window; initially this seems like a taunting signal of having gotten over on the youth, but in fact it is the first indication that Forrester will allow black selfhood (symbolized by Jamal's book bag, which contains his journals with his writing in them) to stand in the former place of the white power to gaze with impunity and thereby to own. Conversely, when Professor Crawford accuses Jamal of plagiarism later in the film (unable to believe that "a basketball player from the Bronx," or in other words a low-income black youth, could write so well), he demands that Jamal write a new paper under Crawford's watchful, judgmental eyes: an attempt to confer ownership over Jamal's work which has the effect of causing the young man to become temporarily unable to produce.

In this sense, the light in Forrester's window (although it is not green) stands as something like "Daisy's light" for Jamal who, watching it at twilight from the basketball court, could be a young black urban Gatsby, not rich certainly and not depressively fatalistic, but still yearning for a desire of his own that could animate that vaguest and most lopsided abstraction, the American Dream. It is the hand-written note that Forrester leaves in Jamal's notebook— "Where are you taking me?"— that first enables Jamal to see Forrester's critiques of his writing not as harsh, unfriendly attacks but as a reaching-out toward shared journey and destination. Before Jamal can grow into the idea that he could lead a reader somewhere with his prose, or lead anyone anywhere, he must have the startling experience of feeling that someone would look to him for such exemplary decision-making, such gravitas, such meaning. Just as Gatsby's impersonal empire of nameless, faceless peons is founded on the slim but touching hope that his wealth could someday enjoy the purpose of taking care of one specific person: Daisy. In *Finding Forrester*, it is not a sexual or romantic yearning that possesses Jamal, but something far more terrible and difficult: that we can only achieve what we have in some way witnessed someone else achieve, someone who consents to welcome us into a circle of human blood and family. Someone who, in allowing his own life to be witnessed by us, makes us feel visible and real in turn.

The conservative literary canon is oppressively literalized in Professor Crawford's classroom, by two large, dense rows of portraits along the rear wall: all famous authors, nearly all of them men, and all of them white. In *Utopia Limited*, Marianne DeKoven strongly implies that the regime of postmodernism was a way for heterosexual white males to retain their dominance of U.S. fiction after the "endpoint of modernism."[17] It was a way of changing the rules of the game, so that skill (often a quality acquired through institutional educational systems, or conferred by fiat) would trump the truth of those other/othered voices attempting to assert themselves and be heard. Likewise, postmodernism seemed to allow these formerly suppressed minorities to have their say, but only in a new era given over to an emphasis on empty, interchangeable identities and meanings, and merely relative truths. This not only invalidated the actual testimony of minorities; it permitted white straight male writers to adopt and ventriloquize the positions of cultural Others without having earned the right to do so. Thus, it allowed those "white male sixties experimentalists who did persist into postmodernity [to be] engaged directly [with] the question of otherness ... that has become central in postmodernity."[18]

DeKoven believes that postmodernism had already begun to flower during the 60s, an era which Van Sant's films, in their politicization of the personal and in their restless quest for expanding consciousness, often seem to evoke. For DeKoven, the 60s "combined, without recognizing a distinction between them, what we now think of as postmodern identity politics — characterized by limited agendas and goals, particular and exclusive to its own identity category — with the universalist, liberatory goals of modernity."[19] The idea, which Van Sant seems to espouse and has helped to articulate with his films, is to acknowledge, again, that fragmented viewpoint of postmodernism, those multiple histories which have replaced the master narrative of a singular history, but to treat these as philosophical and aesthetic advancements rather than setbacks, and to yoke them into the service of a return to human truths and meanings that are not relative but re-universalized in a "liberatory" way.

His films are what I would call experiential texts, in this sense. They are not meant to be hermeneutically paraphrased but to be taken as direct reconstitutions of raw life or experience. This experience can already be mediated or secondhand, as in the case of intertextual usages or appropriations. Even there, it denotes the awareness that someone else has gone before, has seen and felt certain recognizable things. To be a member of a specific oppressed identity can be important, since it enables people, artists, to connect, often over decades or centuries, around the shared experience of how it feels to have such an identity. But all this means, finally, when pursued to its reasonable, logical conclusion, is that the human can be located within any identity whatever that identity's nominal viewpoint; and within any viewpoint whatever that viewpoint's nominal identity. All identities become valid as pure experience. At its best, experiential identity allows one to speak "in his own person" and also "simultaneously, with no sense of self-contradiction, ... as part of a 'we' ..."[20] as part of "the persistence of utopian hope and desire in post-utopian, postmodern culture...."[21] This is what Dr. Outlaw has termed "the recovery of history, of historical meanings"[22] as not merely "deconstructive" but "reconstructive."[23]

The question of authorship, however teased and unsettled by *Finding Forrester*, is allowed to become fixed again, at the end, as words return to their rightful "owners." Jamal is cleared of plagiarism charges when Forrester himself steps forward to hold him up as a uniquely gifted writer, and as a friend. The writing that they did together in the film, and which connects them almost like (I want to say) a paternal umbilicus, gives way to their separate voices, as Forrester the father-teacher affirms Jamal's graduation to being his own man, his own writer, his own voice. The idea of a completely authorless art, or a text whose authorship is uniquely shared, like Burroughs' cut-ups (attractive and subversive as this idea is), finally takes a backseat, in this case, to the idea that the "privilege" of aesthetic theory and cultural production can be extended to the unprivileged — must be extended to the unprivileged. For those who have been historically marginalized within culture (and Van Sant, as a gay man, is no stranger to this), the need to prove themselves in a hostile and biased system often requires that they need all the help they can get. There are few moments in recent cinema as moving as the one in which Forrester tells the astonished English class that the work of fiction which he has just read to them was not written by himself but by Jamal, who sits among them, cast out, disdained, then suddenly lifted up by the support of his famous friend. The idea that language can matter, that, even in the midst of its incessant mutational rearrangements in postmodernism, it can provide an ultimate truth, an ultimate heroism, is an idea which has roots in the more resolute era of modernism and in the radical 60s. Van Sant's cinema may revel in pomo surfaces and nonlinear relativisms, but it knows right from wrong, and furthermore it believes in the difference. *Finding Forrester* may be the clearest and most uplifting proof of this.

— Part Two —
Time Names

These images, unreal, fixed, always alike, filling all my nights and days, differentiated this period in my life from those which had gone before it (and might easily have been confused with it by an observer who saw things only from without, that is to say who saw nothing), as in an opera a melodic theme introduces a novel atmosphere which one could never have suspected if one had done no more than read the libretto, still less if one had remained outside the theatre counting only the minutes as they passed. And besides, even from the point of view of mere quantity, in our lives the days are not all equal. To get through each day, natures that are at all highly strung, as was mine, are equipped, like motor-cars, with different gears. There are mountainous, arduous days, up which one takes an infinite time to climb, and downward-sloping days which one can descend at full tilt, singing as one goes. — Marcel Proust

6. Van Sant and Queer Cinema

I worship a new icon, the dog with wings, god of fun and teenage integrity. —Sam D'Alessandro[1]

Twilight of the Divas

As one of our foremost directors who is also gay, there have been obligatory attempts to place Gus Van Sant within the history of queer cinema, where he does and does not fit. Graham Fuller, one of Van Sant's most perceptive early critics, warned us off this problem of limiting Van Sant to "gay films" back in 1993, calling him "essentially a gay director of films rather than a director of gay films...."[2] But while Fuller championed this distinction as a way in which Van Sant discovered a heightened and more universal humanity in *all* of his characters, the classificatory issues presented by Van Sant remained difficult to wish away. The fact is—as is the case with, say, *Midnight Cowboy*—one misses a lot if one watches Van Sant's films from a non-gay perspective; at the same time, a gay person is not likely to feel especially or consistently comforted by them. Van Sant's films are often concerned with shifting, or lack of, identity (in all aspects) rather than affirming pride in one specific orientation.

Although much of his cinema swirls dreamily around masculine beauty, there is a cooling reserve in the sense that there rarely seems to be lust in the almost neo-classical way that Van Sant's camera watches his male characters. Even when he films them partially nude, Van Sant does not "cruise" his male characters the way Kenneth Anger or Paul Morrissey, for instance, have done in their films—with Anger inscribing himself as a literal cruiser within *Fireworks* (1947), still the ultimate Rosetta Stone of queer cinema. It is a different aesthetic; Van Sant conjures and hovers around floppy straight hair, sweet limpid eyes, fulsome lips, but there is a sense in which the precise question of sex is never asked (unlike the way Morrissey's massaging camera constantly asks this implicit question of the nude Joe Dallesandro). Van Sant is more of a romantic, but not a soft or sentimental one. Frequently, his characters want to love but cannot; want to be strong men without knowing how. Van Sant's films finally place one in a kind of Interzone of the mind, where "manliness" (real and conceptual) is often at stake, where isolation reigns, and where offbeat, doomed, bedraggled tenderness supplants the closed ranks of proud community identification.

For one thing, the (gay) world which Gus Van Sant depicts is not caught up in campy glamour or excess, but simple, even street-level survival, in which love reaches across the boundaries of essentialist or political identity. The few characters in his films who *are* campy — Daddy Carroll (Mickey Cottrell) in *My Own Private Idaho*, the Countess (John Hurt) in *Even Cowgirls Get the Blues* — are indulged as much as celebrated; and significantly, they are also from the older generation, isolated figures from some waxworks past, set off inside diorama-like apartments cluttered with antiques and bric-a-brac. Prior to *Milk*, the closest Van Sant came to depicting an insular gay group is the circle around Bob in *My Own Private Idaho*, and this, significantly, is also given the safe remove of historical distance: it is couched not entirely within a modern moment but a faux–Elizabethan-Shakespearean one; thus it has the effect of "acting a show." And unlike Warhol's Factory scene, this milieu is almost never screamingly high on its own radical chic, but forlorn, hushed, self-doubting. (But, not unlike the Factory, this pseudo-queer scene also doubles or disguises as a druggie scene, a street-kid scene, etc.)

In terms of the question of camp, gay cinema of the postwar years has become, in some ways, as remote from us as Rococo, Baroque and Mannerist painting. Like those genres of classical art, it was a way of willing the physical form into an idealized, or at times freakish, set of gestures — gestures which highlighted the distance between image and reality. The self-willed, self-invented "superstars" employed by Warhol, Jack Smith and John Waters, suggest that for stars in general the problems of life can exist only tenuously, melting away under the scalding glare of spotlights. It is the sacrosanct untouchability of the diva. The diva will do anything to become famous because fame means never having to be lonely. (As if.)

Sam D'Allesandro writes: "She said: I'm gonna make it in this town if it kills me. My name's gonna be in that goddamn cement in front of that stupid theater if I have to pour the shit myself."[3] This is the outrageous, funky power of the diva — vulgar, shopworn, always close to street level, but nevertheless imperious and entitled. The diva speaks; the world listens. A tear glints in the corner of the diva's eye; the world proffers a hanky. The cement is goddamn shit, the theater is stupid, making it will most likely kill her —

she acknowledges all this without batting a lash, at once immersed in fame to the point of drowning while always above it too, scornful that anything so cheap could cost so much.

And the diva does not have to really try, because the thing that commands attention is identical to who she always already is in the first place, a kind of ceremonial essence. Warhol waxes poetically banal over what makes Ingrid Superstar his "favorite" superstar: "My favorite superstar is Ingrid Superstar because, because, because she's just her. She's a real person; she's not phony. She's just her. She's a real person. She says and does whatever she happens to feel like doing and saying at the time."[4]

Where problems persist, they do so deliberately, because the stars themselves cultivate a more eccentric, "spectacularly freakish"[5] presentation: streaky make-up, fright wigs, drug-induced paranoia, etc. So, we learn that Ingrid has "got a crooked mouth and a stray dog face sometimes and she keeps on going up and down through life's euphorics."[6] But even such freakishness is part of the dream of (queer) stardom and exceptionality. The true diva has her revenge when she is seen as trash while still remaining a diva. "She was nothing but a piece of trash — she looked like a piece of trash, but she looks so much better right now."[7]

This having-it-both-ways has often spoken to gay men, unduly judged for behaviors they themselves consider normal and cannot change. Time is not mortal time, in all of its injustice, instead it is always pregnant with an immortality of comebacks and redemptions. The diva *gets away with it all*; she can always finesse a hit out of a flop, an extra curtain call, even the tarnish only adds to her allure. Tinckom writes that Waters' films invoke "the specter of stardom in the everyday" and ask "what it takes to become a star"[8] — yet so many of Waters' films are about literally getting away, or not getting away, with murder. This only signifies an extreme test of glamour's outer limits — what the diva, alone among humans, *can* get away with, *deserves* to get away with, including the most extreme crime of all.

We see Van Sant largely rejecting this strategy, however. Not that he is completely disconnected from other legendary gay filmmakers (ones who still believed in the power of divas, perhaps), but even these connections tend to be problematic; there is a sense, among his youthful protagonists, of the times having simply moved on. For instance, *My Own Private Idaho* specifically evokes both Rainer Werner Fassbinder, in the performance of Fassbinder protégé Udo Kier as Hans, a middle-class sadomasochist; as well as Pier Paolo Pasolini in the Roman street scenes where we see not only young hustlers on the make but a passing woman who strongly resembles Maria Callas. But neither the Fassbinder nor the Pasolini references are appreciated by *My Own Private Idaho*'s teen protagonists. It is reminiscent of Kathy Acker's punk narrators communing with Dickens or Genet, in which the famous cultural icons become altered by the exchange more than their identity-bending interrogators. The "old" gay ways are viewed as simply uncool, or as places of only deceptive refuge (logical, after all, in a post–AIDS world). For example, in the scene where Hans lip-syncs to Krautrock, Scott gets up and clicks off the tape because the decadent, sinister song is clearly disturbing the wary Mike; later, after charging Hans for sex, the boys make a point of laughing about him together, as if to show that they do not care about his excesses, his stylized will to power.

Likewise, the Rome which obliquely evokes Pasolini becomes a place of trauma, where Mike loses the bisexual Scott to Carmella. Van Sant's forward-thinking queer cinema is divested of pious baggage from the past, and invested instead with a spirit of youth caught up in moment-by-moment survival, unwilling to waste time by looking back or venerating. Indeed, one of the most liberating things about *My Own Private Idaho* was the way it presented itself as an offhanded smashing of well-worn idols in favor of current, youthful ones. There is something similar in the autodidacticism of young Will in *Good Will Hunting*, a recognizably American spirit of being oppositional to all institutional authorities. This makes Will, too, a somewhat queer, though not gay, figure, and we can even read his character as a radical transmutation of the diva's self-invention and challenge to social norms even in the figure of the ultra-butch hellion.

In any event, the future of queer cinema did not rest with camp's retro-agonies, but with the literal, teleological future itself: teenagers. Queer cinema was about to merge with youth culture and youth cinema in a radical way, thanks to the pioneering efforts of Van Sant, Bruce Weber, Ron Nyswaner, and a certain cultural phenomenon named Keanu Reeves.

Discovering Youth: Bruce Weber's Broken Noses

One notable turning point in queer cinema was Bruce Weber's documentary *Broken Noses* (1987), in which the tension arising from an openly gay filmmaker delving into the daily existence, both trivial and exciting, of young Olympic boxer Andy Minsker, ended up setting a new trend for "unfiltered reality" as entertainment and for "real people" as readymade stars. Indeed, the day Weber and Minsker found each other was a banner one for gay and mainstream culture alike.

Gay male and straight All-American teen found each other at just the point where both were in need of a kind of makeover. The gay male was trying to overcome the persistence of homophobia in the AIDS era — while the teen male, for his part, bore an even more complex relation to social culture. As Thomas Hine reminds us in his fascinating book *The Rise and Fall of the American Teenager*, the teenager is a social construction who did not exist (at least as we know him or her today) prior to the affluence of postwar American society. From the seventeenth century through the Second World War, it was commonplace for kids to work, marry and reproduce almost as soon as they became physically capable of these things: "A boy big enough to do a man's work would be doing it."[9] Now we regard it as inhumane, for the most part, to throw still-developing adolescents into the adult world too suddenly; and yet, some of the changes in our social customs toward teens were not even strictly motivated by altruism and sensitization: "The movement to restrict child labor, for example, was driven in part by a desire to shrink the labor force and raise wages."[10] What is indisputable is the fact that prolonging childhood into a person's early 20s created a new class of "style setters and consumers"[11]; although this phenomenon came with attendant phobias from the start. "[Teens] are envied and sold to, studied and deplored. They are expected to break the rules, but there are other restrictions that apply only to them."[12]

The male teen of the 80s was the first generation of men to come of age after the feminist revolution. It was this generation that was looked toward as manifesting either a more heightened consciousness or a sexist backlash — or both. In fact, both enlightenment and backlash have been evolving in tandem over the past few decades; but at root, one of the more epochal occurrences of the late 20th century was the way in which the young straight male was sort of "handed off," culturally, to the gay man. Women had their hands full trying to change the already grown men; the "boys" were still something of a sociological non-entity. But as young women began defining themselves, in various ways, as separate from, equal or even superior to their male counterparts, the young men found increasing favor with gay men (and gay artists) who took up the young men's cause. In the off-balance, reviled and (it was thought) sex-obsessed male teen, the gay man saw what he hoped would be a kindred spirit. A connoisseurship of adolescent beauty (James Dean was a too-early, stranded harbinger of this cult) seemed to pick up where Michelangelo and Caravaggio had left off, in the Renaissance; even Dorian Gray would have been slightly too old, but the mood was caught by Tom Cruise's high-school pimp in the suburban fantasy, *Risky Business* (1983), just the right mix of virgin-shy and cocky.

That movie was insidious to some for the way it made prostitution seem golden and cozy; indeed, there was so much focus on whether the women were being exploited (and of course they were) that few paid much attention to the fact that the film was really a landmark for objectifying the teen male and *his* sexuality. Here was a patriarch-in-training, and it was precisely this training status that made Cruise so likable and unobjectionable. He was struggling to catch up, getting a break from life, so to speak; the older woman (Rebecca De Mornay) and her fellow working girls had knowledge to impart, while Cruise looked like the juiced-up toy. Brilliantly, *Risky Business* incorporated early feminist lessons — that a man could and should learn from a woman, that a man can be "used" for sex by a woman — while tending toward a world in which the rich, straight, white male retained an ultimate power and a kind of *carte blanche*.

Still, the teen's shifting status as either underdog or top dog had a threatening and subversive side. Hine writes: "The mere presence of teenagers threatens us."[13] If this panic sounds familiar, it is because we could easily substitute "queers" for "teenagers" and the same statement would apply. In part, it is a problem of classification, similar to the generic "nature vs. nurture" debate about homosexuality. Is adolescence an innate quality that everyone experiences in more or less the same way, or do we need to consider it more provisionally, on a sui generis basis? Also, teens (whether straight or gay) and queers both titillate the mainstream by "breaking the rules" in "expected" ways, then become subject to specific backlashes. In the early 60s, Warhol spoke in favor of teens, calling them "the modern outlaws": "When teen-agers are accused of doing wrong things, it was just the other people who thought they were bad. The movies I'll be doing will be for young people; I'd like to portray them in my films, too."[14] Like homophobia, fear or hatred of teens was just a misguided perception, a projection of one's own "bad" or "wrong" onto an attractive, magnetic target. To make films "for" teenagers — or "to portray them" in one's films — was a kind of guarantor of being new, hip, futuristic.

Except that for teens the future already seemed to be dwindling more than for the rest of the U.S. Throughout the 80s, teenagers found themselves blamed for many societal ills, as their drug and alcohol use soared along with dropout and pregnancy rates. Surveys found teens to be increasingly pessimistic about their lives in general,[15] and even this malaise was held against them, as though, if our kids weren't somehow constantly, mindlessly happy, it was, again, threatening to the social order as a whole. There has been a similar syndrome with gays (the name in itself bearing an ironic relation to the idea of "happy people"): straights still seem to accept us better as funny, fun-loving, empty-headed, sexually frustrated clowns rather than as real, complex, serious, or successful individuals.

In any event, by 1987 the teenager wanted nothing more than to be seen as something other than either a scary delinquent or an Eagle Club conformist; he wanted to be taken seriously, and there, serendipitously enough, was the gay male, ready to hang upon his every word. Again, the ancient Greek and Italian Renaissance taste for smooth, defined, slim bodies and fresh, boyish, even pretty features ("It's tempting to see [the ancient Greeks] as premature Californians — in love with skin and muscle...")[16] returned in the form of advertising, film, and TV, married now to the social-outreach perception that if we just listen to what teens have to say, we can make them feel important rather than "arbitrary and confusing."[17] At the same time, in taking the teen seriously, we made him elegiac, his passing moment gone in the instant it was grasped and named. To be overly aware of one's own youth is to worry that one is losing it, or has somehow let it slip away. (Title of one of the "lost" Velvet Underground songs: "I'm Not a Young Man Anymore."[18])

Recently I overheard a male adolescent on a bus complain to his friends: "I have the worst luck with stuff. I don't know if it's karma, or what I've created, but I have the worst luck." I was struck by his "old-before-my-time" sentiment, and though I would not question the truth of how he felt, I think his lament encapsulates the modern teen's central contradiction. On one hand, he is supposed to be free from the burdens of adulthood, but at the same time, this freedom, being so temporal and temporary, is fraught with a sense of expiration, of one's time becoming arbitrarily "up." And thus, the teen, like some fragile dying swan, could again speak to and for queers, also dying swans in that first decade of the AIDS crisis. Moreover, by championing teens, the gay male could protest against heterosexual society by separating himself from other adults who "are often ambivalent about surrendering their authority over to the young people ... and welcoming them into the circle of adults."[19] One could imagine — or dream — that the teen was fighting our age-old battles for us, within the very families formed around the rejection and exclusion of our gay desire.

It is also possible that the gay man admires the teen's ability to evade classification or to act out: "Because the young people are not quite visible, and certainly not fathomable, adults avert their eyes from what they do. Theft, rowdy and violent behavior, and sexual activity that would ordinarily not be tolerated are condoned."[20] Teen self-contradictoriness becomes almost an aphrodisiac — a perfect covering of all the bases — as when William Burroughs describes young men as "dreamy and brutal, depraved and innocent."[21] Or, as when Sam D'Allesandro writes: "Our sex organs worked now but we were still children.... We were afraid of the adults we were becoming and we didn't want to be children anymore."[22]

The teenager is a living protest. This is why the gay male tends to look toward the straight teen as a younger brother, or perhaps more accurately, however odd it seems, a figure of fatherness, as we saw in the relation between Walt and the Mexican youths in *Mala Noche*, for example. After all, the straight teen is engaged in passing social rites of manhood, some of which (heterosexual sex) were intentionally abdicated by the queer; on the one hand, this confers a kind of superior masculinity (at least in heteronormative terms) upon the teen. Yet, unlike the heteronormative adult, whose role has been cemented by time, the queer does not hold the teen's heterosexuality against him, because the teen is viewed as an experimental creature. He might, or he might not. Like Cruise in *Risky Business*, the patriarch-in-training can be "adorable" where the actual patriarch is just oppressive. In this sense, even the queer view of teen males, though highly sympathetic, nonetheless replicates the judgment of the wider society from whom teens are often almost as isolated as queers: the teen is only going through "phases," blowing with the wind, damned if he does and damned if he doesn't.

Van Sant chose to center his contribution to *8* (2008), "Mansion on the Hill," around casually shot footage of suburban teen skateboarders, while messages flashed onscreen about the staggering numbers of children around the world who suffer and die from extreme hunger and poverty. The teens vouchsafe a certain sincerity; rather than adopting "alien" images of the Third World, which might seem glib or hypocritical coming from a comfortable U.S. artist, Van Sant places on the table, so to speak, one of the centers of his own compassion and human feeling. But the teens do not sweeten or distract (overmuch) from the grim statistics for which they serve as background. We might be tempted to regard the athletic boys, owners of pricey boards and trendy outfits, as designating that folkloric "mansion on the hill" which Third World children are denied; and indeed, that is one meaning of the segment. However, it would be reductive to think that the problems of the world can be solved by skateboarding, or that, just because these American kids own skateboards, that they are fulfilled, hopeful, or even safe. In fact, by virtue of their youth if nothing else, the skate-kids in "Mansion on the Hill" make us think directly about the other children, the ones whom it might be more difficult for some Americans to visualize. In particular, Van Sant makes the short film's climax (coinciding with some of the most dire statistics about mortality rates) a moment in which one of the boys takes a fall from his board, but gets back up and starts skating again. The optimistic nature of this recovery is meant not only to demonstrate the resiliency of youth, but to heroicize it.

The American teen, then, can be given a sort of solidarity, not absolutely commensurable but "felt," with the plight of kids everywhere. As kids, they stand for vulnerability, innocence, the future. Teens have an inherently political element: they are uniquely subject to laws which they themselves never made or voted for. In 19th century literature, it was often women who were depicted as the outsider/other; in the 20th century, blacks, Jews and gays, with all of these minorities being depicted as, among other things, infantilized by persecution and prejudice. Today, in the new millennium, the teen has taken over this codifying role as the emblem of put-upon humanity. Even specifically feminist, racist, queer or anti-Semitic issues are rendered more legible to us, in culture today, when they are presented as happening to teenagers, within teen subcultures. But what is suggested by this — to me, anyway — is not so much that teens have become "serious" (if anything, their infantilization is allowed for, a priori, and taken advantage of, for the purpose of the message-mongering) but that the issues of discriminatory abuse have become more trivial. Like some fad waiting to be outgrown, it could be said that angst-ridden teens have become the sugar in the placebo of social activism.

Thus, is it any wonder that the results of this utopia of angst have been mixed, and have not guaranteed real sociopolitical change? What was a source

Bruce Weber's *Broken Noses* (1987) was an unprecedented documentary about young Olympic boxer Andy Minsker (pictured). The film had a subtext of homo-aestheticization between Weber as gay artist and his good-natured subject Minsker as an icon of straight young masculinity. Suddenly, average teen life was taken seriously in ways that it had never quite been before; the image of teenage man, with his identity conflicts and struggles for power, merged with queer subjectivity's own attempt to define itself within the public sphere, making "queer cinema" and "youth cinema" ubiquitous subsets of each other ever since.

of iconoclastic art for Bruce Weber (and dubious neo-celebrity for Andy Minsker), in *Broken Noses*, has become the bottom line of commercial enterprise: Hollywood has proffered teen adaptations of everything from Shakespeare to *Rear Window* to *Single White Female*, and now, with the blockbuster *Twilight* series and its various offshoots, vampires have never been hotter (what genius to have a clique literally frozen in time at age eighteen, able to experience growing pains and hormonal surges forever). In this whole bonanza of cashing in on teen culture, the queer dollar is treated as the sure thing in this covert bisexual three-way: gays are expected to buy a straight-identified teen heartthrob; straights are rarely expected to buy a gay-identified one.

I seem to be being hard on the spread of teen culture and even its conscious "gay-branding." In fact, real affinities do exist between queer adults and straight/queer teens, although it is often a delicate matter, given to controversy. There is an intriguing story behind *Broken Noses* itself. Weber had been photographing the Olympic boxing team for *Interview*; he was set up by one of the boxers, who went back to the Olympic committee and accused him of unprofessional misconduct toward him. This piqued the interest of another Olympic boxer, Andy Minsker, who reportedly said that the administration tried to talk him out of putting himself into Weber's hands: "They told me that I was forbidden to come meet you. They said that you'd give me a weird haircut and make me wear skimpy see-through clothes, and who knows what else you'd do to me, and I thought, that's all I needed to hear. I'm on my way."

For whatever reason, Minsker was eager to buck the paternalistic homophobes who sought to keep him (and the Olympics) away from anything remotely gay; and from these seeds of subversion a great film — a great collaboration between artist Weber and *objet d'art* Minsker — was born. The film, made in Minsker's hometown of Portland, suggests that the boxer is more good sport than publicity seeker, though clearly he is not shy of the camera's attention; in spite of his quoted statement (used in the film almost a waiver), he is not glammed-up or feminized. On the contrary. It is precisely the purity of Misnker's youthful masculinity that is highlighted as *Broken Noses*' shiny, idyllic centerpiece.

Along with *Mala Noche* (also filmed in Portland, as most of Van Sant's films are), *Broken Noses* marks the true beginning of modern queer U.S. cinema — with the former mode of isolation within an insular, camp-inflected demimonde giving way to sites of interaction between gays and straights, and direct confrontations with homophobia. *Broken Noses*, boldly enough, shows the gay world gazing at the straight world with unabashed if not entirely requited longing; Weber, of course, was star-struck by Minsker himself: he found the boxer a handsome, high-cheekboned lookalike for the young Chet Baker, the subject of Weber's excellent second film, *Let's Get Lost* (1988). In turn, Minsker seems to have been impressed by Weber or by "the star-maker machinery" (Joni Mitchell) that Weber represented. That's why *Broken Noses* works so well, and why its revolutionary premise — that an ultra-straight, athletic kid would consent to be the star of a film made by a hip, sophisticated gay artist — can sneak up on audiences even today.

Like the trophy-cluttered bedroom of the teen himself, *Broken Noses* feels like a site of exciting and forbidden knowledge. The talkative, articulate, friendly Minsker mediates constantly (if largely unconsciously) between the tough, straight world of the boxers and the homoerotic aestheticization practiced by Weber. Occasionally Minsker giggles in embarrassment, but he pushes on, wanting to reveal himself to Weber's camera fully, both physically and emotionally. Weber plays to Minsker's strengths as a subject, taking him as he is — hetero, family-oriented, "red-blooded," even corny and a bit of a redneck — without trying to remake him. The only scene that nearly makes Minsker stumble is when Weber asks him to read a passage from *Richard II* ("...let us sit upon the ground/And tell sad stories about the death of kings....") in the middle of a blossoming rose garden; the flowers and poetry seem to crack Minsker's façade a little, but he gamely completes Weber's fantasy. What is crucial about this moment is the way it establishes the elegiac side of powerful, all-conquering youth: in his ideal state the adolescent is fleeting and doomed, like the roses, like the Shakespearean kings.

Meanwhile, in other, quasi–Kenneth-Anger montages, Weber makes the most of his young boxer subjects (a number of scenes show the members of the Portland Boxing Club), bathing them in romantic sunlight as they jog down the street in a half-naked pack, get their brush cuts and bushy eyebrows combed for a photo shoot, and otherwise flex their muscles. These montages are composed of seeming snapshots, which fade or cut away almost as soon as they materialize, while the soundtrack gushes with incongruous but unironic, sincere love ballads: Johnny Hartman's "Dedicated to You," Chet Baker and Ruth Young's "Whatever Possessed Me," Baker's "Foolish Heart," and (most wickedly) Joni James' "They Try to Tell Us We're Too Young" over a sequence of two eight-year-olds duking it out in the ring.

Not only tapping into one of the last great fountains of material left to the mass media ("ordinary reality"), Weber took the sheer *looking*-ness of Warholian cinema in a whole new direction. *Broken Noses* valorized raw youth as it was, because it saw in that youth a kindred awkward spirit. Much of the footage is as simple as can be: Minsker talking about his friends and girlfriends, talking with his dad, ironing his t-shirt, coaching. The only glamour here is an inverse of traditional sophisticated glamour: a glamour of sweat and tobacco spit, of baseball caps and headlocks. The youth who wonders whether he has grown into a man yet, who strives to prove that he has, and who still lives in the bosom of his family the way the queer lives in straight society, as the blushing, ripening bud of an eternally policed sexuality — this kind of youth was, again, a subversion of the heterosexual family from within. In this sense, Weber was only partaking of a long gay tradition in literature if not quite in cinema. One thinks of Rimbaud: "*J'ai connu chaque fils de famille!*" [I have known all the sons of good families!][23] (Rimbaud was the first queer teen idol.) The height of the irony is reached when Minsker's mom (who has more or less admitted to emotionally and physically abusing Andy in his childhood) drunkenly slurs at Weber, "You oughta come to Portland all the time and straighten families out," after her son has praised his upbringing to the omnipresent camera.

The 80s — the age of Reagan — was a highly conservative time in the U.S. Jingoism and militarism saw a resurgence, along with AIDS-driven homophobia. It was a uniquely difficult time to be gay in America, and therefore we must ask whether Weber's idolization of young, straight, crew-cut jocks was, in part, a reactionary move, a kind of "sleeping with the enemy."

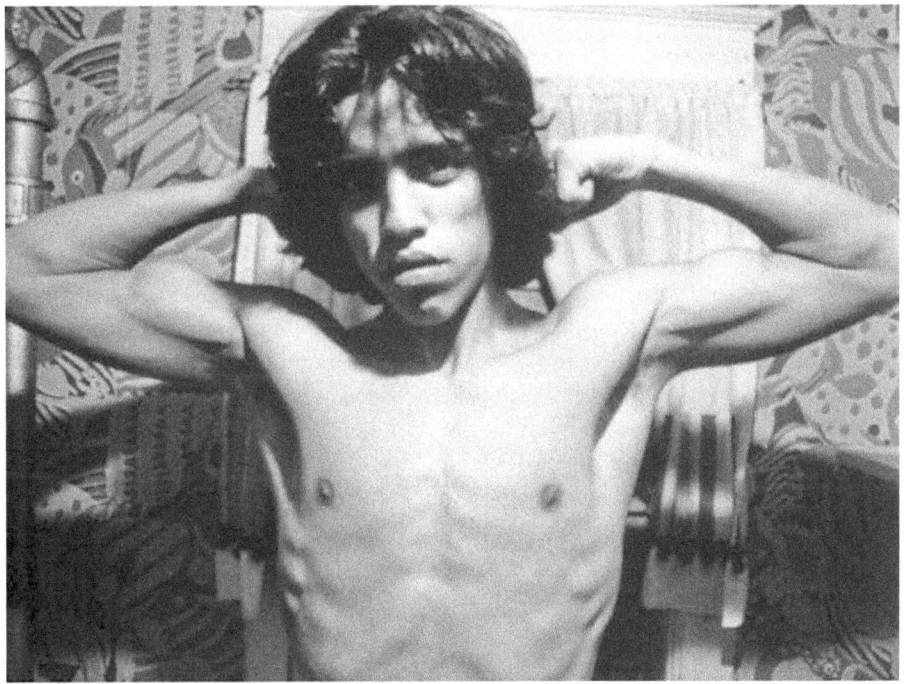

Johnny (Doug Cooeyate) shows off his muscles in Van Sant's *Mala Noche* (1987). The teenage male is an emblem of living contradictions: strong and fragile, happy-go-lucky and touched by automatic elegy, filled with presence yet often invisible, feared as potentially out of control and destructive yet also dismissed as insignificant. In this, he has solidarity with all "underclasses" everywhere.

Only a few years before, in the 60s and 70s, that same all–American jock had been a figure of ridicule to the long-haired hippies of the antiwar movement. Granted, the spread of rock music and pot from the counterculture to the mainstream had made it much hazier, in the 80s, to predict political affiliations based on outward appearances; at the same time these same accoutrements (rock, pot) had ceased to indicate automatic leftism. Perhaps *Broken Noses* was only what it seemed to be, on Weber's part: a way of building bridges between the gay and straight communities, and a radical appropriation of the straight youth as an object of gay desire, a public and an unapologetic declaration that, like it or not, gay men were looking. I am not suggesting that Weber is racist, or even, by indulging so much straight maleness, covertly homophobic; anyway, sexual tastes are always irreducible. Nonetheless, we feel a broader outreach in Van Sant's work, for, although Van Sant and Weber have shared a similar interest in teen life, the two artists are not quite on the same page. Unlike the white, typically Midwestern, butch types who appear in *Broken Noses* as well as Weber's other films and books of photographs, youths of color have often been central to Van Sant's work — as we have seen in *Mala Noche* and *Finding Forrester*—as well as the willowy, floppy-haired, decidedly non-jock, almost androgynous boys who are the heroes of *Elephant* (John) and *Paranoid Park* (Alex).

The Case of Keanu Reeves

Another crucial event along the same lines as Van Sant's *Mala Noche* and Weber's *Broken Noses* was the arrival of a young actor who quickly became a cultural phenomenon: Keanu Reeves — as Paul Burston writes, "not only the most talked about actor of his age [but] an 'icon' whose 'cultural significance' is weighed up everywhere, from the pages of *The Modern Review* to the lecture halls of the Art Centre College of Design, Pasadena, where students are invited to 'use Reeves' films as a departure point for discussing culture and philosophy.'"[24] A large part of this "cultural significance" has turned upon public speculation about the actor's true sexuality: Reeves stands directly at the center of queer cinema's rendezvous with youth in the late 80s. Michael De Angelis coins the word "panaccessible"[25] to describe how Reeves "embodies multiple identities that have been and continue to be appealing within and outside gay culture ... [but remains] always capable of exceeding the constraints that any single image imposes on him."[26]

These images correspond to sexual fantasies in which identity becomes labile, brushed aside in the name of powerful urges and compelling seduction scenarios: he is straight but possibly available; he is posing as straight but actually gay; he is gay for pay, for the right price; he is bisexual; he is open to anything and everything. Indeed, many of the fantasies swirling around the young Reeves had less to do with his Asian-inflected good looks or Rococo shag-hair, as with the fact that a number of his early roles were variations on a classic Valley-boy airhead who seemed like he wouldn't even know if his pants were on or off— someone dumb, juicy and ripe for the plucking. "Young, dumb and full of come" is how Burston puts it,[27] quoting a well-placed line from *Point Break* (1991), one of Reeves' action-star vehicles, which Burston calls a "sperm-fest of surf, sweat and male bonding rituals...."[28]

But Reeves managed to bring a kind of nobility to "idiot boy" roles: indeed, such a cast-off kid can get away with things that a more solemn person cannot, and in this way, Reeves reinvented what a kid is, by focusing on teendom's wild, animalistic (and disappointed) side. To this day, the way he takes Ione Skye Leitch away from Crispin Glover by launching into a lusty, *a capella* rendition of the *Mission Impossible* theme in *River's Edge*, or the full-lunged crow he emits on the rooftop in *My Own Private Idaho*, after pouring his drink down on Bob's head, are two of the great (adolescent) moments in all of cinema.

It turned out that Reeves was impatient to grow up and shed the "stoner kid" image. Because of that fantasy stoner kid's mix of lethargy and abandon, Reeves conveyed a remarkable honesty. He stared; he breathed through his mouth; he stammered a thickly nasal shield of not really wanting to speak at all, not wanting to be put on the spot (by adults). Dennis Cooper has admired the fact that Reeves seemed "incapable of conveying dishonesty," and that he was "always kind of talking around what [he] actually [wants] to say."[29] Sure, he might have seemed hazy, out of it, oblivious, but he registered, with some automatic sixth sense, a true friend from an enemy, a genuine person from a phony. Sincerity as exclusivity is part of the appeal of youth in the first place, the idea that by impressing *him* one has been admitted to a secret club, much harder to get into even than the chicest nightclub, because unlike adults a kid does not care about status, flattery or even accomplishment, but only what one says and does, moment by moment, to express an authentic self. (Some of this is surely an idealization, but it is certainly grounded in truth.)

This plays into gay fantasmatics around the act of coming out: that one will be embraced and loved for one's honesty, that one will be seen as authentic and non-threatening (when the harsh reality is often just the opposite). The thing that the stammering Reeves can't quite say, but which is right on the tip of his tongue, that elusive truth, ties in directly with the gay man's secret sexuality and its revelation. We, too, have felt backed into a corner, tongue-tied, because of straights, *our* version of the adults who are the kid's eternal nemeses. And thus, we can see him as part of our (gay) world even if, rationally, we admit that he might not be: "New 'unauthorized' fantasy scenarios are generated through rumor and gossip discourses that the subculture has used to sustain and stabilize the possibility of the 'if only' of fantasy."[30]

As we emerged in greater numbers as a demographic in the late 80s and early 90s, gays could even imagine that we had solely created icons like Reeves, and that his fame belonged to us. Recognizing that there was money to be made in crossing over to a gay as well as a straight audience, "the Hollywood film industry has often been quite strategic in allowing for star appeal across the often blurry lines of sexual orientation,"[31] while of course insisting that an actor explicitly identify as straight, both in his personal life (tabloids) and the majority of his roles. And we even fantasized that "our Keanu" needed us to liberate him from this industry enforcement of straightness, by supporting him all the more. The pink dollar (or in the U.K., the pink pound) can be counted on by the industry to support a straight-identified heartthrob; the straight dollar is not yet expected to support a queer-identified one.

For this reason, however, there is also a certain price to pay for being a partly-mainstream, partly-queer icon, since the gay community, recognizing itself at a disadvantage and tired of being taken for granted, is often vigilant against getting betrayed by those whom it has trusted. There is an exchange in Cooper's famous 1991 interview with Reeves, regarding a moment from one of Reeves' mainstream films, *Parenthood* (1990):

> DENNIS COOPER: Well, at one point your character does this monologue about how his father used to wake him up by flicking lit cigarettes at his head. It concluded with a statement that could be interpreted as vaguely homophobic.
>
> KEANU REEVES: Really! Like what?
>
> COOPER: He says, "They'll let any butt-reaming asshole be a father these days," which seems to imply that "father" is some kind of godlike state, and "butt-reaming asshole," i.e., gay male, isn't.
>
> REEVES: Oh, that is homophobic. It's weird.
>
> COOPER: Your character does this fantastic double take after that. Some friends of mine interpreted that as you trying to express your discomfort as an actor at having to say that line.
>
> REEVES: Right. Yeah. "Butt-reaming asshole" was a weird line. But no. The character's just dismissing his past....[32]

I wouldn't want to hang too much on this exchange, which is, among other things, "tongue-in-cheek" and even slightly flirtatious on Cooper's part. It is clear that Cooper is trying to sound Reeves' depth of empathy for gays, and also clear that there is mutual respect between him and the young movie star. I also sympathize with the need to be vigilant against egregious and gratuitous homophobia in mass entertainment. Yet the entire pseudo-controversy around the phrase "butt-reaming asshole" opens a window on the fragile longings and crippling expectations of rejection and betrayal which seem to accompany gay adoration of a straight-identified male star. When we "fall in love" with an icon, we sometimes make everything he says and does (even in the context of acting a role) "about us."

First, Reeves is conflated with the character he is playing: though Cooper acknowledges it's "your character," he wants to view Reeves-as-actor resisting and working against a moment in which the character seems precisely to be violently disapproving of gay sex. Most filmgoers, certainly ones as sophisticated as Cooper anyway, would never insist on such a naïve affirmation of the separation between an actor and his role. (As a novelist Cooper has written his share of explicitly gay characters who definitely qualify as "butt-reaming assholes.")

Second, and more baffling, the insult itself, "butt-reaming asshole," is not specifically attached to homosexuals at all. Are homosexuals the only kinds of men who "ream butts"—literally and figuratively? Don't heterosexuals practice anal sex? If anything, "butt-reaming" (a pungent, youthful adjective, in keeping with both Reeves *and* his character) implies that perhaps, at this point in the dialogue, the son is remembering or acknowledging having been raped by his father, therefore making it an indication of pedophilia and incest committed by an identified *heterosexual* character rather than an indication of homosexuality. But what the gay men in question thought at that moment was, "*I'm* being called a 'butt-reaming asshole' (by a male whom I have fantasized about)."

In fact, in terms of his roles, Reeves has played very little as an adult actor to the legions of queer fans in his fan-base, although he continues to defend gay rights in interviews, asserting that there's "nothing wrong with being gay, so ... why make a big deal of it?"[33] Indeed, the "panaccessible" young man grew into a somewhat stiff, terse adult, suited for action films in which he is too busy saving the world and doing other solemn things to declare *any* kind of sexuality. The kid overflowing with too much heart turned into a sometimes heartless-seeming man—but life can be like that, and anyway we are all still trying to read "the real Keanu" too much through his responses in interviews and his choice of film roles; we want to believe that we really know him, and his bare-bones, semi–Zen, tabula-rasa acting only whets these fantasies all the more. Perhaps Reeves' single greatest achievement as an actor is simply to have survived such a complete blurring of person and persona—De Angelis emphasizes the fact that James Dean made such transparent self-giving nearly synonymous with dying young, a tragic cliché which Reeves has luckily managed to avoid.[34] In Reeves' case, and this is why he figures so prominently in this chapter, there was a unique phenomenon of youth intersecting with the suggestion of potential queerness to produce something fresh and exciting—also something too quickly overburdened with meaning.

One of Reeves' most significant early films was *The Prince of Pennsylvania* (1988) by queer director Ron Nyswaner. Reeves plays Rupert Marshetta, a misfit teen on a collision course with his conservative, ex-military father, Gary (Fred Ward). Rupert's mom (Bonnie Bedelia) is equally fed up with Gary; she tells him, "You used to have a wild side. Sometimes I feel like I married Jimi Hendrix and he turned into Oliver North." (The father's response is to defend North patriotically.) Meanwhile, Rupert spies on the adults in his world because "nobody tells the truth." He eavesdrops on his mother's affair with the father's best friend (Jeff Hayenga), and this eventually leads Rupert to concoct a crazy plan to engineer his and his mother's ultimate freedom. When the father shanghais Rupert into working the mines with him, the fed-up kid decides to kidnap his father for a ransom; this will give the mother the excuse to sell the father's land. The mother can then run away with her lover, and Rupert can go off with his lover, an older woman named Carla (Amy Madigan).

Though the plan goes awry, the film does not settle for a contrived ending in which Rupert forgives his father and nuclear family gets reaffirmed. Far from it; the conflict is too deep. As the father puts things in one scene, he had a family only so that he could be "the king" of it; his wife is queen and Rupert, prince. Rupert's need to rebel goes beyond having long hair and riding a motorbike; instead it seems to stem directly from the stifling, dynastic nature of family itself. "My mom works hard, too, right?" he says in one scene. "So why does *he* get to be in charge of everything? Because he's the king? Well, I'm calling a revolution!" Nyswaner identifies with Rupert as a young man struggling for identity and place: the father is a symbol of heterosexual, patriarchal authority; therefore, although Rupert himself is straight, Rupert's revolution can be read as feminist, since he wants to uphold his mother's right to be happy and place her in charge, and even queer, too, since the defeat of conservative masculinity would be a victory for queerness.

In the film's opening scene, Rupert is late for church. The rest of his family sits in a pew, the father seething with anger, the mother trying to defuse the tense situation. The choir sings a hymn significantly titled "This Is My Father's World." When Rupert does come in, he is sporting a new haircut, half his head shaven and the other half still long and shaggy; this "alternative" hairstyle, known as an undercut, was trendy in the late 80s. Rupert's imbalanced hair, half short and half long, becomes a synecdoche, throughout the film, for a possible gender indeterminacy; but sadly, this issue remains hair-deep. The whole film seems to scream out for some kind of bisexual subplot in which Rupert's rebellious sense of not wanting to conform could further manifest itself. However, it isn't difficult to see the father-son conflicts in *The Prince of Pennsylvania* as laying some of the groundwork for Scott's epic battles with his straitlaced father in *My Own Private Idaho*.

There's a marvelously dilapidated quality to the nameless industrial Everytown where Rupert is stuck (the closest city is Pittsburgh). It's not quite a ghost town yet, but it's on the way; by the 90s most of the mining and factory work that had sustained precarious middle-class existences in Pennsylvania's Monongahela Valley had shut down and gone away. The entire town seems to be holding its breath in anticipation of the storm to come. In the film's opening scene, Rupert climbs over a mountain of trash at the local landfill, only to discover a group of punked-out bikers camping on the other side like a cartoon *Road Warrior* (1981). One (teenage) wasteland leads to another in an inexorable chain. Likewise, the ice creamery that Carla hopes to restore as a thriving business is essentially a wasteland within a wasteland. At the film's end, there is simply nothing left for Rupert, and he lights out for Pittsburgh, hitching a ride with a beautiful blonde biker (Kari Keegan). Staring dramatically into the unknown distance of the future, he tells her: "I used to be a prince."

And that's the rub of queer youth cinema. When you dethrone the father-king for being too grown-up to understand you, you cannot be the son and heir, the prince, anymore; so you yourself must change, hit the road, and in short grow up, striving (more or less futilely) not to become the thing that you have defined yourself by rebelling against. Like the straight world who provides the queer with something to fight purposefully against, the father, however repressively and obnoxiously conservative, has his uses. After him, perhaps, the deluge.

7. The Mirror in the Mirror: *Gerry*

> *It is not very many years ago since the first vernacular poets appeared.... The first to write as a vernacular poet was moved to do so because he wished to make his verses intelligible to a lady who found it difficult to understand Latin.* — Dante[1]
>
> *Imagine for a moment that the white blackbird has gone blind — for too great a volume of reflective light is the same as blindness. He is haunted by the idea of a certain whiteness spreading out over his wings which all the blackbirds see and discuss with him, but which he alone is unable to see.... But he could only have seen* himself *if he had been two people. He could see his hands and his arms because the eye and the hand are separate; but the eye cannot see itself. It feels itself and is aware that it is alive; but it cannot place itself at the necessary distance from itself to see itself.* — Jean-Paul Sartre[2]

Nine Heavens: The LSD of Cinema

When his paragon Beatrice died, the lovesick, broken-hearted Dante felt compelled to pinpoint the exact time of her death on as many different calendars as he could: Arabic, Syrian, Christian. His mystical mathematics revealed that the common number in all three time-systems was "nine": she died at the ninth hour of the ninth month of the ninth decade of the thirteenth century. Nine, as in the nine heavens, Dante wrote, a "perfect number" whose root is "nothing other than the miraculous Trinity itself." The beloved's "most noble soul" — for Dante, a qualified source of dreamlike literary visions in Beatrice's brief lifetime — became definable *as a quantity* ultimately only in death; in dying when she did, and revealing her connection with the number nine, she left her last and most compelling message to the poet, proof of a kind of cosmic intentionality and destiny, almost (such is the logic of lyric poetry if not love itself) as a reward for his infinite obsessiveness toward her, his endless parsing of her being, all of his minute interpretations of her fleeting traces.[3] In this sense, and not without a certain noble-hearted creative right,

Dante moves backwards to give his subject creative rights of her own, and to render her indubitably "worthy" (if she would not already be) of his enshrinement of her in verse.

Is death the real identity of love? So much great love poetry is motivated by the absence of the beloved, often in death; so much art in general. The implacable victory of death — what life has attempted to forestall and deny — leaves the surviving lover with no other choice but to inundate the present with memory, the silence with words, the blindness with images. Or, if not exactly coherent, accurate memories, wild fantasies; if not words, crazed, meaningless, private babble; if not images, washes of solid color, anything to decorate blankness. Many of those artworks most fixated by the up-close contemplation of death — including Shakespeare's *King Lear*, Rilke's *Duino Elegies*, Genet's *Funeral Rites*, Picasso's *Guernica*, Verdi's *Requiem*, The Doors' first album, Patti Smith's *Horses* — are also some of those most bursting with the messy energies of love and libido. They are gang-rapes instigated by brutal studs whose snarls we recall long after the bodies have hit the floor: Gloucester the bastard, proud in his damage; that "guilty rivergod of blood" which is Rilke's erection; the backdoor man who awakes before dawn and walks down the hall in his lizard boots; Johnny writing with his switchblade in the snow. The greatest art reveals the delicate feeling of love by violently taking it away, as death, of course, also does. It is explosive bravado that seizes death for our inspection, but seizes it like a violating lover — and there is something finally inscrutable about the way tenderness can only shimmer like an afterimage in the wake of that explosion.

The retinal afterimage — cozened, bedazzled, fleeting — is a strange confusion of clarity and blindness produced by the shock of light, or perhaps the shock of love. The clarity is that we have fixed an element of content, frozen it in our field of vision; the blindness is the inability to see anything else, or even to see that content (afterimage) directly or clearly. It is a metonymy of the lingering survival of love beyond the absence or death of the beloved, what the eye wishes to retain. Those who have sought the afterimage have been themselves motivated by a kind of love, an inability to turn away. In the early nineteenth century, the scientist Joseph Plateau "conduced a wide range of experiments with afterimages," during which he would temporarily blind himself by staring into the sun and then note down the duration of the afterimage, its color and shape. These periods of blindness grew longer, and eventually Plateau lost his eyesight to his yearning to "see" the image of the sun.[4]

Intriguingly, Georges Sadoul, the pioneer film historian, was sufficiently impressed by Plateau's attempt to see and quantify afterimages that he included the scientist among the inventors of cinema in his *Histoire générale du cinéma*

(1948).⁵ The movies always seemed to understand that the privilege of vision was underwritten by a saintly flipside of abnegation, the limits of sight. For example, Derek Jarman's *Blue* (1993), made after AIDS had robbed him of his vision, consists of the director and others speaking over a solid blue screen for 79 minutes, forcing the viewer not to take sight for granted, and suggesting that the most poignant way of mourning and remembering is not to re-view or visually recreate what we have seen but to come face to face with the inscrutability of nothing; of the eyes vainly trying to reclaim the love that has been taken from them.

Gerry, which begins and ends with periods of blue screen, is Gus Van Sant's most inscrutable film. It is also one of his most creative explorations of mourning and loss. This spare tale, based on a true story, involves two young men, both named Gerry, one played by Matt Damon and the other by Casey Affleck, who wander, lost in a desert, for a period of time until, finally, in an act of seeming desperation, the more forceful Gerry (Damon) murders the less forceful one (Affleck). At this point, it is suddenly revealed that they have never really been lost, have never been that far from the highway all along; the surviving Gerry is driven away in a car, an older man at the wheel and a young boy in the backseat.

Essentially a two-character chamber drama (with dramatic landscapes as a kind of third character: much of the film was shot in Argentina), *Gerry*'s resonance comes mostly from the chemistry, by turns spontaneous and easy, by other turns tense and awkward, between the two leads. In some ways, *Gerry* could be said to be a kind of male version of Bergman's *Persona* (1966), in which the constant, dreamlike struggle of wills leads to a blending and usurpation of identities. But while *Persona* created at least a semi-plausible background for its stranded, island-bound female duo — Elisabeth Vogler (Liv Ullmann) was a convalescent actress and Alma (Bibi Andersson) her put-upon, self-sacrificing nurse — we never discover who the two Gerrys really are to each other. Friends? Clearly. Something more intimate and fraternal? Seemingly, at least at certain moments. Or "twin," warring aspects of the same person? Of course, this latter hypothesis is equally possible as a reading of *Persona*, especially when Alma makes love to Vogler's blind husband (Gunnar Björnstrand), or when Bergman fuses close-ups of Ullmann's and Andersson's faces into a mutational blur.

Although Van Sant never blurs the Gerrys' faces as Bergman does with his actresses in *Persona*, the camerawork in *Gerry* does "orient" us toward perceptual disorientation and confusion between the two men. For the most part, *Gerry* is filmed objectively, without subjective point of view shots. When one of the actors looks somewhere, we are usually frustrated in our pursuit of viewpoint by not being shown what he is looking at. This becomes blatant in a dramatic sequence, late in the film — after the Gerrys have been hiking for

7. The Mirror in the Mirror: Gerry

Gerry (2002) is about two men (Matt Damon, left, and Casey Affleck) sharing a single point of view. Psychoanalytically, the film breaks them down through a series of sometimes violent deterritorializations as they wander through wilderness and desert. Throughout the film, Damon-Gerry wears his shirt around his head like a turban and Affleck-Gerry wears a shirt with a Yellow Star on it — possible tongue-in-cheek pop-references to the Israeli-Arab conflicts over Palestine?

days in the hot desert — where the logic of viewpoint is sundered twice. First, we see Damon-Gerry seated on the ground, in close-up, his eyes staring ahead through the shirt that he has wrapped around his head to shield himself from the sun. Van Sant cuts to a medium close-up of Affleck-Gerry, also seated. At first we assume that Affleck-Gerry is sitting somewhere near Damon-Gerry. But then Van Sant begins to execute a slow 360-degree tracking shot all around Affleck, wide enough to show not only Affleck but the lonely landscape for hundreds of feet on all sides of him; Damon is nowhere, not behind or in front, nor on either side. Damon-Gerry was not looking at Affleck-Gerry, but *was*, from a perceptual-view standpoint, Affleck-Gerry. Secondly, out of this nowhere, Damon comes from the left edge of frame and sits down next to Affleck; for a moment we see Damon's shoulder in the frame beside Affleck, from behind, but almost immediately we see another Damon, in the distance, walking toward Affleck. The camera moves to cut the seated Damon out of frame. In both of these shots, the expectation of viewpoint is frustrated not only by the fact that the actors are not where they are "supposed" to be, given the sight-lines, but because the characters are also somehow morphing into each other when they look at each other. Becoming, in a way, fluid mirrors of each other.

Sartre identifies this same usurpation in Baudelaire's work as the anguished drama of consciousness vying with reflected consciousness. According to Sartre, Baudelaire knew very well that his famous look was identical with the thing at which he was looking, that he would never attain true possession of himself, but simply that listless sampling of himself which is characteristic of reflective knowledge.[6]

"Sampling": that resonant word leaps fifty years into the future to connect with the postmodern creative process that we have been tracing, here, in Van Sant's cinema, as intertextuality or Burroughsian "cut-ups." Can sampling ever be enough? Is it always doomed to fall within a kind of pejorative hermeneutic space in which it is deemed inauthentic, a cop-out? It is a moral conclusion, the ephemeral one which Sartre presupposed that Baudelaire had reached, that life, which should be serious and utilitarian, "is nothing more than a game" once "you have begun by *sampling* to the point of nausea this consciousness, which has neither rhyme nor reason and which has to invent the rules which it proposes to obey ... [U]sefulness ceases to have any meaning at all."[7]

And yet, why should that usefulness, that moral seriousness have an a priori meaning in and of itself? Here, again, we join forces with early Sontag to defeat hermeneutics itself, since it sets up these imperative tribal laws and judgments over selfhood and being. The person who already feels himself to be fluid, a changeling of sorts, or someone in need of fluidity with its healing camouflage (this could be any artist, for that matter), is likely to view the sampled and the reflective more generously than those others — judges, critics, trained minds, those with an investment in consistency and structured paradigms — who come along later to assess whether the rules have been followed, whether (false) consciousness has been upheld or "ennobled" rather than subverted and exposed as an already fraudulent performance. Within pseudonarrative cinema the general blueprint for this kind of trippy vision, these seismic shifts of time and identity — I look across the room at someone, I suddenly am the one I am looking at — is, of course, the famous "starchamber" scene at the end of Kubrick's *2001*, whose special poignancy comes from the idea of watching oneself helplessly grow older. And of course, this, too, suggests reflective self-knowledge, since the astronaut is under supervision by the more evolved alien beings who have crafted human consciousness since ancient times.

Furthermore, that scene in *2001* is generally considered to be one which bends time, in the sense that the "cues" — an offstage sound that causes the astronaut (Keir Dullea) to check on the other room, a breaking glass that causes him to look across the room — seem to be linked in an instantaneous relay. Put otherwise, although he ages decades with every one of these relayed "looks," the cues are and seem to be transpiring only seconds apart, during the course of a single dinner, in fact. This continuity is reinforced by the amplified breath and muffled background chatter on the soundtrack.

But these assumptions, startling and heady enough in themselves, can be interrogated. We are in an otherworldly zone where, to quote Hannibal Lecter, "you and I don't reckon time the same way." The cues which Kubrick establishes are only edits, after all; and edits are always meant to compress time, to create shortcuts in continuity or, indeed, to simulate a continuity where none properly exists. Montage can condense epochs into blinks; the LSD of cinema is that we see all the layers of time (past, present and future) in each single discrete moment (shot) of a film. So do the Gerrys when they look—wherever they look. In mainstream films, we viewers feel as though we are drawing the characters into our reality, because everything is normalized to our reality, even though, of course, we are the ones who are being manipulated a priori. In *Gerry*, the characters draw us into *their* reality—which is to say, into the inscrutable, the death of love, the death of sight. A bad trip, needless to say.

Tous les garçons s'apellent Gerry[8]

So, what are we dealing with here? Who are the Gerrys? A major clue can be found in the idioglosssia—the various made-up words—which the Gerrys use with each other. Private languages generally serve four different functions in art (and, naturally, to a similar extent, in life as well). These functions are:

(1) A hermetic, coded slang, typically associated with youth or teen cultures attempting to distinguish themselves from the adult world who are too "square" to understand them, but also associated with the poor, with people of color, and even with revolutionary cabals. There is a pop aspect to such slang, and also a more serious philosophical one. Often, such slang has tendentious, transvaluative meanings, as when "bad" becomes insider lingo for "good." It is deliberately meant to confuse outsiders. But the Gerrys do not ply their slang against any outsiders in the film, so this meaning, although consonant with the youthfulness of the men (who generally act even younger than they appear to be), does not seem germane.

(2) A kind of "baby talk" or interpersonal communication which stems from deep intimacy and the commemoration of a unique bond. There are numerous examples of this in cinema, always denoting a romantic-sexual couple. The romantic dream of such baby talk—the utopia of love which it signifies—is that of two people who have relaxed into a shared denial of conventional linguistic sense. So, pulling a few examples at random, in Spike Lee's *25th Hour* (2002), Monty (Edward Norton) refers to his future offspring with his lover Naturelle (Rosario Dawson) as "chalupas," a word which she pretends to hate but is also clearly charmed by; while in *Eden Lake* (2008),

in one of the last moments where the doomed backpacking fiancés know peace before being attacked, Steve (Michael Fassbender) enacts a private rite with Jenny (Kelly Reilly) by tossing their collapsible tent into the air and going into a mock karate chop gesture, to which Jenny responds by giving a thumbs-up and calling out the word, "Neely!" This ritual is never explained in the film, which makes it all the more potent and realistic as something devised by the couple to relate to a unique shared experience. Finally, darkest of all, in David Lynch's *Wild at Heart* (1990), the perverse assassins Juana (Grace Zabriskie) and Reggie (Calvin Lockhart) who can only become sexually aroused when killing someone, sourly refer to their orgasmic murders as "hunting buffalo."

But are the Gerrys *actual* (e.g., more than symbolic) lovers? They are never shown as such, at least not categorically. Affleck-Gerry brushes Damon-Gerry's crotch with his foot at one moment, and Damon-Gerry flinches and then laughs it off. They share a campfire conversation, but there is no intimate discussion of feelings and no physical contact is established. What they lack is precisely the kind of intimacy that would make their private language shocking or exclusive; indeed, we never feel the taboo titillation of excluded voyeurs as we watch them interact.

(3) Idioglossia is also known as "speaking in tongues," and in this definition it takes on a distinctly religious-cultural significance. When believers speak in tongues, they are affirming a bond with a holy spirit or higher power, who possesses them and speaks through them. The most fluent — most possessed — are often church "leaders," as in Paul Thomas Anderson's *There Will Be Blood* (2007), in which Ely (Paul Dano) makes a theatrical (and sexualized) spectacle of his speaking in tongues, in the scene where he "faith-heals" an elderly woman's arthritis. The Gerrys may view their made-up language as a mode of worship — mysteriously wandering through a desert is a recurring motif in sacred texts. We never learn exactly why they have come there. The Gerrys refer to the reason why they are roaming through the desert as "the thing," sometimes saying "Power unto the thing!" and more frequently saying "Fuck the thing!" The thing, perhaps a gathering somewhere or a sight they wish to see, is thus invested both with faith and with a certain anomie. It may be the putative "reason" why they are there, but it is not exceptional or even necessary.

Also, unlike tongues, the Gerrys' words are matter-of-fact; both immediately understand what they mean when they make up words or "misuse" existing ones. It is neither a cause for puzzlement (the insider-outsider politics of slang) or for wistful acknowledgment of a shared memory (idioglossia as romantic ritual between a couple). Their idioglossia, such as it is, is more akin to a poet's neologisms, or what we might find in the correspondence of Beat Generation writers, for example, where linguistic "weirdness" is understood and celebrated as coin of the realm. "You" will know what I mean, because your own example of weird speech has called out to my own and induced it into being.

Thus, the Gerrys are, as much as anything, sharing a kind of deadpan joke on collective traditional meanings themselves — a hipsterish camaraderie similar to the gay couple in *Go* (1999), where Zack (Jay Mohr) automatically understands and laughs when Adam (Scott Wolf) describes a haphazard series of events as having come together in a "bouillabaisse-y kind of way," or indeed, when Woody Allen jokes to Diane Keaton in *Annie Hall* (1977), "Love is too weak a word for what I feel — I luuurve you, you know, I loave you, I luff you, two F's, yes I have to invent...." These are not cases of the specific romantic idioglossia of the "Neely!" exchange in *Eden Lake*, for instance, in which we are made aware of two intensely shy people overcoming their fear of looking foolish because their shared love helps them do this. These are cases in which love itself is a sort of avant-garde mode of worship, the worship of seeking the edge, of subverting metacultural destiny. Love, we see, requires its own invented language, but unlike modes of worship, seemingly more to prove that it is not a fixed ritual but a spontaneous, overflowing happening.

(4) Which brings us to the last meaning of idioglossia — the indication of a schizophrenia in which a complex rearrangement of reality and its attendant signs becomes the proof of an alternative, "higher" reality which is paranoiac in nature and thus must be kept like a secret against those who would wish to control the schizophrenic's mind with formal and accepted "lies."

Love becomes a kind of obsessive-compulsive disorder in which the spell of magic-thinking cannot be allowed to be broken; the spell, in fact, becomes the love itself, amplified through shared viewpoint. When one partner threatens to dispel the superstitious illusion, the betrayal is against this constructed reality, and a direct assault on the other partner's sense of sanity. Sometimes, love triangles become duels of competing OCD's. In Rainer Werner Fassbinder's *Despair* (1977), the increasingly frequent psychotic breaks experienced by Herman Herman (Dirk Bogarde) involve idioglossia: deranged by the attentions of his wife (Andréa Ferréol) to her lover (Volker Spengler), Herman angrily tries to participate in the adulterers' baby-talk in order to expose it as a code against himself. He will demonstrate that he knows, that he is onto their game, by descending into their utter nonsense and combating them with its illogic. He will revel in, and reveal, the real pain which their playful word games attempt to deny. So, when the wife offers Herman an egg-nog, cheerfully referring it to as a "goggle-moggle," Herman violently counters with another pet-name in order to assert his prior rights as husband: "Since it isn't a chocky-wok, I don't give a damn whose goggle-moggle it is!"

Schizoid idioglossia becomes central to the adolescent love story in Frank Perry's *David and Lisa* (1962), in which two institutionalized teenagers (Keir

Dullea and Janet Margolin) fall in love in spite of the fact that they have markedly defensive psychotic symptoms. He cannot bear to be touched, and she can only speak in sing-song nonsense rhymes. David breaks through to Lisa when he begins to imitate her rhyming speech, literally communicating with her on her own terms and establishing trust. "What do you *see*," she asks him, "when you look at *me*?" "I see a *girl* who looks like a *pearl*." His own individual psyche consents to fuse with hers in a poetic attack on received meanings; trauma ensues when he tries to break her out of her idioglossia by insisting that she speak normally. The love that is defined by psychotic symptoms cannot survive when one of the lovers rebels against the need to distort and hide from reality, or, indeed, when one of them becomes "cured."

In *Gerry*, we are closest to this fourth explanation of a "couple" bonded by idioglossia; two minds, two psyches fused into a schizoid whole which offers them furtive completeness but only outside of socially accepted terms, and only if they keep their mutual pact to dwell in a marginalized, alternative reality. Of course, this is the same as saying they are always already one man — only one Gerry — but divided into halves or split personalities who enter into the same pact in order to bring a phantom of supportive unity into their schizoid isolation. They are the double crutches of a single crippled self. Damon-Gerry seemingly escapes from this pact in the end, while Affleck-Gerry is sacrificed to it. Ironically, when things are going relatively well for the Gerrys earlier in their trek, before the hardships of the desert become too grueling, it is the Affleck-Gerry who seems more lively and more in charge. When things become much rougher, when the lifeboat gets leakier, so to speak, Affleck-Gerry becomes demoralized and falls behind, while Damon-Gerry emerges as the leader.

If the Gerrys are actually multiple personalities of the same schizoid being (borne out by the fact that the only other tourists they encounter in the film greet the Damon-Gerry and seem not to even notice the Affleck-Gerry), then their recurring, pejorative use of the word "Gerry" itself (both as a noun denoting a snafu or mistake — getting lost is "a total Gerry" — and as a verb synonymous with "fucking something up" or "ruining something" — "You Gerried the rendezvous"; "we Gerried off the animal tracks") becomes the expression of the divided, self-loathing self, unable to see itself as good or whole, or worthy of forgiveness, understanding and love.

I'll Be Your Mirror

Arvo Pärt's electronic composition, *Spiegel im Spiegel* (1978), accompanies the beginning of *Gerry*. The title means "The Mirror in the Mirror," and refers to the process of enfilade: the creation of infinity by setting up two mirrors facing each other in a regress of doubled reflections. Mirrors, of course, are not strictly essential to this process. The history of painting contains clever examples of enfilade, notably Velázquez's "Las Meninas," which depicts a studio in which there is a painter standing beside his own self-portrait, in which he appears in the same studio again, standing beside the same self-portrait, and so forth and so on. The sense of infinity with two mirrors or with perspectival labyrinths like "Las Meninas" is more theoretical than tangible or experiential; it exists at the limits of actually being able to discern the last "visible" reflection, the point where vertigo sets in, washing over the eye and substituting for actual sight the abstract knowledge that infinity remains a mental rather than a physical-optical production. There can be no end to enfilade. The death of actual sight is the birth of abstract, intangible consciousness; we must take on faith that "something" is there. In many ways, this relay between evidence and faith is the vast boomeranging of human evolutionary development itself; we move forward as a species by intuiting something out there that cannot as yet be perceived. Telescopes and microscopes confirm what exists beyond the naked eye, and lead to the development of ever more sensitive equipment predicated on the intuition that something else exists to be seen beyond even those frontiers. The atom is split because we know the atom can be.

Gerry is about the exploration of a geographical frontier; the film's heroes wander in unmapped, uncharted space. Simultaneously, it is about those invisible, internal frontiers which arise from that shifting tango of evidence and faith, where what is discovered only points toward a further, as-yet-undiscovered edge. Again, there is a point at which our understanding of these natural mysteries must be more theoretical than tangible. An enfilade *suggests* infinity, but remains contained within the very finite space of three-dimensional mirrors in a three-dimensional room, and within the scopic limits of what the naked eye can see.

Love operates like this. Like infinity, our knowledge of love can only be an approximation, compromised by spatial and temporal limits; also, like enfilade, love is predicated on the coming-together, face to face, of two objects. Two mirrors. Two views. Two persons. It is where the naked eye begins to fail (in its capacity for gathering evidence) that the faith of love must begin — "when the lover goes away," a frequent motif of art, especially popular art. Again, as in the science of infinity, or the practice of enfilade, a higher consciousness obliterates sight and inaugurates something post-optical in its place.

Van Sant dedicated *Gerry* to the memory of Ken Kesey, the great celebrant of psychotropic hallucinogens, especially LSD, as means for unlocking internal boundaries and seeing "through" the mere trappings of existence. LSD and cinema can both function as extenders of sight; they crash the party, so to speak, of the literal real. Although relentlessly materialist and literal (the recording of actual objects and sights), film can lend itself to a kind of extra-sensory perception beyond actual vision: as we considered earlier, in passing, Bergman's *Persona* and Jarman's *Blue* are two such examples of this. Whether complex or matter-of-fact, or even nonexistent (as in *Blue*), images can take on a life of their own, whereby we are no longer sure of what we are seeing; like eyewitnesses who must recall details that happened in a flash, there is a tendency to invent things to fill in the gaps — this is one of the explicit subjects of Errol Morris' *The Thin Blue Line* (1993), even as this very process is an implicit subject of *Persona* or *Blue*. Similarly, *Gerry* is an ambitious attempt to reconfigure filmic vision between the lines of what is really there, not through surreal special effects but through the transcendent attempt to construct symbolic enfilades within the space of the frame: for example, the two Gerrys standing on opposite hilltops facing each other.

The mirror is not a reflective surface, it is not even a surface at all. It is the space between bodies or rock formations, or the space between night and day perhaps. (There is a sensuous sequence in *Gerry* where time-lapse photography shows the passing of several days and nights over the film's desert landscape: during this sequence, darkness and light can barely be separated out from each other, but rather continuously morph into each other.) Van Sant has employed actual mirrors in his films — Bob in *Drugstore Cowboy* has an epiphany when he views his bloodied, exhausted face in a mirror, and Lila Crane has a start when she glimpses herself in a mirror in Mrs. Bates' eerie bedroom in *Psycho* — but in general, Van Sant's sense of mirrors is far less literal, and less cynical and constraining, than we are accustomed to seeing in the work of Sirk or Fassbinder, for example. For those great exponents of Marxist melodrama, in which immanent spaces are laid-out cadavers dissected by social relationships, mirrors are the objective metaphors for claustrophobia, mortality, delusion, denial — all of the human dysfunctions that we would expect to result from the capitalist vanity of attempting to double any living space the way one might double one's riches. Infinity is denied within the Marxist-melodramatic mirror, simply because everything is brought back to the "founding crime" of something less trying to become more, or to become too much in an unearned or a dishonest way: Sirk's and Fassbinder's characters are shown as lonely within mirrors, and even lonelier still when they share the same mirror with someone else who does not love them as they hope to be loved. So, in Sirk's *Written on the Wind* (1956), Dorothy Malone is a thin-eyebrowed gargoyle on Robert Stack's shoulder, inducing him to douse their double reflection with bitter bourbon. She does not "see" *them*, but rather, as she heartlessly puts it, "the end of a marriage, and the beginning of a love affair." In Fassbinder's *In a Year with Thirteen Moons* (1978), the violent lover of a transsexual (Volker Spengler) beats her and holds her face up to a mirror in order to cruelly force her to see that she, as *Dasein*, as person, no longer exists. The genus of such images is familiar from ghost or horror stories in which someone looks into a mirror and suddenly sees a threatening apparition from out of nowhere, antimatter which throws the "real world" into question.

Not so in Van Sant's cinema, in which mirroring and (so to speak) mirror stages are not automatically tortuous. Indeed, people can easily mirror each other in ways that are inevitable (in the sense of romantically predestined) and unselfconscious. In *Restless*, the lovers Enoch and Annabel come to physically resemble each other more and more as the film progresses, with their cropped yellow hair and skinny frames; in one scene they are dressed in matching hospital gowns. Sympathy is not the wish for resemblance, it *is* resemblance itself. Similarly, the courtship scene in *Good Will Hunting*, where Will and Skylar surprise each other with different masks in a costume shop, uses heightened, superficial masquerading to counter the moment's obvious subtext, that they are falling in love and therefore in reality becoming *more* akin and *more* visible to each other rather than more "disguised."

At the same time, one of my favorite shots in Van Sant's cinema is centered around a truly scary mirror, the forlorn moment in *My Own Private Idaho* where Scott, alone in a bathroom, looks at himself in the mirror above the sink. The harsh overhead lighting completely pulls down his features, making his eyes seem sunken and washed out; he looks frail, skeletal, distinctly feminine. This is bad-acid-trip lighting, and of course it is not merely the lighting that casts a pall over Scott's self-image but the fact that he has recently had sex with Mike, thereby acknowledging the "weakness" of gay desire within himself. Now, looking at his face for the first time since that revelatory sexual encounter, he slouches, pouts, shrugs, afraid of being or appearing irrevocably changed by what has transpired, and by what is still transpiring within him (the terrifying extension of gay desire into the possibility of loving Mike). At this moment Scott literally "loses face." The moment itself seems to pass — when Scott returns to Mike in the other room, it is as if he has crossed from winter back to summer: indeed, Scott is more himself again, filled with his usual bravado — although the never fully spoken judgment of the bathroom-sink mirror will haunt and eventually doom the young couple's chances for happiness. Van Sant suggests this by filming Scott with the same, downcast expression in the later restaurant scene where he formally rejects homosexuality in favor of heterosexuality.

Love's mirror needs to be fairly constant, then; the instant that one drifts away from the eyes of one's adorer, as Scott does in the bathroom, self-doubt begins to creep in. One sees oneself through one's own harsh eyes, and also through that literal materialist mirror which Sirk and Fassbinder always depicted as capitalism's campaign of fostering distrust in visual evidence through forms of commodification. Perhaps only the fragile, neurotic self

Scott (Keanu Reeves) makes the mistake of looking at his face in the harsh light of a bathroom sink mirror in *My Own Private Idaho* (1991).

needs such a constant, affirmative mirroring — but doesn't love, in a way, make us all feel fragile and neurotic? I cannot help but think of the Velvet Underground's "I'll Be Your Mirror," the most beautiful and important love song of our time. Like all great lyric poets, Lou Reed broke through to a universal truth about love by flinging himself directly into his own quirky needs and obsessions. As in Dante's visionary sonnet where the poet watches Love feeding his burning heart to his beloved Beatrice,[9] Reed plunges headfirst into the retrograde and potentially fatal narcissistic projection which we are inclined to read, psychologically, as morbid, unhealthy and dysfunctional — for there is something schizoid albeit undeniably tender in wanting to be someone else's mirror. Where do the selves go, not only the self that consents to do the mirroring but the self that, in being reflected, becomes other than what she believes herself to be in the first place? Yet we can all identify with sparing a beloved the pains of reality itself. As the song states, when she hates herself, i.e., sees herself badly, the lover will not stoop to plying her with trite, phony compliments; rather, he promises to take away the eyes with which she sees and leave her "blind." In love, the blinded will lead the blinded, at each other's mercy. Complete subjugation will bring the lovers to that paradise whose entrance can be gained only by a kind of a murder-suicide pact. Finally, it is never infinity itself that is infinite; instead, life and love are fond, familiar illusions of the infinity that we hope for, but which always end too abruptly with the factual but wholly unimaginable infinity of death.

8. Queering the Iconographies of Fashion and Militarism in *Even Cowgirls Get the Blues* and *Elephant*

We've all got an identity. You can't avoid it. It's what's left when you take everything else away.—Diane Arbus[1]

Collecting Specimens

In *Specimen Days* (1882), Walt Whitman frequently expresses love for the young Civil War soldiers who lie maimed and dying in the army hospital where he volunteers. It is not a naïve love, he understands these men are (or were) combat veterans, hard and rough; yet his love sees tenderness in them as well. It is a beginning point for the queer iconography of American youth which I have been tracing somewhat fitfully in this book as it appears in modern cinema, in the work of Bruce Weber, Larry Clark, Gus Van Sant and others. Whitman, too, discovered that same mix of beauty and hopeful tenderness, along with sometimes murderous toughness, in the young men he tended and helplessly watched die. And Whitman's feelings were not unusual, or specific only to him, but instead struck an obvious chord with other men whom we would probably consider gay today (such categories of sexual orientation were not as much in vogue in 1882). About the young Charles Caswell, for example, we learn in *Specimen Days* from a letter sent to Whitman by his friend John Burroughs and extracted "verbatim": "He had the sweetness of a child, and the strength and courage and readiness of a young Viking."[2] John Burroughs states that this apparent contradiction is in fact something that Whitman "would have loved.... He was like one of your poems."[3] Admiring such a boy is already an aesthetic experience (just as admiring certain poems, Whitman's for example, is already an erotic experience).

Elsewhere in *Specimen Days*, Whitman himself uses seemingly contradictory terms to describe young soldiers. In one passage he comments on a regiment temporarily barracked on Fourteenth Street in New York:

> There did not appear to be a man over 30 years of age, and a large proportion were from 15 to perhaps 22 or 23. They had all the look of veterans, worn, stain'd, impassive, and a certain unbent, lounging gait.... They were all of pleasant physiognomy; no refinement, nor blanch'd with intellect, but as my eye pick'd them, moving along, rank by rank, there did not seem to be a single repulsive, brutal or markedly stupid face among them.[4]

The knowledge that these veterans have seen and done brutal things does not escape Whitman; but as his eye "picks" them (a beautiful verb in this context, connoting not only a visual survey, but also freely made aesthetic and erotic choices), he does not see brutality in their faces.

In fact, the apparent contradiction here is really not a contradiction at all, since without either the tender beauty *or* the veteran brutality, these young soldiers would not appear as the amazing "specimens" which they do in Whitman's prose. The two qualities work completely hand in hand. If the youths were merely children, untouched by life, they would be uninteresting; if they were haggard and dragged-down, old before their time, they would be pathetic. Instead, they radiate, alongside their youth, a strength that tragic circumstance has given them, or brought out in them; an unbelievable power beyond their years. In this sense, they are the *forced-to-become*; forced by life into an early awareness, an early endurance of hardship. And it is not difficult to connect their fraught puberty with the puberty of the homosexual, in which he discovers his gay desire and is also, in some ways, forced to become something that requires strength and courage, something that he might not always want to be.

Thus, although Whitman did not think in our current sexual-political terms of clearly labeled orientations, we can read *Specimen Days* as an incipient project of queering the military, especially the young military. War has only added to the young men's beauty a new and seasoned readiness, a toughness that makes them recognizable to a homosexual, for whom the ineffable traces of experience, of having crossed some internal or external Rubicon, are more precious than the blank, unformed look of inexperience.

Whitman bears "the heart of a stranger that hover'd near" a "poor death-stricken boy," obliquely equating his heart with the boy's — in this case a particularly tough young Irishman named Tom Haley, whom Whitman, keeping vigil at his bedside, particularly longs to view as a mirror of his own desire. "Sometimes I thought he knew more than he show'd," Whitman writes, these

8. Queering the Iconographies of Fashion and Militarism   161

words superficially describing Tom's awareness of his own mortal condition, and of his surroundings (Tom is drifting in and out of consciousness), but also charged with a larger, furtive resonance, e.g., Whitman's hope for Tom's ability to respond to the love which the poet finds difficult to hide in his presence.

> One time as I sat looking at him while he lay asleep, he suddenly, without the least start, awaken'd, open'd his eyes, gave me a long steady look, turning his face very slightly to gaze easier — one long, clear, silent look — a silent sigh — then turn'd back and went into his doze again.[5]

Tom may have been merely wary or defensive of the older man who watched him while he slept; and Whitman is not naïve about this possibility. "Little did he know,"[6] he concludes, referring to the heartfelt communion which the poet sought with the dying warrior.

Whenever such a communion occurs between, or with, tough young men, it is noted by the queer sensibility as a moment of transcendence. The immortal and the mortal brush against each other, and jostle into visibility. So John Burroughs' letter about Caswell builds to a deathbed kiss which Caswell gives to his brother, S.: "In the morning ... S. was standing over him, when Charlie put up his arms around S.'s neck, and pull'd his face down and kiss'd him. S. said he knew then the end was near."[7] The kiss of brothers, like Nietzsche's description of the overcoming of shame at intimacy in "men who are hard," is precious[8] — and it is also, significantly, the kiss of death.

Today we are the heirs of Whitman's vision of youth. The possibly gay school shooters in *Elephant*, Alex and Eric, are modern teens; the special, life-changing circumstance of war is not required to give them the same sense of occupying a provocative middle ground between childhood and adulthood which Whitman saw in the young Civil War soldiers. They both wear recognizable teen fashions (sleeveless T-shirts, hoodies, etc.); Eric has a crew cut; Alex can play a little Beethoven on the piano, but also gives the score the finger when he has had enough of it. They rebel in all the small, ordinary ways that make teens current figureheads of social rebellion, but in addition to this they also rebel in one major way, extreme to the point of being deadly: their strong, obsessive identification with military culture. They are Whitman's teen soldiers gone wrong, gone bad, or perhaps merely with an exacerbation of that brutality which Whitman cannot, or does not always choose to, reconcile with the handsome lads trooping past him in the street or filling the beds of the sick wards.

In fact, for Alex and Eric, war *is* a circumstance of their lives: they are pointedly waging a war against their school, and they go about it like military strategists. Before the shooting massacre, they go over a detailed map of the school, with Alex pointing out to Eric which parts to attack: "we should be able to pick off kids as we traverse the east wing.... Then, after that, you'll hit your yellow line here, which is your plan B...." Military command-structure even operates within their close friendship: Alex issues the orders, Eric follows. Earlier, Alex had studied the school cafeteria, writing down his observations in a little notebook, like a General studying a field of battle.[9] Finally, when Alex and Eric show up at the school, stalking toward it with their weapons and ammo in heavy duffel bags, they are both dressed from head to toe in camo gear and armed to the teeth: a Tek-9, an automatic rifle, a shotgun, a .223-caliber, and on top of this, a couple of pistols, a knife, and "enough explosives to last us all day." Alex says these last words with a grin on his face.

"That's Hitler, right?"

They order the automatic rifle only one day before the massacre, from a gaudily patriotic website called "Guns USA"; the weapon is delivered on the morning it is to be used, arriving while Alex and Eric, ditching school and left alone in Alex's house by his working parents, are transfixed by a documentary about Adolf Hitler. From the dialogue they exchange during this documentary, it becomes clear that their understanding of Hitler and Nazism is sketchy and ahistorical, but that this is irrelevant to the obsessive pleasure they take in it:

ERIC (*referring to a German official in the film*): Who was that?
ALEX: I don't know.
ERIC: This was made in Germany, right?
ALEX: Yeah.
ERIC: Can you still buy Nazi flags?
ALEX: Sure. If you're a nut.
ERIC: Who's that guy? That's Hitler, right?
ALEX: Yeah.

These terse questions and answers further establish Alex as leader and Eric as eager follower. Moreover, Alex is a kind of autocratic, indeed Hitlerian leader: when he says "I don't know" about someone or something, it is not meant to indicate a deficiency of knowledge; it signals that the matter itself is unimportant. Eric is waiting only to "spot" Hitler in the documentary, like a forlorn son looking for glimpses of a father he never knew. By recognizing and affirming which one Hitler is among the other uniformed Germans, Alex not only points to the symbolic father but substitutes, in some ways, for that father. Again, it is through Alex alone that recognition and knowledge come.

But why would one have to be "a nut," in Alex's words, to purchase a

Nazi flag? After all, they are about to go out and do something infinitely more destructive and illegal. Apart from the delight these friends take in militarism and Nazism with each other, the fact that Alex would not fly a Nazi flag in public seems to indicate that perhaps he would still prefer to blend in with the school population which he and Eric are about to assault. We have seen that they exist within this school largely as targets for the bullies, athletes, popular kids, etc. The brutish openness with which these other kids prey on Alex and Eric might in fact reinforce the shooters' wish to remain covert, since openness is the mark of the "enemy."

This also ties in with the exploratory gay sexuality which they reveal only furtively, to each other, when alone. It also ties in with a sense of integrity, perhaps, by which they can declare their essential difference from their bullies. The bullies, who represent the social order of the school, are one-dimensional, uncomplicated, unmysterious. Displaying a Nazi flag openly would be, perhaps, like publicly having the kiss which Alex and Eric share only privately, in the shower: a declaration that would become phony and meaningless, since, if it was something they could get away with so openly, it would no longer be worth doing; it would no longer hold that lonely but potent charge of defying the social order.

Like the stand-off between the cowgirls and the troopers over the endangered whooping cranes in *Even Cowgirls Get the Blues*, the defiance of authority represented by Alex and Eric's massacre is a kind of allegory for the growing pains of nonconformist sexuality faced with its exposure to a hostile world. The cowgirls' inspirational rallies and speeches are a way of giving each other courage to carry on with their takeover of the Rubber Rose Ranch; because they are going against centuries of ingrained patriarchal oppression, they need to reinforce this courage as women, among themselves. Just as the cowgirls are attempting a construct a self-sufficient world without men (and dealing with the attendant internalized shame of being *sexual* dissidents, *sexual* revolutionaries), Alex and Eric are attempting to construct a world not only without women but without any "others" at all.

This is the traditional world of militarism at its most extreme: the militaristic mind conceives itself as "safe" only when everyone else, every potential threat, has been killed. However, even if the social order of their own peer group gives Alex and Eric a lot of negative attention, outside that group, in the larger society as a whole, the two boys are all but invisible. Behind the TV where the Hitler documentary is playing, there is a picture window that shows the arrival of the parcel delivery truck and the uniformed delivery man (we note that the agents of the capitalist system wear quasi-military uniforms) bringing the automatic rifle to the door. He casually asks the kids why they're not in school, and when they lie and tell him they don't have school today, he merely says, again casually, "Well, good for you." The camera hovers closer and closer to the image of Hitler on TV as this bit of free and irresponsible enterprise plays out, and the delivery man innocently puts the package with the automatic rifle into the hands of the unsupervised teens.

This invisibility is, in some ways, not the flipside of the negative attention and bullying which the boys receive at school, but a further component of it: it is an extension of their isolation. Later, before he shoots the principal, Eric lectures him that he should have responded when the boys came to him with their problems. With the massacre, Alex and Eric welcome not only an end to their abuse, but an end to their invisibility (though they also understand that the real end will come only with total invisibility, in the form of their own violent deaths).

Alex and Eric unpack the newly delivered rifle right away. It is probably the most excited they are about anything during the entire course of the film; even the killings themselves will be committed in a somewhat impassive, stoic manner, not as if the boys' feelings were dead or nonexistent, but almost as if they did not dare to let themselves express feelings of satisfaction or triumph. Looking at and holding the firearm, however, they grin and enthuse that it is "awesome" and "sweet," immediately carrying it out to the garage for target practice, taking turns firing it into stacked cordwood.

The material presence of the gun, and the loud explosions it makes, reduce their invisibility: this is a major part of Alex and Eric's militaristic fixation on weaponry; it is not beneficence or peacemaking which they idolize about military life and its gear, but instead the power to noisily declare one's (superior, inescapable) presence. As transfixed as they are by the Nazi regalia in the documentary, we see that there is a further reason why Alex would not buy a Nazi flag: deep down, he and Eric only care about what Hitler and his troopers *did* with the enormous power they had, not the tokens they wore or displayed. True killers—as opposed to soldiers, or even killers with the pretense of being soldiers (Nazis)—have no flag.

Alex and Eric are many things, but they are not hypocrites: this is probably the most important thing about them. Although excluded from the teen cliques at school, they exist in the same light that we have been considering adolescents throughout this book, as figures of a purity that verges on queerness in contrast to the compromises and deceptions of the adult world. They have been hurt, so they want to get revenge by killing; the lack of impulse control, which in adults, such as the alcoholic father or the punitive principal, automatically becomes frightening or creepy, is a further sign of sincerity in youth: "children of America are seen to be irrevocably formed by violence, warped by that failure of love that lies at the heart of individualism and turns us all into freaks."[10]

Diane Arbus as Blue Cowgirl

We know from *Even Cowgirls Get the Blues* that "freaks" are simply the politically oppressed and not yet radicalized. Nonetheless, it is somewhat different for men than it is for women. There is also an entirely separate set of cultural industries (fashion, feminine hygiene) which are identified in *Even Cowgirls Get the Blues* as specifically exploiting women by constructing the female condition as a state of automatic shame: repulsive if they are overweight (the Countess' ranch doubles as a fat farm) or undeodorized (in spite of cancer warnings about the vaginal douches and deodorants he manufactures, the Countess makes his money off concealing the natural scent of women, which repulses him personally).

Thus, the fashion plate is, for heterosexual women, the equivalent of the iconic military man for heterosexual men: it is the ultimate archetype of (comforting) gender extremes. Before she becomes a cowgirl, Sissy was a cover girl, a model for feminine hygiene products, and we are shown a photograph of her from those days (the mid–60s) looking much like Edie Sedgwick: short platinum hair, a silver mini-dress, and a heartbreaking, bewildered, lost-little-girl look in her eyes. This visual reference to Edie necessarily conjures up the fate of a fragile woman mishandled, controlled and even abused by a series of men (some of them gay), although, of course, much like Sissy herself, the real life Edie had deeper problems than the ones that surfaced during and after her stint in the Warhol Factory. But, as the photographic reference makes obvious in Van Sant's film, Sedgwick's gay gurus found her suffering picturesque; she broke like a little girl, and they helped her dress up like Barbie.

It is dicey, and for me uncomfortable, to pit women against gay men, even if the fashion industry has often operated in just such a schematic way, with gay men sculpting female iconography in ways that have sometimes been devoid of innate love or sympathy for women. For the drag queen is traditionally tortured by the fact that she is not a real woman; nonetheless, her reckless, playful cavorting is sometimes an indication of what women themselves could be if they did not possess bodies that menstruated and got pregnant, bodies more innately vulnerable to patriarchal oppression. And no one ever expects a drag queen to be truly beautiful, or truly happy. Drag queens do work hard to become what they imagine women really are, but women still struggle more with the expectations placed upon them (including the drag queen's expectations).

Diane Arbus certainly understood the visceral nature of this female struggle. Seemingly as if to specifically subvert her early fashion photography, and its complicity in heterosexist standards of beauty, Arbus sometimes made a point of taking seemingly candid snapshots of unposed "average women," such as "Girl with a cigar in Washington Square Park, N.Y.C. 1965," "Puerto Rican woman with a beauty mark, N.Y.C. 1965," "Lady in a rooming house parlor, Albion, N.Y. 1963," "Woman with a locket in Washington Square Park, N.Y.C. 1965," and perhaps most extraordinarily, "A woman with pearl necklace and earrings, N.Y.C. 1967," in which the subject is not only not classically beautiful but elderly and angry-looking.

Arbus seems to have intuited that male sexism could only be combated by women making a compact to love themselves and each other, and that this could begin with one of the prime weapons of that sexism, photography itself. This "love" was pointedly at odds with the aesthetic standards that she herself had internalized and had to un-teach herself. She wrote, about a series of photos of a female that at first she thought had "sort of missed" their subject: "But there was one that was just totally peculiar. It was a terrible dodo of a picture. It looks to me a little as if the lady's husband took it. It's terribly head-on and sort of ugly [in fact this could be 'A woman with pearl necklace and earrings...'] and there's something terrific about it. I've gotten to like it better and better and now I'm secretly sort of nutty about it."[11]

Becoming "sort of nutty" about female (and perhaps artistic) imperfection is a kind of political liberation, here. The eros of art may always be that we are led to fall in love (become "nutty") over the "wrong" thing — the anti-classical, somewhat shameful subject of misfit adoration — simply because the artist has had the temerity, and offbeat taste, to incorporate it into art; queer art is founded on such subversive erotics and misidentifications. Also, this is not only a barrier that women can, and must, overcome. Similarly, many of Arbus' nudists and transvestites are proud, shocking exposures of people failing to meet male-defined standards of physical perfection and yet being revealed as all the more human and loveable as a result.

Likewise, in *Even Cowgirls Get the Blues*, Van Sant seems to celebrate the natural, unreconstructed humanity of women (Roseanne Barr, a pioneer in the attempt to make heavy women acceptable to TV audiences, has a significant cameo) and at the same time remorselessly implicates gay style-makers (such as the Countess) in the conversion of women into tools, or human dolls, inauthentic and ridiculous. In another scene, a flamboyant director (Udo Kier) dresses Sissy in a silly whooping-crane costume for a TV commercial about the plight of the endangered birds: instructing her how to flap her wings, he leaps and flutters about the set, vicariously feminizing himself through the spectacle of Sissy's hobbling bird disguise. She can barely move, paralyzed by the weight of aestheticization, and he is dancing.

By making the real woman more unreal and artificial, also more fragile and ludicrous, the gay man hopes, here, to come closer to being like her; to meet her halfway, so to speak, on a battlefield of mediation. Of course, there

8. Queering the Iconographies of Fashion and Militarism 167

In *Even Cowgirls Get the Blues* (1993), Sissy Hankshaw (Uma Thurman) spends much of her life as a fashion victim and put-upon model, fulfilling the misogynistic fantasies of powerful gay men. It is not until she embraces her own queerness, her female masculinity, symbolized by her outsized thumbs, that she finds freedom and selfhood.

are gay men who do not strive to imitate or become women; Van Sant is not implicating *all* gay men in this syndrome. One might say that *Even Cowgirls Get the Blues* relates to a battle of institutionalized representations: to the extent that gay men, via the fashion world, have gained power as style-makers, it has sometimes been at the expense of the self-esteem of the women who become their "fashion victims" (as well as at the expense of gay men who do not wish to become feminized, either directly or by proxy).

Misogynistically, fashion brands women as freaks in their natural state, then, only to make them over as even bigger freaks. Arbus herself thought of freaks as privileged beings, suggesting, again, a politicization of standards of attractiveness, and a liberation from those standards. "Most people," Arbus wrote, "go through life dreading they'll have a traumatic experience. Freaks were born with their trauma. They've already passed their test in life."[12] If, in *Even Cowgirls Get the Blues*, it is the female fashion models who are presented as freaks, constructed from man-made standards of beauty and thinness, and fragile in their corporeality, then the escape from becoming such a freak, for a woman, is precisely to pursue alternative, but more natural, images of being human: the rugged, self-reliant, no-nonsense cowgirl, who stands in opposition to the fashion industry and its manufactured ideals.

Thus, Van Sant extends Arbus' sense that those we condemn as "freaks" are the true beauties, and the people who are most alive. In one scene, Delores

Jellybean Bonanza (Rain Phoenix) becomes the love of Sissy Hankshaw's life in *Even Cowgirls Get the Blues* (1994). Cowgirls, empowered and masculinized, counteract the fashion industry's attempts to control women's bodies with willowy, anorectic, submissive "ideals." Expert marksmanship with guns completes Bonanza's identity as heroic Phallic Woman.

Del Ruby uses her skill with the whip to lash a stray fly off a black-and-white pinup of a 40s-style fashion plate, as if to imply that the female model — and the fashion industry whom she represents — is already a kind of corpse drawing flies. Jellybean Bonanza speaks of having seen pictures of cowgirls in a magazine when she was little and being inspired to become one when she grew up, her destiny as a woman pointedly in opposition to the iconography of the fashion industry. Freakishness is not so much in the eye of the beholder, as in, or under, the skin of she who must face limited options in "a man's world." Independence, as a masculine trait, makes the cowgirls out of step with heterosexist society; but it makes them in step with the progressive vision they have of themselves as whole human beings, exempt from male patriarchal control.

The Freak Test

For Arbus, the "test" which distinguished a freak from a bland, normal person simply consisted in surviving as a freak; but mere survival does not constitute whole selfhood. The journey from being a freak to becoming a whole person (in one's own eyes) hinges on the ability to love and be loved; yet it is easier to follow the default option of destructiveness and self-destruction, kill and be killed. Hitler, for example, would have rejected Arbus' work as degenerate and undermining in that all-important nationalistic pride whereby normative standards of physical beauty went hand in hand with glory and patriotism. For Hitler, beauty conveyed the right to kill, and vice versa; and this, too, is a queer position albeit a transgressive and inhuman one, as explored famously by Jean Genet in his novel *Funeral Rites*. The position is queer because it summons up a vision of gender coding by which masculine honor, virtue and justice become synonymous with masculine beauty (and violence). Institutions that once seemed to connote an impervious integrity become awash in the impulsive passions of attraction and bodily worship. Like having a sexual "type," one need only assemble the designated attributes (blond hair, blue eyes, etc.) to signify that one has found what one is looking for.

The physically anomalous and unconventional were considered subversives, and targets a priori, under the Reich, because (among other things) they did not make for convincing, self-justifying killers. This was not strictly a male issue; however, it is true that for males (though also for the cowgirls) violence itself is already one of the socialized tests that can transform the "freaks" of this world into supposedly complete persons. The military might be thought of as corresponding, for gender-conventional men, to the fashion industry for gender-conventional women: a site of institutionalized representations in which a certain extreme ideal of gender in itself is purveyed to people uncertain of their own natural status.

Like artificial beauty, hyper-violence makes some feel real and powerful, though this violence is ruthless in its logic, as is the need to escape from the label of being freaks in the first place. At the same time, the shooters in *Elephant* reclaim the label itself with a vengeance: if you despise me, I will become capable of fulfilling your worst nightmares; if you condemn me as gay, I will become gay, to punish heterosexuality; I will use feminization as well as machismo to complete the picture of myself as outlaw, as avenger, as a freak perhaps but a freak who nonetheless "rules" the social order through a code of honor so rigorous and pure it will justify massacre.

The dark irony is that Alex's prolonged damage from being unloved and despised, from being viewed and treated precisely as a freak, will require him not only to sacrifice the other kids whom he views as enemies, but Eric as well, his best friend, lover, and only ally, whom, in a pungent moment of Genet-esque betrayal, he suddenly shoots at point blank range during a lull in the massacre. We note that none of the cowgirls would betray each other in such a way, not even to ostensibly protect them from falling into the enemy's hands, or preserve them at their greatest moment of beautiful, incendiary rebellion.

What this says about the ultimate optimism or pessimism of Van Sant's view of men (or gay men) is somewhat difficult to discern, if it even says anything categorical or definitive. But we can further note that a distinct paranoia of falling victim to male violence seems to go with the territory of bonding with, or declaring love for, other males in Van Sant's cinema, in which trust and vulnerability and generally punished with an onslaught of the assaultive violence which they have presumably courted. So Pepper, who allowed himself to become the lover of Walt, is shot and killed by policemen who seem to corner him in a moment of obliviousness. In *Drugstore Cowboy*, Bob is beaten and shot by younger thieves and dealers whom he had formerly taken into his confidence. People reach for guns frequently in Van Sant's films, and the guns go off. One of the most resonant scenes in *My Own Private Idaho* is the one where Mike's brother drunkenly relates the story of how their mother shot and killed one of her lovers. Jellybean Bonanza is shot at the very instant that she tries to end the stand-off with the state troopers. *To Die For* is based on a notorious lovers' triangle and gun homicide, the Pamela Smart case.

Even the non-gun-related homicides are centered around slow buildups of tension, followed by sudden, ecstatic releases; the killer's whole body becomes a gun, and once again, it is intimacy that is being punished and revoked — or perhaps just viscerally acknowledged as having transpired? Norman Bates' "mother" kills those hotel guests who have made her jealous by opening up to her son. One of the Gerries murders the other after the two men have seemingly bonded during a frustrating desert trek. And the guns return: in *Last Days*, Blake is shot and killed by someone whom he greatly fears, possibly himself. And Harvey Milk is shot and killed by Dan White because he repeatedly underestimates White's rancor and because there is a part of Harvey that wants to be friendly and open toward his colleague; although specifically warned to avoid White, Harvey follows White into an empty office as if this was finally their chance to be alone together.[13]

The pact between men, the pact with vulnerability and same-sex love, is depicted as exceedingly lonely on the other side, so to speak. And the sheer number of homicides by guns is striking in and of itself. The gun, a complex emblem of father-son bonding through shared phallic mastery in the early short, *The Discipline of DE*, turns into an object which tends to recoil upon male love. The surreal gunplay which marks the death of homoerotic love in Luis Buñuel's *Un Chien Andalou* (1929) seems to be stamped on Van Sant's unconscious like a recurring nightmare or obsessive fantasmatic; one glimpses

In *Milk* (2008), Dan White (Josh Brolin, left) assassinates his City Council rival Harvey Milk (Sean Penn), the legendary gay activist, even though Milk has tried to reach out to the less diplomatically adept White. The ultraconservative White is depicted not merely as a deranged zealot but as a fragile, frustrated man, burdened with having to uphold Irish-Catholic standards of manhood and desperately afraid of failing. Brolin and the Oscar-winning Penn led a stellar cast in one of the most powerfully acted films of the 2000s.

also, perhaps, the "sexy" gun-slinging in so much of late 60s U.S. film (Arthur Penn, Sam Peckinpah, etc.), in which guns become a sort of new language among people, a language in which messages get registered and meanings get conveyed.

What is probably most unnerving in Van Sant's adoption of gunplay and killing is that one is often left wondering whether to empathize with the shooter or with the shot, the killer or the killed. Both seem to have their reasons; if anything, the killers' reasons are often clearer and more direct than the victims who place themselves into lines of fire. Perhaps the truest character is Blake, the bizarre martyr, the murdered suicide, who could be effectively behind *and* in front of his loaded gun. (To be shot with one's own gun is always a sign of dishonor in westerns.) Rather than a demarcation of "sides," a gun might finally be an enclosure which entraps two people within the same explosive destiny.

Professional Tough Guys

Again, this is part of the contradictory nature of male queers and male teens which have made them complementary, in so many films, of the same struggle: gay men's poignant attempts at love often fail because of pressures and lack of support from the heterosexual society. The very struggle (because it is a struggle) undermines love and brings about its inevitable defeat. Put otherwise: both teens and queers derive their individual identities from a collective identity whose rages and difficulties often make individual loves impossible, and nearly compel the betrayal of those loves by forcing them to play out against a background of constant struggle. Whether as a mass-market or boutique commodity, hustling or true romance, love is a species of damaged goods. In *Milk*, Harvey, two of whose boyfriends have committed suicide, is torn between anger at a homophobic society which gave those men fragile egos and the wish to die, and also personal guilt at not having been able to love them enough, e.g., not finding a way in which his love could have transcended his own individual warping at the hands of the homophobic society.

In *Elephant*, Van Sant literalizes this connection between teens and queers in the moment which Alex and Eric have in the shower (making out and presumably having sex with each other). This moment seems to belie their anger at being taunted by other kids and accused of being "gay." But in this gay sex we also detect a certain contempt of Alex and Eric for their bullies, since they are actually doing, actually having, the real thing, which the other kids bandy about as insults without really knowing what they are talking about. The often unacknowledged part of gay sex has always been that it requires a certain toughness of body and mind: anal penetration can be, at first anyway, painful for the partner who receives it, while performing oral sex can require a measure of determination and discipline. Like the female role in heterosexual sex, there is a process of overcoming, of relaxation, of learning. Of course, some of this is also in the mind; homophobia is about building up the bogeyman of traumatic anal or oral rapes, a heterosexual imaginary of same-sex activity without desire, love or mutual arousal. But this only shows how being gay also requires a certain mental as well as physical toughness, since it is still reviled and persecuted by many.

The jocks in class cover Alex in wads of wet paper that are meant to suggest them putting their semen all over him; but just as the jocks could never really kill, while Alex and Eric can and will, so the two shooters are the only ones who can cover each other with real semen. Their guns and militaristic prowess are not a simplistic substitute for a lack of phallic mastery (the way those things might be read if there was no sex scene between the boys), but a clear extension of that mastery. And this homosexual intimacy does not lead them into society or pacify their urge to kill; it exists (like the gay sex in Burroughs' or Genet's work, for instance) outside of or beyond socialization. Van Sant devotes a long sequence to a meeting of a student Gay-Straight Alliance organization, but we are given to understand that Alex and Eric would never take their problems *there*. Instead, their sex is simply another of the ways that they have set out to prove, on this day, that they are the real tough guys at their school.

Is male toughness a sort of absolute which contains all trials and tests of body and mind? The military man, in our society, is often considered the *ne plus ultra* of toughness, not only because he kills but because he faces the constant threat of being killed. He is under threat; thus the military man's toughness derives not only from strength but from the acceptance of a general "weakness" as well: he could be killed at any moment. The soldiers in the documentary *Restrepo* (2010) call themselves "professional tough guys," and indeed they are brave men. But some of the most disarming and compelling moments in *Restrepo* occur when these professional tough guys show emotion, weeping bewilderedly at the death of a comrade, for example. There are even one or two very interesting moments in which some of the soldiers behave, one might say, queerly.

In one scene, three soldiers in the barracks get excited about hearing an MP3 of a techno-house song; they rush together and begin to dance furiously. "Touch me," the androgynous singer repeats like a mantra, "I want to feel your body." The image is instantly familiar to anyone who has ever been to a gay club; we don't even have to make any allowance for their army fatigues, since military gear has always been fashionable "butch attire" for gay men at clubs. One of the dancing soldiers gets in the middle of the other two, who begin to simulate sexual penetration on him (also a common scene on the dance floors of gay clubs). As if to underscore that something queer is happening here, directors Tim Hetherington and Sebastian Junger cut in some reaction shots of other soldiers on their bunks, looking askance at this spontaneous bacchanalia. The frenzy escalates when the dancers recognize a fourth soldier heading into the barracks and try to drag him into their circle; instantly, this fourth soldier becomes wary (of the men themselves or of the presence of a camera?) and runs away. The dancing ends only as the three dancers go chasing after this reluctant fourth.

In another scene, the men have come to mess hall for chow. Out of sport and playfulness, three men suddenly hug a fourth by placing him in a chokehold from behind. Tickling him, they surround him on all sides. "Don't fight it," one of these subduers keeps saying to the man in the chokehold, who gradually allows himself to be pulled down to the ground. Someone asks why the soldiers always mess with certain guys, and one of the soldiers gives this answer, "He's a beautiful man. I'd fuck him back in the States," making explicit that sexual tension and even attraction play a role in this free-floating atmosphere of— of what? It's hard to know what to call it. The forced tickling and subduing are not malicious or threatening enough to qualify as hazing; rather, they seem to be the need to prove, moment by moment, that, as brothers in arms, these men have a right to touch each other's bodies in ways that civilian (straight) men would not have a right, or even feel the need, to do. I am not suggesting that all of this is, by definition, gay, or that the soldiers in question are (still less that they are all having sex with each other); but it is an outsiderness, if you will, born hand in hand with the toughness required of these soldiers for survival.

The complexity of the soldier's statement about "fucking him back in the States" is immediately echoed by a prolonged laugh from another soldier. The laugh feels like a way of offsetting or expelling any tension produced by this remark, but the remark itself does not seem to be uttered as a joke, at least not entirely. The soldier's matter-of-fact comment, "He's a beautiful man," has the slight vocal quaver of a man admitting to something that might not be easy to admit. We are being let in on military argot and military thinking (and humor) here: to "fuck a man back in the States" means doing it not because one is desperate and without heterosexual options (because there are no women around); it means doing it because one is queer for that man. Again, this does not mean to say that these soldiers are gay or engaged in male-male sex; however, they have an ease with the thought of it that would not come as naturally to a straight male civilian.

In this sense, militarism and war do not exclude and cancel out homosexual feeling, but instead create unique human situations in which that feeling becomes comprehensible and even necessary. This is only a theory; but perhaps barriers do break down in situations of life-and-death stress — the barriers between different "kinds" of people and also ones that are internal, within each man himself. Celebrating precious life and desire in all its forms might become an essential survival method to someone under constant threat.

What do these moments *really* mean? Nothing? Everything? Does queerness become inevitably *more* visible within those social institutions which have been most vociferous in banning and excluding it, since the presumption is that no one, here, can ever really be queer? Is the queer soldier a kind of oxymoron, where queerness (even where it truly exists) would be normalized by militarism itself? Although silenced for a long time in the military, queers are already there, and they have already adapted to life within heteronormative institutions; queer soldiers look, speak and behave like any other kind of soldier. And increasingly, of course, civilian gays are just as masculine and "straight-acting" as anyone who has been through Boot Camp — although not, perhaps, with that experience of physical and psychological extremity by which a male soldier might freely acknowledge the beauty of another male soldier.

Again, as in *Elephant*, tenderness between two men does not necessarily lead them to put down their arms and renounce killing; far from it. This is ultimately the most discouraging aspect of a military that allows itself to be queered but goes on fighting nonetheless, for those of us who might want to believe that a more openly gay world would be a more peaceful or less violent world. Of course, this must remain an unanswered question. And the sense of contradictoriness may be because the queer feeling, to the extent that it exists in wartime soldiers, is dependent on conditions which the soldiers themselves understand are not universal. (Things remain different, after all, "back in the States.") But this might only be to say that the queer feeling is an embryonic one, not fully developed and liberated.

Nonetheless, we see this also in recent fiction films about Iraq and Afghanistan soldiers. It becomes part of the awkwardness of returning to civilian life in *The Messenger* (2009), whose veteran hero Will (Ben Foster) is searching for meaning in his post-combat existence. Having witnessed and survived so much, he is no longer held by the same taboos that are enforced in "straight society." Queerness is part of this same syndrome of the tough military man having gone so far beyond the pale of everything that he is no longer frightened of the implications of that queerness. In *The Messenger*, a different young veteran, at a welcome-home party in a bar, shocks and ices the conversation of his non-military friends by telling a story from his service-time about his offbeat friendship with an Iraqi civilian. This story has open, matter-of-fact gay overtones, and culminates in the abrupt, equally matter-of-fact death of the Iraqi in a sectarian killing. The friends—speechless, uncomfortable, suddenly out of their element—do not want to disapprove of the veteran, but end up becoming wary; Will, however, drinking by himself at the bar, overhears this story and nods in complete understanding.

Militarism, not to mention war, might be so all-encompassing and life-changing that it makes certain prejudices seem petty and irrelevant. As another damaged vet (Woody Harrelson) says to Will, later in *The Messenger*, "Civilian life's for people who ain't seen shit. It's too late for you. You already seen the shit, you can't unsee it anymore." Of course, this "shit" is not referring to homosexuality, but to larger issues of life and death: it places the veteran beyond the petty ways in which "civilians" divide up experiences, and create artificial prejudices and taboos in lieu of real experiences.

Even the trained Marines who have not yet seen combat, in Sam Mendes' *Jarhead* (2005), seem to have an ease with themselves, their bodies and each other, which allows them to spontaneously simulate an enormous gay orgy, for the benefit of a female news anchor and her camera crew, in the amusing "field fuck" scene. We understand that sexual deprivation, and the sight of the attractive female news anchor, is what drives them; but this does not feel like a full explanation of why they throw themselves into the act of grinding their crotches into each other so lustfully. It is hard to imagine most men behaving this way; but somehow it is plausible to imagine military men, those "professional tough guys," being able to get this close to gay sex without losing face. Even so, the anchor and her camera crew are hustled away by a nervous commanding officer, and the men are punished by being made to stack sandbags all night in the rain; so, ultimately, the gay implications in *Jarhead*, as in *The Messenger* and *Restrepo*, are disturbing to the social order *just enough* to make them feel genuine and subversive.

Apocalyptic, Gun-Toting Youths: *Jarman's* The Last of England

Derek Jarman was a filmmaker who often explored the intersections of queerness and militarism, queerness and macho violence, in daring and provocative ways. Scholars are still grappling with the issues raised by his films, I believe because he often centered his films around questions that had no definite answers. It was the asking of the questions, and the exploration of possible answers, which seemed to interest Jarman most.

The Last of England (1988), one of Jarman's best and most formally experimental films, begins with an extended elegy for lost youth. As Jarman remembers "the boys who died at Flanders" in voiceover, we see a butch-looking teen, tattooed and shirtless, in tattered jeans and military boots, wander across Caravaggio's *Cupid* (1601) in a landfill and proceed to stomp all over it. The boy does a kind of stylized, destructive dance, something like a punk rocker in a mosh pit; the image of the boy is already homoerotic, but the boy's violence seems to be directed against the homoerotic imagery of the painting (a full-length, naked boy with genitals exposed). The violence may also be directed at "culture" in general; the entire film takes place in a sort of wasteland where all vestiges of civilization (and of "beauty") seem totally extinct. After stomping the painting, however, the boy seeks a surprising tenderness from it, laying on top of it and humping it furiously, then rolling over with his arm extended and seeming to fall asleep beside it.[14]

The homoerotic masculinity of the boy implies a circularity of destruction and tenderness, strength and weakness. The tenderness and weakness (like the gay desire itself, for the naked cherub in the painting) can only emerge after the boy has proven his toughness and strength through destruction. To the male psyche, Jarman seems to be saying, being a creative, nurturing god is not enough; he must first be a wrathful, scourging one. Only after his powers of annihilation are established does something like love become possible in any way, shape or form. This may be a phase in an individual life (or society), or it may be a cycle that repeats ad infinitum, with no end in sight. But it is clearly established as a cycle in the staging of this scene: the boy's posture and body language move entirely from the vertical (aggressive stomping) to the prone (surrender to the need for love or tenderness).

These images resonate with so many others in Jarman's work, in which aggression between men leads to love (and then sometimes back to aggression), that it is impossible not to view it as the director confessing to his own impulses. (The cycle includes self-aggression, too, as we see the boy retire to a dank underground hovel where he ties off and injects himself with narcotics, bleeding from his arm and lapsing into blissful, if artificial, oblivion.) Jarman seemed to view military values of might-makes-right, of butch toughness, inflecting all of humanity: not an option which men could choose to adopt or discard, but a way of life which spelled masculinity itself, and therefore had to be simultaneously confronted, embraced, purged if possible, again in endlessly repeating cycles. But that ultimate goal of purgation would necessarily involve relinquishing the worship of masculinity as a categorical absolute; therefore, it is often common in the work of gay male artists (Caravaggio, for example, as well as Jarman) to find contradictory images that celebrate male violent power while at the same time acknowledging its terror and limitations.

Later in *The Last of England* we see a group of soldiers; it is impossible to tell who they are or what "side" they are on, since they are sheathed from head to toe in ski-masks, military gear, leather gloves and boots. They do not represent a position that could be articulated, much less defended; they are a faceless, anonymous outcropping of the same male aggression that the boy manifested earlier, stomping on the painting. They represent anonymity in the same way that sex can be anonymous: one gives oneself not to person but to a series of acts and gestures, and to the gender which the person represents. But compared to the boy, these soldiers are on a much higher, more organized plane of aggression: they set fires, tote around rifles, and stand guard over bands of bedraggled refugees, some of whom they execute by firing squad. Are they resistance-rebels, government mercenaries, mere apolitical thugs? Are they exacting justice, vengeance or planned genocide against their victims? The open-endedness of these questions ultimately casts Jarman and the viewer as complicit in the violence which these soldiers wreak. Again, it is the same cycle of masculine aggression and tenderness, writ larger now, that we saw with the boy and the painting; it does not matter who the executioners and who the victims are, only that they exist in an exchange which enables the exhaustion of male brutality (which is never fully exhausted, only susceptible to moments of less guarded respite).

We see that the gun-toting masked soldiers are part of this cycle of violence and tenderness when we arrive at the scene where one of these soldiers is sleeping on a bed draped with the Union Jack and scattered with empty bottles of lager. A young man, who has already killed a whole fifth of alcohol in a seemingly macho display of hard drinking, staggers in, strips naked, and climbs into bed with this soldier. The soldier responds, making passionate love with the naked man while never removing any of his own concealing "armor." The gay fantasy of having sex with a figure of totally straight masculinity is allegorically teased here: on one side, a completely exposed, vulnerable, identifiable naked man (we see his face and his entire body), and on the other side, a sinister, hidden, unidentifiable figure. The gay man has declared himself, put himself on the line; the soldier has indulged in the same gay fantasy without making the same irrevocable declaration.

Abruptly, Jarman cuts to the young man, now half-dressed (as if the soldier's shame of self-exposure were suddenly contagious), standing in a corner smashing bottles against the wall in anger. This anger seems to relate to the young man's consciousness that he has given himself to a man who only used him. This is why Jarman often highlights gays as sacrificial victims: the masculine, straight-identified shame of wanting to fuck other men incognito, so as to preserve heteronormative power, is an enemy whom only an extreme degree of gay pride can overcome. All too often, gay pride still stems mainly from the constant reinforcement of the fact of homophobic oppression. And even in spite of the anger he subsequently evinces after surrendering to the ski-masked soldier, the young man in *The Last of England* cannot overcome his own moment of surrender, the fulfillment of his passing fantasy. His sexual "collaboration" with the soldier buys him nothing. Like the other refugees, he is summarily led away by the ski-masked soldiers and executed.

These are shifting, overlapping definitions of masculinity being offered simultaneously by militarism and by queerness. Neither one is identical with the dominant culture; both are aberrational (by the more moderate standards of the dominant culture), and both exist in an unconditional realm where proving that one is a man becomes the only thing that matters. The soldier needs to prove that he is a man in order to function as a soldier (at one point in *Restrepo*, after urging two young "cherry" soldiers to fight, one of the older soldiers states: "Vaughn here is very cherry at life, but we're making him into a man. That's all that's important here"); whereas the queer needs to prove that he is a man in order to become desirable to other men, and to function in the experience of gay sex. The logic is irreducible: a real man shoots; a real man also gets shot; both take it "like a man."

Hitler: A Cameo Role

The recurring images of ballerinas pirouetting around bonfires in both *The Last of England* and Jarman's earlier *Jubilee* (1978) suggest the potential emergence of non-macho, indeed ambiguously-gendered culture rising phoenix-like from the ashes of the old, excessively male and militarized culture. (In *The Last of England*, the ballerina is a transsexual.) However, these dances are lonely rituals in Jarman's films, and they are far from being as pervasive, or persuasive, as the recurring images of male violence. As in Van Sant's *Elephant*, everything in *The Last of England* seems to lead back to Hitler, one of whose declamatory speeches is heard on the soundtrack as the ski-masked soldiers prowl around their pyre. We think again of Eric's question, "That's Hitler, right?" as if asking permission to enter that illicit pact we all enter into, whether eagerly or in spite of ourselves, whenever we see or hear Adolf Hitler. It is as if Hitler stands for ground zero of masculine-militarism trying to assert itself as normative rather than aberrational and therefore queer: Hitler, king of freaks, and also their remorseless exterminator, the one who drew relentless lines around who belonged and who didn't, what constituted a freak and what did not; and the one who spoke to that threatened masculine need for such lines. Actual military veterans may have learned a kind of tolerance which only the nearness of death and the fragility of life can teach; but those men who still fear their own status, who fear being "freaks" deep down, can still be lulled by the Hitlerian rhetoric of cleanness and contamination, of all-powerfulness and all-powerlessness. From long beyond the grave Hitler goes on conferring certain exclusive rights upon men, to be aggressive, self-righteous, violent, arbitrary, even as both *The Last of England* and *Elephant* remind us that the Reich was nothing but a tenuous moment, a voice on the air, ultimately collapsing and going under.

With its vision of gun-toting boys engaged in a total war in which masculinity and queerness are inextricably linked, *Elephant* may be Gus Van Sant's conscious homage to *The Last of England*. In both, the future rises up against past and present; maleness consumes itself in a death-frenzy. We are helplessly exhilarated by the spectacle of a cathartic violence that is both macho and queer. And at the same time we hold out a distinctly queer desire for the kids to be "all right," even as we see with our eyes that they aren't.

9. Back from Interzone: Reading William Burroughs' Sexual Politics Through the Films of Van Sant

Would it be possible to write a novel based on the actual facts of Interzone or anyplace?— Burroughs[1]

A creation of author William Burroughs, "Interzone" provides the setting for some of his early fiction. Short for "International Zone" and modeled on the section of Tangier where Burroughs lived in the 50s — a polyglot haven for all manner of expatriates and refugees — Interzone is a mutant place. On one hand, it seems to be a place of special freedoms, antibourgeois, antinationalistic, libertarian, evasive of centralized control. Life there is a hedonistic bazaar, a non-stop party (though nothing, of course, is free). Robert Horton writes of "a zone whose immediacy remained uninsulated by middle-class protections, whose reality could not be shielded by bourgeois euphemisms and hypocrisy...."[2] For this reason, criminal activities run rampant in the Zone; so do dissident sexual activities. For example, we learn from Burroughs that the outlaws "holed up in the mountains of Interzone" manage to "evade the sex census."[3] Even more important than the avoidance of detection as a criminal — and interlinked with this criminal identity — is the avoidance of detection as a sexual dissident; one might prefer (for reasons that have to do with male ego, shame of weakness, etc.) to be known as a criminal rather than as a homosexual. In fact, one's status as a sexual dissident becomes a prime reason why one finds oneself in Interzone.

And of course, homosexuality has itself been a category of criminalized behavior. Burroughs grew up gay in early 20th century America, where homosexuality was not only socially unacceptable but subject to virulently enforced laws. This kind of persecution persisted into the 60s: "Homosexuality was just not mentioned in the early sixties; it was an illegal, hidden secret business," Burroughs biographer and scholar Barry Miles writes, "and for Burroughs to so casually reveal his preference for young men was seen as appalling."[4] In Burroughs' writings, American vice and narcotics squads are often characterized as bumbling, redneck versions of invasive, punitive, state police-apparatuses like the S.S. or the KGB. Burroughs was the first artist to blur the line between the addict and the law, both "job-holders," as it were, operating under the same system of control; both drawing the main part of their identity from something illicit. In Van Sant's *Drugstore Cowboy*, a narco agent on stakeout begs his chief to let them plant drugs in a junky's apartment; the agent is like a junky himself at this moment, pacing the floor and clasping his arms around himself, with a lurid expression on his face.

Vice is not a job in Interzone the way it is in the U.S., because there is virtually no correlative, in Interzone, to the kind of narco agents who flourish elsewhere. Lax laws create a condition in which one can separate crime from punishment, pleasure from routine. Indeed, the main thing about Interzone is that it is not the U.S. And yet, Interzone is not quite a place, as Paul Burston writes, "where moral judgments, like disbelief, are willingly suspended."[5] One brings one's baggage wherever one goes, and even in Interzone there is disapproval of homosexuality; thus, there is reason to be as wary of living there as anywhere else. (Some of the disapproval is, naturally, old-fashioned self-hatred. This doesn't make Burroughs himself a homophobe, although, like Genet, he is often cited as one of homosexuality's "problem authors," taking us so deeply into a world of nasty transgressions that love and loathing become the strangest bedfellows of all.)

In the end, one may have "more freedom" in Interzone, yet, simply by being *in* Interzone, one has declared oneself an oddball, guilty of something. Thus, far from being an earthly paradise, Interzone, in its most paranoid permutation, is a makeshift utopia for outcasts which ends up doubling as a dystopian glass gulag for keeping the wrong people "in," identifiable, under surveillance. In Burroughs' writing, the special horror of surveillance is transformed by a positive aesthetic method that begins somewhat like spying or eavesdropping: the cut-ups purport to be a process of uncovering secret meanings in texts that have come into one's possession more or less at random. One thinks of code-breakers, interpreters; Burroughs shamanizes espionage and incorporates it into his art so as to fear it less. In a number of films, Van Sant replicates the idea of Burroughsian surveillance by having his camera relentlessly follow the backs of his protagonists as they walk (also the backs of cars as they drive down highways), a visual trope which resonates with Burroughs' sense of being hunted and watched.[6]

Surveillance in Interzone can be relatively high-tech but is, in fact, more likely to be extremely primitive. Indeed, eyewitness, evil thoughts, and word of mouth are its main modus operandi. Vicious gossip about any little thing which someone has been caught doing is a characteristic feature of the Zone; at the same time, usually next to nothing is ever formally done about any of this anecdotal information.[7] As a result, "surveillance" is often no more than a kind of smear campaign — half Kafka, half bedroom farce — as when Burroughs (as his early alter ego and pseudonym, William Lee) feels himself about to be arrested by the cops for sleeping with a teenage hustler; however, it turns out to be only the boy's mother and the boy's jealous lover (another gay man) putting the screws to him.[8] Of course, in other texts, mainly *Naked Lunch*, Interzone takes on a more fearsome Orwellian cast, and we see that the real criminals are not the anonymous street-level freaks but the shadowy powerbrokers who truly run the show. At the same time, street-level gossip can be demoralizing in itself: let us not forget how certain types of paranoiac situations move from random sightings and casual-sounding conversations to dense, widespread conspiracies — situations in which the highest and lowest members of society share a power which is equally powerful and sinister, equally absurd.

Nominal "freedom" becomes a trap, a set-up or con game, in which one is given enough rope to hang oneself, so to speak. By making one's freedom visible, one gives anyone at all the anonymous power to restrain it by informing to the police. Here, persecution (real or imagined) enables the fantasy that it is the presence of others which creates problems, not a sickness within oneself: the sickness of "perversion" or the sickness of self-hatred, that vicious circle in infinite regress. Thus, there can be freedom perhaps but no independence. One cannot be one's own man; the best that any "agent" can hope for (Burroughs uses the word agent to denote people on either side of the law) is not to get caught. What is an "interzone," after all, but a region symbiotically connected to other regions, whose boundaries are in-growing, hidden, subject to constant intrusion and interference? Not a state of independent existence, but an interpenetration of subjectivities, a parasitic set of relations to one's immediate neighbors.

Also, Interzone is a uniquely *internalized* place: it is not difficult to read "inter" as shorthand for the psychological condition of "internalizing" the judgments and values of others, thereby literally *becoming* one's own worst enemy. (Interzone disappeared from Burroughs' texts as his sense of well-being and self-acceptance as a gay man seemed to increase.) Again, the atmosphere of persecution seems born from the persecuted one's guilt and self-loathing. Likewise, the police investigation in Van Sant's *Paranoid Park* finally serves only to inconvenience and irritate Alex more than anything, while the real guilt and terror which Alex feels stem entirely from his own troubled conscience. The enemy is, famously, within. It is Nietzsche's "minotaur of conscience," lying in wait to sabotage anyone who wanders too far into the labyrinth of his or her own freedom.[9] Even here, the labyrinth metaphor positions freedom as an enclosed space, and a solitary one. In *Paranoid Park*, Alex has no real "room of his own": at his mother's house, he sleeps on a mattress in a corner of the basement. Only in the security of his car, driving around by himself aimlessly, do we see him evince much freedom of self-expression. This is not to say that Alex, for example, has no reason to feel guilty for having accidentally killed the guard; but there is helpful guilt which enables us to see problems more clearly before solving them or moving on, and then there is unhelpful, blinding guilt which keeps us stuck, holds us back, often for less valid reasons than we might believe. Self-actualization, particularly for those marginalized by society, is usually about the management of these various forms of guilt, and learning how to distinguish them from each other. Interzone punishes its residents to whatever degree they themselves feel the need to be punished — but for this same reason, when looked at in another way, it can provide lessons in self-acceptance for gays (and other social outsiders). As long as one can turn down the voices in one's head, and provided one doesn't expect *total* acceptance from the status quo, one can be as free there as anywhere, i.e., as free as one allows oneself to be.

Finally, Interzone is a region characterized by that harshest, and at the same time most nebulous and interdependent, of economic systems: laissez-faire capitalism. Interzone is, in fact, a small-scale model of global capitalism. In Burroughs' writings, laissez-faire capitalism is a villain, but not an automatic "strawman" villain. This is because laissez-faire capitalism is the only arrangement which enables sex between gay and straight men, or between men and adolescents, via prostitution and economic hardship.[10]

Because it depends on a localized condition of widespread deprivation, this sexual commerce is a prototype of what has come to be called, with chilling accuracy, "disaster capitalism." Yet, in contrast to how we judge most cases of exploitation, such sex is also deeply personal, even invested with feelings of (at times mutual) love. Being a respecter of nothing but the color of one's money, capitalism, in its indiscriminate bypassing of moral questions and considerations, can also bypass the moral reservations which homophobes wield against gays.

Let me make this clear. Burroughs himself was no blind defender of capitalism, or any kind of system for that matter. There is something malign in humanity that undermines not only utopian dreams but the basic management of ordinary resources and functions. He writes: "What form could rebellion take if the communists took over the country they would either have to keep the present bureaucracy in place or provide a new one to fill exactly the same functions. All paths are blocked by numbers, by what we have too much of already."[11] Typically with Burroughs, distorted, experimental syntax helps to reinforce the basic anarchy of the thought which the syntax is expressing. We tend to create the same limiting, distorting traps for ourselves, no matter what name we call it. Escape begins when we "unblock." Likewise, in Burroughs' writings there is nothing glamorous or romantic about poverty: he foresaw the cheapening of life under a privatized healthcare system, for instance, in his early routine about "Friendly Finance" repossessing a woman's iron lung.[12] Andrew Hussey writes of Burroughs' "acknowledgment that beyond the economics of sex traffic, there is a symbolic order—the United States, the 'System,' the 'West'—that must be opposed or destroyed ... not in strict terms of postcolonial vision but rather, more accurately, a postnational vision."[13] Desire becomes a transcendent nation unto itself, with its own laws and customs, its own economy.

Bodies, which suffer under capitalism, become exalted in Marxism (the body of the worker) and in homosexuality (the body of the lover), but for essentially different reasons, the latter at odds with the former in its willingness to objectify and even commodify the bodies in question. Homosexuality is also perhaps more directly and enthusiastically exalting of the body than the pseudo–Puritanism of communism will allow: for Marxists the body is a site for the deserving redress of injustice, for gays a site of pleasure divorced from moral categories such as "deserving" or "undeserving." Not that gays are constitutionally insensitive to issues of economic exploitation, or resistant to Marxist analysis. But the fact is that gay desire (as expressed in the arts) has always cut drastically across sociopolitical lines, and revolutions of desire do not always match up with Marxist-economic ones: Paul Morrissey, Andy Warhol's protégé, filmed ruminative studies of Joe Dallesandro's face, body and genitalia, but was by all accounts a reactionary conservative, a kind of gay Archie Bunker.[14] Perhaps this is because, although one accepts, as a gay male in a straight world, that one must to some extent "fight for" one's desire, there are many ways of carrying on this fight, and some people may place greater trust in individual circumstance than in collective organization — again, even while acknowledging, as Morrissey does in his films, that being gay can be lonely and alienating.[15] Yet Morrissey's own viewpoint is not beleaguered or victim-identified, but rather one positioned between swaggering lust and barbed outrage at human stupidity; the only attitude which comes off well in his films (apart from physical beauty, usually male) is that of hostile aggression.

Just as Morrissey's camera sought to "possess" Joe, and his narratives highlight Joe as unattainable to his many admirers, somehow off-limits, so desire in general creates a wish for exclusivity which is also in keeping with laissez-faire capitalism and at odds with the communist ideal of "sharing things equally." Indeed, Morrissey covets Joe with his camera the way a billionaire stockbroker covets gold bonds. By this, I don't mean anything as banal as that Joe is turned into an object or a commodity, or that sex becomes businesslike — I mean the opposite, which we are still loath to square with the identity of an artist, perhaps especially a queer artist, that business itself can be a kind of sex or sexiness, as well as a kind of art. Warhol colleague John Giorno *was* a stockbroker, and Warhol himself said that "good business is the best art."[16] Also, like certain power-inflected sexual scenarios, business might be "good for" one partner in the exchange but not the other.

Another Warhol Superstar, Eric Emerson, helps us rethink the nature of the commodity-form as consumable item in his monologue from *The Chelsea Girls* (1966). After peeling off his clothes for the camera under colorful lights, he begins to say, "I wish I was a piece of sweat, or a drop of sweat being licked by someone, dripping down their neck and having a tongue creep along and pick me up," and we think, "Uh-huh, there it is, the Warhol people were *exploited*. Their expenditure of creative energy, their sweat, was consumed by 'creeping' tongues!" But all at once Emerson's speech takes an unexpected and more visionary-romantic turn: "Then being taken into the body, completely in. To go that far into someone's body. That'd mean you were all them, or they were all you — whoever was the controller. I guess they'd be all me, because usually I'm the controller." What is consumed has ultimate power over whoever consumes it. Emerson is also slyly advertising in this speech his status as a sexual top: it is his body fluids which go inside his partners and make the partners "all him." His speech has even more resonance in the AIDS era, when the free exchange of body fluids is far riskier than it was in 1966; yet this power does not have to be ruthless, it can be a kind of harmonious oneness with others. Emerson's drop of sweat and its journey through the other's body touches upon what is most sacred and profound, not only in sex but in all forms of human communion. Even if we could regard Emerson's entire monologue and simultaneous striptease for the camera as self-commodification, it is finally revealed as the commodity's empowerment, to be consumed. (It is also Emerson's major claim to cultural and aesthetic immortality.) Sometimes we reach too quickly for abstract words like "commodification" to explain exchanges that seem disturbing in their openness and freedom, or which defy (political) categorization because they stake out a place for desires that have been barely named, let alone classified. We brand everything as cautionary or harmful or inhuman, because, in witnessing the inevitable gulf that opens up around anyone's individual desire, *we* become the alienated ones.

Coming into contact with naked desires of exhibitionism and "exploitation," the sensitive onlooker expresses this alienation in two ways: (1) *I do not want this* (meaning, it isn't for my benefit that this body in question is being exploited or exploiting itself); and (2) *this body does not really need to be doing this* (meaning the body in question wants this, and is actually content with the situation). The extent to which these responses are mere measurements of personal discomfort and bewilderment can be seen in the live-sex-acts section of Sam D'Alessandro's "The Zombie Pit." The narrator and his friends are on a quest to become habitués of the most disgusting dive they can find, and one night they end up at "the sleaziest I've ever seen in this town."[17] A regular named Little Ricky jumps up on the bar and begins to perform a striptease, which culminates in him bending over and "letting these old men stick quarters in his asshole."[18] "He starts out with dimes and then advances up to quarters later on," another regular explains to the narrator. "Every once in a while he goes in the back room behind the bar and empties out."[19]

The money earned by Little Ricky's naked dancing body literally penetrates (fucks) him, and in its passage from outside to inside to back outside the body, it becomes a grotesque metonymy for the consumption of nourishment and its later excrescence. It is a more appalling version of Eric Emerson's drop of sweat and its quest to penetrate someone else's body and make it "all me." It is also mercenary, or cash-driven, in a way that Emerson's pansexual body worship is not. Here, prostitution cuts out the middle man, so to speak (the client's genitalia), and makes the monetary exchange directly substitute for sexual penetration. The urgent need for money, even small change, becomes not a furtive rationale behind a sex act but the entire trick, suggesting that this trick itself has meaning for Little Ricky as a kind of public expression of his identity. Seemingly puzzled and unable to distinguish between the economic need that might drive Little Ricky to do something like this, or the kinky thrill that might also drive Little Ricky, the narrator responds with an attempt to block out what is happening: "I've had enough of this place ... [W]hat I'm really trying to do is get away. Distancing."[20] But during this distancing, he says, tellingly, "I take possession of the rest of Sid's beer."[21] (Sid is one of the narrator's bar-hopping friends.) On some level, the narrator does not deny his own complicity in power exchanges, raw need, even forms of aggression, in the "taking possession" of his friend's beer. The alienated response—*this is not for my benefit, I do not want this*—is displaced onto, and belied by, the exercising of a different kind of desire, consumption, satisfaction.

Yet, there is a sex act even more horrifying to the narrator, "a nightmare I can't get out of my head." This is an "overweight woman with pasty skin" who balances pieces of fruit between her breasts and offers customers "the chance to snare one of the edibles by mouth." Here, the nakedly perverse need is seen more clearly on both sides of the exchange, since, wanting to eat of this forbidden fruit from its human fruit stand, "various men and one woman are smeared with juices dripping from their chins."[22] Just as the anal insertion of money conflated payment for sex with sex itself, now we see a metonymy for breastfeeding which involves the desperate consumption of real food. Are the bar patrons starving, perhaps after having stuck their last quarters into the orifice of Little Ricky? Does *his* kink soften up the clientele and prepare them for the gratification of *her* kink? (Will they, too, go behind the bar later to "empty out?") First "give till it hurts," then "all you can eat." Feast or famine.

The fruit stand lady does not seem to charge for her produce, at least we see no money changing hands. In fact, she instigates the second alienated response—*she does not really need this, she actually wants it*—when she corners and attacks the narrator: "Bending menacingly toward me, her swaying chest aims at my head and in one swift maneuver entraps my face between the two enormous balloons of warm, sticky flesh. I'm suffocating, literally, my mouth and nostrils filled with her expanding skin and the remains of a cantaloupe. Using only her breasts, she shakes my head viciously from side to side, in the same way a dog kills a small rodent...."[23] Again, this may be a naked dancing body on display; but there is no question that *this* body controls the sexualized activity she performs, as well as all of the sexualized and non-sexualized activity surrounding her. It is her need which is being satisfied. The client becomes *her* prey. Once he escapes her "suffocating" flesh, the narrator's response is precisely to imagine a back-story, a kind of alibi, for the fruit-stand lady "in which she's an everyday New Jersey housewife who just does this two nights a week for a little exercise and pocket money,"[24] i.e., *she does not really need this, she actually wants this.*

It is not so much whether these alienated responses to desire are accurate or inaccurate, or whether the displays of desire themselves are or are not exploitative of *someone*; it is more the fact that they describe the inability of any person to ever measure or fully understand the world of desire within another person, or indeed, within himself or herself. Not only do we construct fantasy scenarios for why someone might be performing this way in a bar (when we are not outright looking the other way), but we construct, at the most general level of society and culture, elaborate ideological systems (Marxism, Freudianism, religion, etc.) precisely to explain away the existence of such forms of sexuality, as well as our own ambivalent reactions to them.

Increasingly, as gay activism moves away from the murkiness of individual desires and toward a consolidation of collective social power, and as capitalism

In *Mala Noche* (1987), Pepper (Ray Monge) occasionally sells himself as a street hustler to survive in Portland's poverty-ridden Old Town. As we see from William Burroughs' depictions of Interzone, a fictionalized Tangier, hustling is often inflected with elements of bad faith from imperialism, colonialism, and laissez-faire capitalism.

becomes increasingly fundamentalist–Christian, it becomes strictly a point of historical irony that the inherently subversive desires of gay men have often made common cause with the marketplace and the market's demand that one possess money. Working-class gays remain invisible and powerless; one of the most ubiquitous gay stereotypes of the 20th century, and one of the last to retain any sort of widespread cachet, was the *faux-riche* gay, who evinced class snobbery and even a certain juicy nostalgia for aristocratic manners and breeding.

Why were generations of commentators — even Susan Sontag in "Notes on 'Camp'" — spellbound by the image of gays as some hypersensitive race of blue-blooded aristocrats? Perhaps because it made gays seem weak, defeatable, a relic of bygone history. But the hiddenness of middle-class and working-class gays should never have blinded us to their existence in the first place.

Camp's "snob taste,"[25] its outlandish bad taste, then, is not really "about" the cherished tchotchkes or *objets d'art* themselves, or even the money required to collect and appreciate them, but instead an ideal of off-limits power lurking behind all taste-making and monetary exchanges. For some homosexuals it simply feels safer not to mix with the "rabble"—and to promote excessively drawn lines between that rabble and some supposedly ultra-refined elite that can stem a feared tide of coming barbarism. We see this in Interzone, where one is only as safe as the cushion of wealth one can inflate around oneself like a life-jacket. Indeed, Burroughs, or William Lee, has enough money to live fairly well in Interzone, he can buy a certain level of respectability and tolerance. So, too, a number of gay characters in Van Sant's films are or seem to be well-to-do, with material advantages that set them apart from the various people whom they hire to do their bidding: this is true of most of the johns who cruise for hustlers in *My Own Private Idaho*, as well as the ranch-owning Countess (his name literally an homage to the aristocracy) in *Even Cowgirls Get the Blues*. Not that these characters are depicted as being comfortable with themselves or even literally safe from harm (there's a lesson there: money can buy only so much protection, after all, when one is flagrantly gay in a straight world); nonetheless, although American, they seem like denizens of Interzone, where money facilitates desires that might otherwise find themselves denied.

One fantasy of laissez-faire capitalism, especially as it relates to gay desire, is that everyone has a price tag, and money can bridge the gap between average older guys, say, and handsome younger ones. Money substitutes not only for something as banal as romantic love, but for laws and moral judgments: a straight man selling his body can ostensibly have no complaints about the transaction as long as he is remunerated to his satisfaction (which, since Interzone is a third world country, usually does not require much). According to this fantasy (and perhaps valid in some ways even beyond the fantasy), the hustler is an operator, too, as well as the john; the native a capitalist as much as the Ugly American. An indigenous boy who attempts to fleece one's wallet with a sweet, come-hither smile is both an anarchic challenge to (Protestant) capitalism's constricted, self-abnegating energies, and a kind of triumph of those same energies: the hustler openly performs the kind of paid seduction which U.S. multinationals, Wall Street or Madison Avenue take such pains to render subliminal. This is not to say that the Arab natives become anything like Protestant Americans. "The racial groups of Interzone are not ... 'absorbed into more collective identities' ... but preserved in all their human variety and uniqueness."[26] (Besides, as Ian MacFayden notes, the Zone "embraces ethnic diversity because it's great for business"[27]—multiculturalism as marketing strategy in the secret history of U.S./global capitalism.) In any case, they retain their own culture, their own personality (which is partly what makes them so exotically attractive), and if anything, it is the American, Burroughs, who picks up more from them than they do from him. He is broadened by his exposure to the more ancient and pure culture, the same way we will see Walt broadened and sensitized by his encounter with the Mexican youths in *Mala Noche*.

The natives learn capitalism (often the hard way) but without becoming creatures of it. Yet they can be excellent studies. Indeed, a good hustler, like any good capitalist, knows how to make his smile go a long way, so he can sometimes get paid without even having to follow through. If the need is pressing enough, if the fantasy is all-consuming enough, buyers will attempt to satisfy it with entirely inadequate remedies (for which they will even pay top dollar, in their desperation), thereby simultaneously increasing both the efficacy of duplicitous business methods and the agonizing need itself.

We can follow this logic to its end, for it is finally equivalent to the logic of romantic love, no matter how sardonically mediated by money or homophobic laws. (It is also, in some ways, the current state of capitalism in the U.S., where the working and middle classes largely cling to a broken system whose rules have changed, whose powerful have abandoned them, and whose job opportunities and healthy infrastructure will most likely not be coming back.) Getting knowingly cheated by a hustler is a way of declaring one's love for him, and moreover, almost a superstitious way to "manufacture" future good karma, even a kind of sainthood. One can end up pursuing a martyr fix, addicted to swallowing the snake oil as if it were a real remedy. Interzone is a snake-oil capital, with "cheap counterfeit goods of every variety. Adulterated shark repellent, cut antibiotics, condemned parachutes, stale antivenin, inactive serums and vaccines, leaking lifeboats."[28] As well as hustlers too straight to perform with their male clientele, perhaps. One demonstrates one's highest love for the "object" in question by paying him the going rate while at the same time allowing him the liberty not to perform, not to render the advertised services, e.g., to remain human.

When there is nothing inside the vaunted package, charisma becomes crucial. Under laissez-faire, everyone is blatantly out for his or her own self-interests, yet there is also some incentive to winning people over, getting on people's good side, so they may be happily suckered in, and protest less when they find themselves ripped off, the way K-Y floats brusque penetrations, or again, the way true love looks the other way when it gets cheated. In this sense, hustling is laissez-faire not only in terms of the market bearing whatever it will bear, but in terms of personal charisma adding its irrational, impulsive element to enterprise. Thus, in *Mala Noche*, Walt is so in love with the straight young Mexican Johnny that he offers him fifteen dollars to sleep with him; but Johnny, macho and proud, with no intention of actually sleeping with Walt, holds out for twenty-five, which Walt insists he does not have. Finally, it is Johnny's friend Pepper who takes the inducement. Pepper more or less rapes Walt, anally penetrating him without lube, then plucks the extra ten dollar bill from Walt's pants pocket. In the end, the full asking price of $25 finds its way to the hustlers in spite of Walt's attempts at negotiating — and this lying on both sides is the gesture of bad faith which could be said to begin this saga of Walt's love for Johnny under an inauspicious sign. Nonetheless, Walt falls even harder for Johnny, settling for being able to have him only through very distant and attenuated proxy, and leaving himself open to further liberties and predations.

Indeed, blame is far from Walt's mind on the morning after, when he is able to rationalize getting robbed and more or less raped by Pepper since he admits to having asked for a reckless night and in a sense (happy and proud to have gotten fucked by someone so desirable) only got what he wanted. The hustler must lose some face (he is sacrificing his "total straightness," what he tells himself about himself), and so must the john, who nearly always ends up paying more than he wanted or expected to, but is still content (again) as long as that high-priced, laissez-faire charisma fills him with a glow that cannot be reckoned in dollars. In fact, hustler and john are often each other's "contented victims."

In Burroughs' writings, we see teenage hustling from the john's viewpoint: suspicion, wariness of getting cheated, sometimes a kind of love, sometimes an offhand guilt,[29] and the feeling of being reduced to an object (a gringo tourist with a wallet full of U.S. dollars). In *Mala Noche* and *My Own Private Idaho*, we see the same process more from the viewpoint of the hustlers: degradation, dangerous street life, vulnerability, sometimes a kind of love, sometimes an offhand bravado, and the same feeling of being reduced to an object (a body hired for someone's pleasure). Of course, Burroughs also speaks of having known at least a few "sweet" hustlers (Kiki, for instance[30]). But on the whole, these viewpoints of hustler and john tend to exclude each other: which one is correct? *Both*, because, like any laissez-faire transaction — like any transaction in Interzone — buyer and seller are schizophrenically fused as ideal partners by their shared recklessness, that element of risk by which each "has" something on the other. Buyer *and* seller beware.

Still, there must be something better, nobler, more honorable, than all this chicanery? In many of his films, Van Sant keenly (and fondly) observes moments in which his characters refuse to participate in any capitalistic exchanges at all. When Sissy Hankshaw, whose outsized thumbs have made her the world's greatest hitchhiker, comes to New York City, she is like an innocent adrift in Interzone; she is appalled at the idea of paying for a ride in a taxi, and before her newfound friends drag her into the cab with them, she stands in front of it, making her patented waving and swaying movements with her hips and thumbs, as if to assuage her outraged conscience by at least going through the motions of getting the cab through artistry rather than commerce. In *Drugstore Cowboy*, Diane, an avid reader, shoplifts a paperback from the book rack on her way out of a pharmacy after one of the junkie gang's drug raids. In *My Own Private Idaho*, Mike is teased by another hustler for never having been to a rock concert. Rock 'n' roll comes up again in *Last Days*, as something "free" which has been corrupted by a ruthless business model: Blake, a belated rock star in a post-rock era, is in trouble with his record label and his management for dropping out of a multi-million dollar tour for reasons of depression, exhaustion, and personal burnout. It is capitalism which enables the two killers in *Elephant* to purchase an automatic rifle online and have it delivered the next morning, in time to commit the massacre. In *Paranoid Park*, Alex must prove his alibi to the police interrogator by being able to remember the cost of the meal he claims to have ordered at a restaurant on the night in question; the interrogator asks if he still has the receipt, and Alex says, "I don't keep Subway receipts." In a moment that verges on black humor, his very liberty or life might be at stake if he cannot prove his participation in capitalism.

Likewise, Burroughs exposed an infamy of capitalism that seems all too easy for people to accept: the way it leads to rampant, appraising judgment about anyone and everyone, an immediate, ongoing cost-benefit analysis replacing human interactions. Interzone is a "miasma of suspicion and snobbery.... Everyone looks you over for the price tag, appraising you like merchandise for immediate or prestige advantage."[31] Theoretically (martyr fix aside), exploitation is never without psychic fallout or what we might term a species of uniquely bad karma: what goes around comes around. But in Interzone, this kind of karma cycles so quickly that the malevolent air is nearly thick enough to be cut with a machete; one learns to cope with it, it becomes business as usual. "The market of psychic exchanges is as glutted as the shops."[32] Or one *tries* to learn to cope. Economic and emotional depression go hand in hand, as one finds oneself reduced not only to object status, but even worse, utter uselessness. Because information is always a buyer's market, Interzone is "a vast overstocked market, everything for sale and no buyers."[33] (This is why people who come to Interzone expecting to strike it rich usually have another thing coming[34]: in this sense, we can see parallels between Interzone and U.S. history, pursuit of the American Dream as a false promise held out as enticement to immigrants but usually denied. The Mexican immigrants in *Mala Noche* have little honest work to go around, and it is always menial, unstable and underpaid.)

With personal information devalued to the point of meaninglessness, only the extremity of the information (and the behavior that lies behind it) determines value, if any. For this reason, those behaviors which are most antisocial or which carry the highest negative judgment in Interzone — homosexuality, drugs, youth itself— become the only ones that still retain value as sources of gossip and, beyond that, action taken in the name of "Control." "There is," Burroughs writes with characteristic perspicacity, "always money in hate."[35] This abject behavioral extremity, which makes one a target of gossip and control, is what Robert Horton calls "inverse social capital"[36]: every rebel's status is based on it. But if the wages of hate are exploitative, and if love is bankrupt, then the real currency, the real life energy, stems from something like indifference. Indeed, sheer indifference is like gold in a crowded Zone where it's every man for himself. "A.J. claims to be an 'independent,' which is to say: 'Mind your own business.' There are no independents any more.... The Zone swarms with every variety of dope but there are no neutrals there."[37] In cinematic terms, neutrality can be defined by Van Sant's observant, unobtrusive and usually distant camera, and by the use of "real time" to show events unfolding in an ostensibly natural, non-manipulated way. This instinct for neutrality surfaces in the way Van Sant chooses to pull back and finally cut away from the violent moment, near the end of *Gerry*, where the two Gerrys wrestling turns into mortal struggle. A different director would have zeroed in on the crime, participating, cheerleading, taking control; whereas Van Sant abdicates control and minds his own business as a kindness to his harried characters.

Interzone is infected, Burroughs writes, by a particular sickness of Control[38]—and always behind Burroughs' loathing of societal and state control is the vulnerability of the homosexual (and the drug user as well) to police intervention. But somehow this becomes the homosexual's fault, by being too obvious. Hence, again, the ubiquity of internalized homophobia as a prime mover of social history, however bizarre: Burroughs becomes nauseated by witnessing a gaggle of effeminate queens, then, as if in atonement for his own reactive judgment, immediately embarks on a suicidal mission to assassinate the mysterious "Holy Man" who runs Interzone.[39] To make a common enemy of the self-righteous dealers in control is the only way Burroughs can be comfortably *gay like the others*— not registering passive protest through some form of auto-feminization, but taking up arms in a perilous struggle against the heterosexual strongholds themselves. A manly gayness which is all the more violent, righteous and invested in death for bearing within it an essential kernel of homophobic (self-)hatred.

But this manly posturing is instantly unmasked. It is revealed to Burroughs that the Holy Man is not the true enemy but rather he himself, and he weeps. What divines homosexual desire in a man is always a "telepathic penetration" which targets the guilt and need for concealment latent in the desire itself.[40] Because of man's inhumanity, this telepathy nonetheless ends up being the functional equivalent of gossip, and spurring behaviors motivated by panic and guilt; thus, the would-be enclosed community reveals itself more than it realizes in everything it says and does, and can therefore be studied from the outside, like an ant farm. "It is frequently said," Burroughs writes, "that the Great Powers will never give up Interzone because of its value as a listening post. It is in fact that listening post of the world, the slowing pulse of a decayed civilization, that only war can quicken."[41] Interzone is every city's red light district, a demarcated, even protected realm where the illicit is sanctioned for a price. It is also, as it turns out, popular culture, which entertains, shills, distracts and, along the way, occasionally "liberates" (again for a price) what can and cannot be represented, what is and is not acceptable.

Selective enforcement: confusion about this double nature of Interzone, as benign playground *and* lethal police state, where each man is, again, given enough rope to hang himself, leads Burroughs to wonder, in one vignette, if he'd be better off living in the absolute repression of an actual police state where at least all the cards are on the table — the cold war-era Soviet Union, for example.[42] At least there, what is verboten is usually physically off limits and thus removed from temptation. But as usual, temptation takes on a life of its own. The narrator witnesses the slaughter of "a legion of embattled queens behind a barricade of Swedish-modern furniture," and still imagines that he can infiltrate this "Russian sector" to pick up a boy at a bath house.[43] The "great histrionic gestures and pathic screams" of the dying[44] obsess him, but act, if anything, as a kind of goad for him to persevere in his personal mission to accomplish gay sex even in the middle of such a vastly homophobic place: anyway, again, he is not *gay like the others*. (In this case, not subject to abject, squalid, pathetic martyrdom.)

Many of the characters in Van Sant's gay-themed films follow Burroughs' distinction of insisting on a life outside of gay community; insisting on not being gay like the others. In *Mala Noche*, poverty and perhaps pro–Mexican feeling form a larger part of the circle of friends' solidarity (Walt included) than Walt's romantic feelings for men or the men's occasional situational bisexuality (hustling for money). In any event, Walt's friends are mainly fellow artists rather than fellow queers. *My Own Private Idaho* is even more complex: the film depicts gay desire as a difficult, unstable, makeshift refuge outside of, and against, society. Daddy Carroll, the elderly john who picks up Mike early in the film, goes through a nearly complete transformation as he pays Mike to act out an elaborate fantasy of dressing like a Dutch boy and scrubbing his apartment with steel-wool. "That sound!" Daddy Carroll enthuses to the scratching of the steel-wool on a kitchen surface. "Harder! Harder!" Dancing and writhing out of his conservative male attire, he literally "lets down his hair" and appears, finally, in a kimono and make-up, with distinctly feminine gestures. During this extended transformation he also seems to rejuvenate, from elderly male to more youthful-seeming femme. Gay desire is a refuge within a refuge (the apartment itself) within a hostile environment (the heterosexual world). As in Interzone, it is not actually sex or drugs but refuge itself which is being sought and paid for, nothing more or less exalted, and nothing more tangible. For his part, as seller of refuge, Mike must faithfully and patiently submit to this coded and superficially non-sexual ritual before earning the trust required to see Daddy Carroll's indeterminate, vulnerable sexual body fully revealed.

Later in that film, after the threesome which Mike and Scott have with Hans, Van Sant cuts to Hans driving their motorcycle and getting pulled over by a cop for speeding. Hans is in an erotic memory trance, caressing the motorcycle and barely able to answer the policeman's questions. Successfully realized gay desire is such a leap outside of social conventions that it makes the gay man vulnerable to forgetting other "laws" and being penalized. Inversely, crime of all sorts is a metonymy for gayness. In *Elephant*, the school massacre is linked with gay desire. The two shooters, Alex and Eric, feeling alone against the world and sharing the bond of knowing this will be their last day on earth, are seen showering together and kissing; it is implied that they have sex with each other before going out to commit their massacre. But what does this sex signify, and does it make them gay? There was some controversy — or, more accurately, the touchy fear that there *might be* controversy — over Van Sant's "daring that some will call irresponsible,"[45] in depicting two hated mass murderers as gay. Why suggest it at all, particularly if their sexual encounter in the shower is not intrinsically meaningful to the plot but instead ultimately irrelevant, and can be discarded as one more false lead in trying to "lay blame for an act that at its core is absolutely senseless?"[46] But there are nuanced reasons for the sudden physical intimacy between the boys (we examined some of them already in Chapter 7). They may want to experience physical closeness with someone before dying; they might be trying to imitate the Nazis they admire (often Nazis are culturally coded as "gay"); or they might feel, as best friends united against a hostile world, that sex is an appropriate extension of their friendship. Sam D'Allesandro writes about finding a special, protective intimacy with a lover: "Together we formed one large womb providing a safety neither of us possessed on our own."[47] Eric and Alex might also *be* gay, with a concomitant sense of doom, however — incapable of viewing their gayness as anything other than a kamikaze mission against the straight world. Put otherwise: no matter what the reason, we are again led by gay desire definitively outside of, rather than back into, society. And theirs, too, is that manly gayness which seeks revenge against heterosexual society, like Burroughs' self-appointed mission to assassinate the Holy Man — violent revenge rather than a passive, live-and-let-live acceptance which would, first, make them complicit in the social order as such, and, second, make them feel *gay like the others*, e.g., ordinary victims born to hurl themselves into the trap of their own victimization. Instead, they and other Van Sant heroes may well hurl themselves into certain traps, but as a distinctly poetic, heroic quest. One thinks of the line Van Sant added to *Drugstore Cowboy* (this line is not in the novel) during Bob's voiceover when he is being beaten up: "There's nothing more life-affirming than getting the shit kicked out of you." Moreover, this celebration of duking it out might be partly why Van Sant sets a no-holds-barred playground brawl to a particularly pretty pop ballad in *Good Will Hunting*. This kind of sentiment is one that we have come to regard as anathema to current gay orthodoxy, which is, of course, anti-gay-bashing and, as a result, condemnatory of all violence (Bob is not gay, he is attacked for the drugs he is assumed to be holding); and which also reads traditional expressions of masculinity (such as violence) as the benighted, regressive capitulation to a tautological ("a-man's-a-man") and repressively homophobic code. But if elements of traditional masculinity survive in the modern-day homosexual (and of course they do), then gays are products of heterosocial conditioning in spite of themselves. Where, then, is freedom — freedom from being beaten or bashed, freedom as that universal head-start given by the ostensibly stronger (straights) to the ostensibly weaker (gays) and which is meant to bring a certain equality to social relations? Or is this definition of freedom as something granted to the disempowered by the powerful essentially outdated and in need of revision?

Burroughs lived most of his life on the run, in a way few of us are existentially (or perhaps financially: the cost of traveling and living anywhere has skyrocketed so much since the 50s and 60s) prepared to do today. Perhaps this is why freedom in Interzone is not to be legislated, regulated, and doled out equally to all; it is only for those wily or insane enough to try to seize it. It is also, at times, inadvisable to pursue, and blatantly incompatible with living. Hence, the stakes are high, as high as they are for the Nietzschean "free spirit": "Independence is for the very few; it is a privilege of the strong. And whoever attempts it ... proves that he is probably not only strong, but also daring to the point of recklessness."[48] And the blame for "losing" always rebounds upon the gambler, the adventurer who could have merely gone, like any other modest tourist, "back to the hotel...."[49] "Nor can he go back to the pity of men"[50]: there is no one to cry to if one falls victim, no one to protect the abused homosexual (or junky). Anarchy prevails in all relations outside of society, and though there is always some honor among thieves, this courtesy is not automatically extended to homosexuals, who are perceived to be conspicuously lower, Others among Others.

To live in Interzone is to be (at the very least) a tourist without a guide — in fact, "guide" is one of the filthiest insults one can level at anyone in Interzone.[51] This is presumably because there simply is no negotiating this double-edged world — only an outright con man or a double agent (or worse yet, someone who proffers sympathy to those "beneath" him[52]) would present himself as a guide, and no such person is to be trusted. The visitor to Interzone ends up in the space between two things: freedom and entrapment, being useful and getting used, staying sane and going crazy, human and alien, as well as an entire host of ambivalent, paranoiac sexualities — straight passing for gay, gay passing for straight, someone's phony john or someone's phony trick. No one *chooses* Interzone, as no one chooses to be gay, but making it one's home is a self-revelation of sorts. To be there is to be, in one way or another, forced to be there; and one is always alone there, with one's case history of abnormalities, dysfunctions and crimes. It is a place of "deterioration and final loneliness, a dead-end setup where there is no one I can contact."[53] Yet it *is* an identity, however isolating, however precarious and far removed from easy comforts or consolations.

One might think of Interzone as an anachronistic relic of the oppressive past, to be dismissed as a living museum of demonic, toxic pansies, vicious straights, and faithless double agents — except that gay artists, especially the few who manage to cross over into the mainstream, like Van Sant, always dwell within a kind of Interzone. The paranoiac clouds of Interzone hover over them: their work is often disparaged for obscure reasons, it gets accused of being either always too ubiquitously gay or never quite gay enough, simultaneously. And these artists understand too well the double agency endemic to Interzone, "attacked" from both sides as it were, the gay audience with its expectations and the straight with its own.

To be sure, Van Sant's temperament seems suited to withstand many of these onslaughts. Like Burroughs, Van Sant bears very few "feel-good" messages, very few homilies about pride and the will to overcome; in this regard *Milk* was an almost complete departure from his previous gay-themed films. Likewise, Van Sant is immune to the politicized call of the happy, or even hopeful, ending: he composes films like romantic poems around the presence of beautiful young men, only to dryly surrender them to a seemingly inevitable death. In his films, romance is filled with pain, and love likely forlorn, occurring between misfits.

Moreover, love almost never develops naturally in Van Sant's films: it is always conditioned by larger circumstances which help define and often destroy it. Love needs an objective correlative, a reason for being that stems from outside of itself, and which is stronger than any love could be without such a reason: Walt believes he is helping to redress the plight of Mexican immigrants; the junkie lovers in *Drugstore Cowboy* are strongly connected through their addiction, and remain together only as long as the addiction endures. Street life, with its perils and codes, lends the love between Mike and Scott in *My Own Private Idaho* a powerful sense of mission; but the love is undone when Scott Favor comes to reject living on the streets. Sissy Hankshaw and Bonanza Jellybean in *Even Cowgirls Get the Blues* share a similar sense of mission, in liberating the Rubber Rose Ranch and in protecting the endangered whooping cranes on the ranch's property; their love grows out of these quests, and vice versa.

This pattern continues in the later films. In *Gerry* the two Gerrys — symbolic lovers who are also subsumed to an extreme degree in each other's identity — fail in their quest to find their way out of a desert they are lost in, so their "love" comes to a grim finality. In *Elephant*, Alex and Eric are united in their purpose to kill as many students at their high school as possible; even so, Alex will finally betray Eric by shooting him along with all the others. In *Last Days*, rock 'n' roll stardom connects Blake with his wife and his entourage, while ultimately dividing him from them as well; while in *Milk*, political commitment initially unites Harvey and Scott, until its hurly-burly and time demands come between them.

Love is a potent, temporary name given to a feeling that transcends individualism and therefore is doomed by the individual's inevitable commitment to self — a pattern very similar to the one which Nicholas Garnham identified in the films of Samuel Fuller. Even though Fuller and Van Sant are very different filmmakers, Garnham's words could equally apply to the films of Van Sant:

> Love means the death of individuality, love is both the highest expression of individualism and also its violation. The concept of romantic love is based upon frustration, upon the idea that the structure of society makes such a love impossible and that if the love is fulfilled the lovers will be punished as transgressors. America is a society based more and more on self, on individualism.... In such a society love comes to be seen as a transgression of the self. So love is a trap, a relaxation of the tensions which keep the self together and protect it....[54]

"America" comes to look more like Interzone, where (sexual) freedom can become a trap for the would-be free individual. But although sex and love can both be traps (like anything which breaks the individual out of his enclosed self and forces him to become dependent on others), love is much closer to being the true opposite of freedom. Time and again in Van Sant's films, there is one in a pair of lovers who dies directly or indirectly for the other one (Nadine in *Drugstore Cowboy*; Mike in *My Own Private Idaho*; Marion in *Psycho*; Gerry; Eric in *Elephant*), or who simply dies leaving the other one to mourn (Pepper in *Mala Noche*; Bonanza Jellybean). The free individual resists the power of love to literally kill him or to symbolically do so by dislocating him from himself. One thinks also of *Paranoid Park*, where Alex is reluctant to take his girlfriend's virginity because he knows that, if he does, things will get "all serious" between them.

At the same time, some of the lovers in Van Sant's films recognize that by loving they are engaged in a kind of protest which will have far-reaching implications, if not directly in their lives, then possibly for a future as yet unseen. The extent to which they fail (in the present) should not exclude the potential for someone else's success in a distant or not so distant future; such is the nature of sexual dissidence, or love outside of society. So Eric speaks of how the school massacre that he commits with Alex will help bullied kids in the future to be listened to, before they take matters into their own hands; Sissy burns the dead Bonanza's love letters but retains her memory and goes on with their shared cause; Scott Favor hints at a future time when he might turn back to the gay lovers he has spurned for the sake of wealth and power; most dramatically of all, Harvey Milk's martyrdom spawns a new unification of the gay rights movement, in which the complex, fraught love of individuals becomes sublimated into group solidarity and collective action.

While in pursuit of an elusive freedom often as poignantly small and fleeting as an embrace or a moment of shared emotion, Van Sant derives the real expressive tension of his art from what remains "taboo" or "unspeakable" in gay identity (even though his solidarity and identification with gays are unquestionable) and from that frustration and disappointment of individual human feeling. Here, we might listen to one of Sam D'Allesandro's characters speaking: "I like small things, that's where my pleasure comes from. The big things disappoint me, but there is something small to enjoy for a moment, to look to for keeping life pleasurable."[55] There can be pleasure, but it must not be confused with "big things" or, far worse, sustainability. That way lies heartbreak.

This may sound self-defeating, but Van Sant's films do not celebrate self-defeat. I never feel defeated or dispirited watching his films; on the contrary, in the lucid testimony they offer about the problems that arise from social marginalization, they can have the effect of turning down the self-destructive voices in a viewer's head. *Even Cowgirls Get the Blues* is his most tender allegory of overcoming the shame of being sexually different from the norm (being a sexual dissident). And even when his characters end up slipping down some horribly wrong path, this fate is never glamorized. Unlike Hollywood's desensitizing violence, the meditative, stylized *Elephant* and *Paranoid Park* achieve their catharses without pandering to manipulative cheap thrills. Van Sant's films offer not only a passport to Interzone but a round-trip ticket back, even if some of his characters pointedly do not make it back, instead becoming "sacrificial victims" and exposing the implicit dangers faced by all of us.

10. Secret Histories

In a sense, abstraction presupposes fiction, since it consists in explaining things by means of images (and in substituting, for the internal nature of bodies, the effect of those bodies on our own). — Gilles Deleuze[1]

For mankind does not want to take the trouble to live, to take part in the spiritual elbowing of the forces that make up reality, in order to pluck a body from them so that no tempest could ever harm it again. — Antonin Artaud[2]

One of the points that William Richert's *Winter Kills* (1979) makes explicit is that in our time power has passed definitively from the hands of individuals to the hands of systems. The details of an individual life have largely become irrelevant, not only because everyone is a pawn, whether President of the United States or a lowly janitor, but because these details have already merged with the control effected by corporate systems. This has to do with the branding of mass-produced consumer goods, which infect nostalgia itself, the timeline of a life, with corporatist identities. Nick Kegan (Jeff Bridges) has a "Rosebud" moment when he asks the elderly butler to bring him a mug of Ovaltine, which he remembers as having been a comfort to him when he was a boy. But no sooner has he tried to explain his craving than he realizes that the memory has been falsified by what he now knows about the systems that have manufactured this memory and all of his others. (Anyway, the butler has no idea what Ovaltine even is.) Likewise, the young doorman at the posh hotel, who declares that for all of his life people have looked ugly to him and who attacks Nick physically, would have been a child when President Kegan was assassinated. His reality has also been manufactured, as a side-effect (cynicism) of ruthless hegemonic systems.

In *Citizen Kane* (1941), "Rosebud," however debased, was still a token of a 19th century world in which artisanal, handmade products coincided with the sense that an individual's life could be uniquely sculpted for him or her alone. One's experience, whether bad or good, was ostensibly untarnished by anything ersatz or shamming, nor by anything totalitarian. Lives, identities, were not mass-produced. Kane himself, handed over to capitalism as a boy, does not so much take over the entire system (by becoming the richest and most powerful man in the world) but rather gets completely taken over by this system. At the heart of Orson Welles' vision of materialist evil in *Citizen Kane* is the pathos of the rich man glimpsed as a stooge of his own empire, which existed prior to him and which outlasts him (in the cluttered warehouse of abandoned things, in which "Rosebud" gets exterminated along with art treasures of the ancient world).

Gianni Vattimo's assertion that postmodernist doubt always calls for the existence of a weak subject[3] (one who is unformed, unknown and unknowable to himself) is accurate, since the individual is only useful in terms of how he or she reveals the ubiquitous omnipotence of systems; hence, a final way of understanding the importance of adolescent heroes in current cinema, particularly, here, the films of Van Sant. The growing pains of youth are a way to read and measure modern history. Trauma and self-doubt, along with the reckless, messy energy of struggling (briefly) against disillusionment and foregone conclusions — these patterns of childhood and adolescence have become metonymies, writ small, of a U.S. society fixated at the moment where it was forced to "come of age." In *Citizen Kane*, this moment is the abandonment of artisanship for industrialization, and simultaneously the expulsion of the boy Kane from family and into the arms of businessmen. In *Winter Kills*, that moment is the assassination of a popular, idealistic leader.

Although *Winter Kills*' vision of conspiracy may be exaggerated, there are ways in which it certainly rings true. Watching it today, we shudder at how the structures of organized crime, corporate business, and "democratic" government are presented as being perfectly identical, perfectly aligned. Money is their ruling principle, ruthlessness and expediency their modus operandi. Small, human gaffes and vices are blown out of all proportion, contorted into agonizing morality plays for the evening news, so that the true systemic evil can grind on unabated. Moreover, all three structures — crime, business and democracy — refer to, and substitute for, each other at will. Although Richert succeeded in making the film a vigorous Buñuelian comedy, "a kind of political *Alice in Wonderland*," he acknowledged this as a conscious strategy for dealing with the material's potential for overwhelming audiences with too much grim truth: "[*Winter Kills*] said a lot of things about powerful people, in code, but the code was identifiable to anybody."[4]

Part of that "code" was to have characters articulate the irresolvable and ultimately futile outcome of seeing behind the conspiratorial veil, so to speak. The lies of the powerful snowball, by design; even as they perpetuate the fear that the meaning of our collective narrative has been forever altered or lost, the multiplicities of possible lies and spins cancel each other out and function, like one too many plot twists in a thriller, to annihilate the search for truth in a barrage of unlikelihood and unreliability. It is Hitler's doctrine of the Big Lie, the lie so boldfaced and all-encompassing that not to swallow it would unravel the threads of life itself; as others have certainly noted, reality is always the ultimate enemy of dogma and fascism. Or rather, reality-principles must be overturned and defeated *first* before fascism can gain hold. "Because reality is terribly superior," wrote Antonin Artaud, "to all history, to all fable, to all divinity, to all surreality."[5] It is the watchman at the gate, who must be taken out before thugs can commit any coup d'état. Once disordered, these reality-principles prove difficult to recuperate. Some people who grow up during particularly disordered and truth-deprived eras may be scarred by it as by collective traumatization, an evil which Artaud calls "civic magic."[6] It is the voodoo of the upright and uptight. In *Winter Kills*, a character speaks about how "they" (the people who run things) will pile up so many falsehoods that one can no longer tell the truth from a lie, and, more sinisterly, "won't even want to."

If a regime can grow more powerful by openly parading its crimes under an anti-reality doctrine, then it becomes unassailable. Whatever evidence could be used against it, in a reality-based society, becomes merely evidence of the regime's power (the Patriot Act, Guantanamo Bay). Thus, the total enervation of the political will to change, of revolution, stems today not from ignorance of scandal and corruption but from their comprehensive public revelation, the mish-mash of concepts invoked to justify the scandal and corruption, and the numbness that ensues in the sphere of discourse. As Artaud wrote: "Things are bad because the sick conscience now has a vital interest in not getting over its sickness."[7] The system has made a spectacle of its own flaws, thereby giving even venality or slaughter a place within the machinery and creating a way of sustaining itself no matter what, sustaining itself by its own abuses and mistakes as much as anything.

Finally, there *is* a purpose for corruption: to assert that power remains powerful even where it is most supremely arbitrary and nihilistic. Like postmodernism itself, this aspect of power is reflexive and nearly semantic: the end of history comes because no one point of view can be privileged to tell the story (already, as we saw in Chapter 5, a false syllogism); so power is unassailable because it has rendered reality so thoroughly disposed to support it. It exists beyond what we thought of, idealistically, as the nature of truth, to "set one free." Just as Cerutti (Anthony Perkins) overwhelms Nick with multiple hypotheses in a short span of time, all of them equally preposterous and equally imaginable, so the crippled imagination itself is walled up in the dead end which it has reached, precisely through this exploitation of the (learned) tendency to nightmares and anxiety.

The dead end of the imagination and of the will to change becomes further symptomatic of the sense of living in post-historical times. In fact, what postmodern theorists have termed "the end of history" is actually the end of *a* history, driven by individuals, and the beginning of a history of systems, whose power exists prior to and long after any given figurehead or fixer can survive. Experientially, there is little difference, however. Welles, in *Mr. Arkadin* (1955), when his lifelong hatred of the rich had sharpened to a point where it no longer had room for even the tinge of pathos given to the forlorn figure of Kane, depicted an egocentric magnate who kills off all the witnesses to his empire's founding crime. *Winter Kills* is structured similarly, but with shadowy organizations and cat's-paws doing the dirty work. Just as Arkadin (played by Welles) wished to shield his tainted past from his daughter Raina (Paola Mori), in order that she would not lose her illusions about him, so the systems are also engaged in trying to preserve illusions which pacify the masses. The only real difference is that individual histories allowed for finite, graspable scapegoats (and heroes); systems are nearly impossible to pinpoint in the same way, since they become like the very air that we breathe. We cannot simply stop breathing even if we suspect the air to be polluted and poisonous.

How do we tell the histories of systems? This is one of the great questions of the late 20th century and now the 21st. Like individuals, systems can be highly secretive and paranoid of the truth; they can also be open to betrayal and sabotage from within or without. The clues and traces that they leave behind are generally in the form of perishable humanities, which then become classified as aberrant. The various conspiracy theories surrounding Kennedy's assassination are mirrored by the ones surrounding the death of Marilyn Monroe; she has absorbed much of the neurosis which would otherwise attach itself to politics or business. Thus, in *Winter Kills*, Monroe is paraphrased as a contradictory, ghostly anecdote: one character states that she committed suicide after her presidential lover left her, thereby bankrupting her movie company; another, that the movie company was already losing money over her and had her killed to save face. Either way, the system emerges as more functional (and enduring) than the individual who serves it.

In an age jaded by the loss of unified, preeminent subjectivities (my truth is no more or less valid than anyone else's, on an experiential level), the only histories that still have validity are secret ones. At least what is secret has not already been overdetermined, it is hoped, by conflicting viewpoints. The revelation of a secret stands as an existential moment that can preempt the stalemate of meanings that comes with the need to give equal weight to both sides of an equation. The phrase "coming out," once exclusively gay in its meaning and still used for the public revelation of homosexuality, has become a blanket term for any moment when individual action or speech seems to temporarily jam systemic gears, and to stake a makeshift place of unvoided truth.

But naturally, the time of coming out — like the time of adolescence, perhaps — is fleeting and bounded. And yet, this inevitable mortality and decay of truth often have a special poignancy which gives the truth a kind of life after death. When individual lives have secrets, we sometimes expose them, biographically, in the putative aim of making other "misfits," suffering mutely, feel more normalized. This is the ideal, at any rate. When systems have secrets, they are called conspiracies (necessarily, since they involve more than one person moving covertly), and we talk about them only at the risk of throwing everything into an extreme crisis of instability. Individual secrets normalize; systemic secrets radicalize or destabilize. To a great extent, our sense of the former has become confused with, preoccupied and conditioned by, our sense of the latter, and vice versa. (As JFK has become "unthinkable" without Marilyn.) Basic human emotions will always be tatted up in shopworn costumes to dissolve destabilizing conspiracies into manageable, understandable episodes of "coming out" — and there is every reason to believe that this is a deeply ingrained, even pre-modern tendency of human socialization. So, the fall of ancient Egypt was ascribed to the couple, Antony and Cleopatra; Anne Boleyn's beheading overshadowed the malfeasance of government and church collusion; the French Revolution was explained by Marie Antoinette's self-centered greed; and so on. Nearly always, the true "secret history" is not the messy human foible, easily registered and lending itself to mythic narratives, but instead the systemic shifts — of which our knowledge is always more difficult to perceive and pass down.

Longtime activist and Harvey Milk compatriot Cleve Jones has praised Van Sant's *Milk* for the timely way in which it "informs the newer generation about the history that they were absolutely not taught, even in San Francisco."[8] Put otherwise: a secret history, and a systemic one. Always interested in real stories, real characters, non-actors, actual locations, Van Sant has become increasingly involved with forms of documentary. By absorbing techniques of documentary (archival footage, actual testimony, etc.) Van Sant enlarges the envelope of narrative to be able to tell stories which resonate beyond individual human players. This is something he was clearly always intent on doing but he is getting better and more precise at it. In some cases, he has recast documentaries as fictionalized or biographical films: *Last Days* has direct aesthetic ties to Nick Broomfield's *Kurt & Courtney* (1997); *Milk*, to Robert Epstein's Academy-Award-winning *The Times of Harvey Milk* (1984).

These are not just generalized ties but entire images and scenes which make their way into Van Sant's films. For example, the scene in *Last Days* in which two men search for the missing rock star at his estate, calling his name over images of green forest trees around the shed where the star's body waits to be discovered, is patterned on the same scene, itself an eerie recreation of actual events, in Broomfield's film. In keeping with what we have already uncovered about Van Sant's intertextuality being a kind of shared testimony between or among likeminded artists, we see that Van Sant has not referenced, here, the factual, archival information from Broomfield's documentary but also Broomfield's own matter-of-fact vision of the dense Pacific Northwest foliage, lush and serene, in contrast to the morbidity of the human events transpiring in it. That vision was already akin to Van Sant's, therefore able to be incorporated. This is the sense of incorporation which Deleuze describes as the effect of bodies (the trees, the calling voices act corporeally) being the conduit between factual abstraction and narrative fiction.

Likewise, *Milk* is filled with verbatim recreations of news spots, interviews, and public debates. These, too, are the bodies of history, already images, resurrected as new images based upon the old. Actual archival footage of the candlelight vigil for Milk after his assassination, filmed by Epstein and included in *The Times of Harvey Milk*, was licensed to be inserted directly into Van Sant's film. This was footage which Epstein says he had often been approached about licensing but had never agreed to, until *Milk*, because of the great trust that he had for Van Sant.[9] Even Sean Penn becomes a kind of living quotation: the image of him as Milk, wearing a white "I'll never go back!" T-shirt and waving his fist in the air at a rally, is a direct quotation of Milk himself at the Gay Freedom Day parade in 1978.[10] Van Sant has called all of these references "information flowing back into the fictional soup."[11]

Van Sant has also produced the amazing *Howl* (2010), directed by Epstein and Jeffrey Friedman, a tribute to Allen Ginsberg woven together from historic texts: Ginsberg's long poem; its censorship trial; an interview with the famous Beat poet. To the extent that our knowledge of the real is bound up in visual representations (images) and cause-and-effect progressions (narratives), documentaries often find themselves engaged in renovating or revising one set of truth claims in favor of a different one, and always circumscribed within the same tools of knowing. A film that punctures the inflated meaning of one image only does so via another, substituted image; a film that attempts to unweave a given narrative only does so by constructing another narrative. But what is most fascinating about documentaries is not the noted way in which they subjectivize the "truth"; it is, ultimately, the way that they objectify the already subjective process which formulates individual and shared perceptions of truth in the first place. If totalitarianism, as we supposed earlier, is always a direct assault upon reality, then documentaries adopt the same tactics to

10. Secret Histories

Howl (2010), starring James Franco as Beat poet Allen Ginsberg, suggests that a key turning-point in Ginsberg's personal and artistic life (coming out as gay) coincided with a key historical turning point in 20th century U.S. culture (increased liberation of thought, expression and lifestyle).

mediate with reality in ways that are (generally but not always) opposed to totalitarian thinking.

The full implications of this are beyond the scope of this book. Again, we must speak largely in ideal terms. There is no act of looking that is not attached to a point of view. Thus, as Godard and other filmmakers and film theorists have presupposed, the best films always mingle, consciously and unconsciously, the techniques of fiction *and* documentary, until the two forms become nearly indistinguishable.[12] Robert Epstein himself has said: "I always thought of [*The Times of Harvey Milk*] as a narrative film, as a nonfiction narrative film, and I think that's been my approach for much of the feature documentaries I've worked on since: that, bottom line, you're creating a narrative movie, and it just happens to be a documentary.... I feel less embracing of the categorization of 'documentary filmmaker' as opposed to 'narrative filmmaker' because, to me, they're one in the same." Indeed, a "poetic novelist" was brought in to help sculpt the background narration of *The Times of Harvey Milk*.[13]

History is an ambiance as much as a set of facts. Richert has said that he deliberately cast the most iconic actors he could find for every role, in

Winter Kills, so that the characters themselves would be immediately legible to the viewer. The glamour and charisma of show business — a kind of parallel history, and sometimes a secret one — are finally the clearest way by which we discern modern history at all. The allegorical, which was once a way of staging events so as to assign them fixed readings and meanings, has become destabilized and ephemeral in its new function as a constant, running paraphrase of postmodern society's reflexive schizo-ing. So, John Huston, as the patriarch in *Winter Kills*, is the already mythic "John Huston" and, finally, the Surface, visible to all, even those who have never seen or heard of him before, based on automatic physiological cues: Wry Rabelaisian Cynic, Imposing Old Man. Put otherwise, he is instantly coded as someone powerful and someone not to be trusted. The double-sidedness of everything is taken in with a yawn, and somewhere, too, the relief that one does not have to make a decision because all viewpoints have been equalized. One cannot help but "like" Huston, after all. Hollywood tricks of casting have become universalized in how we now read everyone whom the media or, indeed, daily life presents for our inspection. The surface is the essence; the "stereotype" (cut loose from the political and made to rejoin its origins in superstition and folklore) reigns as the only discernible truth.

One can trap historic truths only by pretending not to look at them, or by not looking directly at them, for if one does try to meet them head-on, one meets only the stereotype, only the conditioned postmodern schizo-ing of viewpoints. This has become true of all histories, but especially secret ones, where nearly mystical methods are required in order to give shape to evidentiary traces which exist everywhere and nowhere. Van Sant, like the 60s, that era which helped spawn him, is intrigued by secret histories, at a place where the stories of individuals intersect with the stories of systems. Individuals are charismatic leaders who galvanize and crystallize events, and also become scapegoats; systems are interested in reigning in, and profiting from, the energy of these individuals. The individuals are not always aware that they are being "used" (as the Affleck-Gerry does not realize he will be killed by the Damon-Gerry, perhaps). The systems sometimes are or seem to be shaken up by individuals who attempt to evade control. This is also the inherent process of "fame" in an increasingly fame-driven culture.

The secret history is not only a favorite mode of Van Sant's, but one that he has associated with the empowering of minorities. In *Finding Forrester*, there is the memorable exchange in which Jamal, always wary of white people underestimating his mental powers, "schools" Forrester's assistant (Glenn Fitzgerald) on how BMW's were first designed, as a result of German engineering being forced by the victorious allied powers to channel wartime airplane technology into peacetime private enterprise. Thus, like Arkadin, the founding crime tells the real story of any empire, whether political or economic; such crimes often have social outcasts as their victims, their stepping stones. And let us note how there are no individual players in this history, only nameless people acting on behalf of systems: the players are "engineering," "allied powers," "technology," "enterprise." The stage is always already set for allegorization, since the appearance of any human figure becomes a way of pointing back toward these and other systemic, nonhuman forces. The BMW story is, finally, not so much a secret history, meaning one that has been deliberately hidden or (like a criminal conspiracy) hushed up, but a camouflaged one. (Typically, the black Jamal, as a member of a minority, is forced for the sake of his own survival to learn more about white history than even whites do; pointedly, even a white who can afford to lease a BMW.) It is a history that counts on the passage of time and on the prestige of the BMW-product itself to reduce the likelihood that someone will research it, or even care if they do. Capitalism thrives on these camouflages, really the euphemisms of history, the way totalitarianism performs its assaults on reality-principles.

In part, this is because we are understood to be living in an age that is post-innocence, *after* the possibility of absolute moral perfection. What is actually occurring is a constantly updated remapping of what can and cannot be countenanced. In many ways, this process is as necessary and natural as it is also jarring. And the supposedly prelapsarian time of innocence is actually a trick of the mind: the Golden Age, we saw precisely in *Finding Forrester*, is a mirage constructed by a complacent, backwards-looking nostalgia that wants to shrug off the demands of living in the present. But all ages contain their exiles, their defectors. It is from a mix of people struggling to update the past and other people struggling to preserve it that history has always moved, fitfully and, unfortunately, as we know, not without bloodshed.

Secret histories are always histories of death or deaths. They would probably be public already if lives were not at stake, or rather, the way we wish to remember the celebrated dead. In *Winter Kills*, the conspiracy all revolves around the President's past, and his father's; nothing lives in the future anymore that is not made to order to control the past. The future is like the empty air which the father plummets through in his climactic fall from the skyscraper penthouse. And it is a crucial turning point of Richert's film when Nick discovers that he, too, could be killed for digging into these secrets, in the same way that Van Sant often builds into his films similar turning points where the stakes suddenly become much steeper and more lethal for protagonists who have been more or less drifting along with their luck: the death of Pepper in *Mala Noche*; the death of Nadine in *Drugstore Cowboy*; Mike's loss of Scott in *My Own Private Idaho*; the rainstorm that causes Marion to seek shelter at the Bates Motel in *Psycho*; the moment in *Good Will Hunting* where Will realizes that he must act or lose everything. Of course, many of these films have nuanced progressions, or tiers, in which the stakes rise steadily, as in a cosmic poker game. *Gerry* is a staggered series of worsening moves and narrowing options; *Milk* is a seesaw where Harvey rises as Dan White sinks, etc. These losses and deaths are covered up by the characters, who are guilty, ashamed, or impossibly ruined and sad. Van Sant's films are elegies to the human energy — creative energy, perhaps — which gets siphoned off by the chronic need to hide, the constant fear of some exposure, the refusal to acknowledge a wolf at one's door, or, to refer to a famous Ginsberg poem, "The Lion for Real," starving and accusatory in one's living room.

That lion is partly Ginsberg's reclamation of his right to be a poet, an artist; his drunken fondlings and rows with ex-lovers and bemused straight men bring out the scary, threatening lion. But this process transcends sexual identity. Artaud wrote, "No one has ever written or painted, sculpted, modeled, built, invented, except to get out of hell."[14] In Ginsberg's case, homosexuality was the lion. By embracing his selfhood openly, Ginsberg defeats — starves — the regretful monster of the past, and makes room for himself in a future where he will commit to telling his experiential reality (in the same way that his poem "outs" recalcitrant male figures from his sexual history). Just as *Finding Forrester* insisted that there could be a real, experiential truth in the life of an artist, something that would not be reducible to the vagaries of interpretation (in Forrester's own case, the slipping-away of a beloved brother through war, alcoholism and eventual suicide), it also interrogated the reasons why someone like Professor Crawford would choose to impose his own un-experiential reading upon a text, thereby concealing messy human truths in neat, cloistered abstractions. Crawford cannot forgive Forrester for conquering, and then moving on from, a past in which Crawford remains stuck, the prisoner of his own bitter failures. So, although he is Jamal's official teacher, he can finally teach him far less than does Forrester, who is far more open to living not for the dead past but for that frontier-like promise of the future which Jamal inhabits. Those people, who live among us but in the future, often cannot sustain their lives; they are also people who change the world. Meanwhile, those who seek to enshrine, or return to, a hallowed past often do great damage in the name of maintaining an ostensible "stability." Usually, worshippers of the past are directly in flight from current struggles of social liberation. (As is said of the prep school professors in *Finding Forrester*, particularly Crawford: "The teachers here aren't all that into student participation. They're more concerned with listening to themselves talk.")

But of course, although this is generally true, the reality is never that simple. The figure of the future, the one engaged in struggle, might also yearn to worship the past like others; might prefer to belong within rather than to agitate, by his mere presence, the life of his own time. Also, various struggles of liberation, although they seek emancipation from similar forms of oppression, might actually collide or fight against each other inadvertently. Both of these phenomena are investigated in Van Sant's film, *Last Days*, in which the secret history of a fictionalized rock star becomes a secret history of (pop) culture itself. Blake is tormented by his own failings and quirks; talking to himself almost constantly, he refers to the problem posed by going deep within oneself, because when one tries to "come out" again, there is nobody one can talk to. The loneliness that settles on Blake is presented as the price he pays for his musical art, and also for the way he refuses a conventional identity. He is inscribed as a figure of queerness in the way he derives comfort from dressing in women's clothes (he wears a black cocktail dress in several scenes of the film) and the way he maintains a druggy, bisexual entourage, including fellow musicians Luke (Lukas Haas) and Scott (Scott Green).

The three great and ongoing projects of social liberation in our time are: people of color; women; and gays. We can already see how these categories can easily triangulate and demand conflicting loyalties. Women of color, for example, might be hard pressed to say whether racism or sexism is the more powerful of their foes. But issues of sexual preference complicate things even further. Straight blacks do not always feel solidarity with gays; gays, in their "rejection" of women, are often seen as unsympathetic to female emancipation. Moreover, the sexual objectification that is a natural currency among gay men is anathema to most feminist and lesbian communities, who view any kind of sexual objectification as one of their single largest obstacles to selfhood. Whereas in gay male communities, the harsh standards of beauty — one must be excessively thin, excessively fit, excessively young, excessively libidinal — which progressive women have tried to expunge from heterosexuality, find their nirvana and reign supreme.

The confusion brought on by these conflicting practices has had the effect of de-consolidating any efforts, on the part of minoritized groups, to effectively form a united front. What is also difficult is the attempt to create art which gives equal weight to all of the main struggles. Much identity-based art tends to highlight only the experience of a single identity, narcissistically blurring out nuances in a wash of "guided" consciousness-raising; we end up with the answers we expected all along, in fact the answers precede and predetermine the questions being asked. Symptomatic of postmodernism's fragmentation of viewpoint, identity-based art, while ostensibly telling real and even secret histories, helps in the breakdown of historicity, the end of history, by foreclosing on any attempt to intersect with other viewpoints or to achieve a holistic dialectic.

Nonetheless, there have been brave attempts to look at eras of history more panoramically, resulting inevitably in a pessimistic pitting of minority viewpoints not only against the background of a normative hegemony but against each other as well. A case in point is Todd Haynes' *Far from Heaven* (2002), which I have grown to admire and enjoy after being initially troubled by what I saw as its "triangulation" of feminist-black-gay awakenings. So, in a 1957 small-town, a closeted gay man, Frank (Dennis Quaid), struggles with his sexuality, with his very sanity clearly at stake. His wife Cathy (Julianne Moore), recessive and demure, begins to wonder why her own selfhood and liberty are being held hostage by her unstable, self-consumed husband. Nonetheless, she continuously stands by him, even when he lashes out and hits her. Eventually, she turns to a kindly black man named Raymond (Dennis Haysbert), who seems to understand and love her, but racist pressures from both the white and the black communities drive them apart.

In the end of Haynes' film, Cathy bids a sorrowful farewell to Raymond who is leaving town with his young daughter Sarah (Jordan Puryear) to make a new start somewhere else. Cathy is alone, her marriage over, her friends turned against her. Only Frank has found any semblance of fulfillment, in the person of a young lover (Nicholas Joy) with whom he has begun living. Haynes depicts homosexuality as nominally "winning out" in this triangulated battle of oppressions, largely because, we assume, the gay man is white and wealthy, although Haynes does not exactly articulate this. As the film stands, the woman's unhappiness and the black man's unhappiness are not able to be overcome, and if they are not direct results of the gay man's (relative) happiness, they are at least shown, by contrast, to be even further outside of society and less assimilable. I still find this aspect of Haynes' film to be somewhat reckless and disingenuous, although I commend him for attempting a view on history which tries to oppose fragmentation by revealing all of the parts that are normally isolated from each other. Like the characters themselves, *Far From Heaven* always feels like it is hovering on the edge of breakthrough, and this is what gives it its fascination, its sense of being more than a movie.

What might be missing from Haynes' film is the representation of a united conservative front that is simultaneously racist, sexist *and* homophobic. Haynes' affinity for ambiguity and nuance (such as Raymond's painful revelation that his own black neighbors have turned against him) is better suited to uncovering internalized turmoil than blunt, external confrontation; indeed, one of the clumsiest scenes is the one in which white kids pelt Sarah with rocks. Apart from this, the "opposition" appears only in the wife's best friend (Patricia Clarkson), who bears the pressure of having to bring various hatreds to bear at different points in the film. Indeed, she must be, from scene to scene, anti–Semitic, anti–communist, homophobic, racist, and incipiently misogynistic in the way she refuses to stand by Cathy in the end. But this is part of the real problem which Haynes' ambitious film attempts to define: the hateful enemy is consistent in his or her hate, and also definitively "within." The gay husband has no problem being sexist and racist; the women in the film actively participate in sexist oppression by masochistically supporting crazed men and by judging each other; the black man's black circle abandons him for courting scandal with a white woman, etc. In seeing another Other as a more abased object, one can perhaps avoid recognizing the extent of one's own Otherness. Thus, the various Others often cannot bond even around the cynical logic of "the enemy of my enemy is my friend."

In *Last Days*, Van Sant offers glimpses of a similar triangulation of minority interests, but set in current times and, in marked contrast to *Far From Heaven*, with the queer figure ending up as the martyr and sacrifice at the end of the film. The points of intersection among the various minorities in Van Sant's film are not emotional and melodramatic, as they are in Haynes' film, but coolly focused on the pervasive demands of capitalism and commercial enterprise. The African American door-to-door salesman (Thadeus A. Thomas) who tries to interest Blake in purchasing an ad in the phone directory, is hard-working and polite, a striving businessman. Even though he has Blake confused with someone who manufactures locomotive parts, he sits and talks with Blake, trying to find out about his advertising needs. The biggest dif-

In *Last Days* (2005), a door-to-door salesman (Thadeus A. Thomas) tries to interest the rock star Blake (Michael Pitt) in purchasing an ad in the phone directory. During this scene, Blake is wearing a dress and appears high. In general the scene is created to feel like they are talking about two very different things.

ference between the black figure and the queer figure is that Blake, out of politeness, boredom or loneliness, indulges Thomas' sales pitch passively without attempting to assert that he is not a manufacturer. In the end, Thomas returns to a reality that is in congruence with his determined work ethic, and leaves Blake nodded out in a chair.

Blake is always playing whatever role that others see him in: this passivity, which extends into an implied masochistic deference to his wife Blackie, is the greatest mark of Blake's queerness. Two of the songs featured prominently in *Last Days*—Boyz II Men's "On Bended Knee" and the Velvet Underground's "Venus in Furs"—both invoke male submission to female dominance in sexual/romantic terms, and even contain the same central image of a male kneeling before the woman whom he worships, to beg forgiveness or to receive punishment. But whether this is a shy, bizarre, courtly form of chivalry, or a twisted neurosis, it creates a situation in which Blake becomes prey instead of predator, unfit for this harsh survival of the fittest which reigns in the drug world, the music business, and even interpersonal relations.

It isn't only that blacks or females manage to "get away" with this or that at Blake's expense; at any rate, it is debatable whether they actually do get away with anything. Rather, they are presented as having a naturalness which Blake pointedly lacks. This naturalness is an asset, indeed it is very nearly a commodity. It enters a strange new terrain in which something organic can be converted to commodity-status simply by coming into contact with a different kind of commodity (Blake) which finds itself endangered because its un-naturalness has fallen on hard times. Ultimately, nothing is as tormenting as Blake's own demons. In the club scene where a music scenester (Harmony Korine) apprises an impassive Blake of rumors circulating about Blake having become sexually impotent, we are made to see that Blake's popularity always depended on a kind of tightrope act by which his queerness could be yoked to the social authority of heterosexualism. He could liberate queer energies precisely because he was (seen as) straight. This liberation was, for various, complex and fateful reasons, short-lived, unstable, implosive. Just as *Howl* depicts Ginsberg's epochal poem as a positive turning-point in both his personal life and the life of his society, so *Last Days* could be said to depict a setback, which occurs simultaneously for a queer icon and for queerness itself.

Capitalism is shrinking down to the increasingly surer and surer thing. Although not flower children by any stretch of the imagination, the characters in *Last Days* sometimes evoke the 60s as a time when new and exciting things could still happen. The music scenester tells Blake how he played Dungeons and Dragons with Jerry Garcia after a Dead show, and Garcia was the best dungeon-master: "We captured the winged Pegasus." Scott is fixated on the first Velvet Underground album, which he sings along to, trying to sound like

Lou Reed. But of course, what is implicit in the film is the fact that Garcia and Reed have had an enormous longevity and staying-power, surviving and growing as artists, unlike Blake's self-destructiveness. In part, the 90s are shown as being less open than the 60s; even the best rebels have trouble breaking through, partly because, as products of the 90s, they, too, are colder. When Scott sings Reed's lyrics on "Venus in Furs," he tellingly drops certain words to highlight the song's brutality. Reed sings: "Taste the whip, in love not given lightly./Taste the whip, now bleed for me." Scott sings: "Taste the whip, not given lightly — bleed for me."

In *Last Days*, the young male rock star is already a dying dinosaur, not only because he is too decadent, although hard drugs play an enormous role in the film (*Last Days* is terrifyingly anti-drug, a stark vision of people whom heroin has driven almost completely insane), but because his liberation, allied with queerness, has become less fashionable, and is eclipsed by the more normative claims of blacks and women. Blake's gender-bending fits less well into capitalist schemas. Popularity in music intersects, usually, with that kind of naturalness which is exemplified by traditional gender. Music that succeeds as commodity or communal experience can invoke nihilism only as something that can be instantly comforted and placated, the way aspirin relieves a headache. Even so, Blake's truly subversive cultivation of femininity is belied as posturing by the female record executive (played by musician Kim Gordon) who inhabits herself in a way that is both naturally tough and naturally maternal. The queer male's submission to female power (in the form of wanting to be a woman) is sincere and well-intended, but finally a losing strategy in what has become not merely the schematic triangulation of *Far From Heaven* but an all-out war, with blurry frontlines, between competing minority identities.

The closest we come to sensing how Blake himself really feels are the scenes in which he sings and plays music by himself, sometimes screaming at the top of his lungs. First, there is his tentative "grunge" rendition of "Home on the Range," the classic western ballad of tranquility and happiness, ironized, of course, by Blake's depression, beside a lonely campfire in the woods. Later, there is a session in which Blake overdubs a demo where he is playing all the instruments (the song, called "Fetus," is credited to actor Michael Pitt). Finally, on the last night of his life, we hear Blake, alone in his studio again, seemingly improvising a long song, "Death to Birth" (also credited to Pitt), with soft/loud, slow/fast dynamics reminiscent of Nirvana's sound. It is in these moments that the usually wordless or mumbling Blake vents his anguish in lacerating shrieks and howls, and slurred, menacing, plaintive melodies. The fact that both of these songs reference birth is not merely coincidental: we know from *Kurt & Courtney* that Cobain himself was obsessed with the prenatal and the birth process, which he found both disgusting and fascinating. "Death to Birth" is resonant as a title, in the same way that many Cobain lyrics are, sardonic, twisted puns which detonate in the brain. It could mean "down with birth"; it could also mean reincarnation or rebirth through dying.

It seems poignantly essential that only we, as the audience, witness these final performances of Blake. Is something a performance — is it even art — if no one witnesses it? We are meant to understand that making music is the most natural state for a musician, like meditation or even something more basic like eating. Anyone who is a musician or has spent time among musicians knows that the music they officially release in their lifetime is an almost arbitrarily filtered sample of the sum total of music that they *make*. Within *Last Days*, there is a nice tension between the long, steady takes that accompany Blake's music-making, attended to as moments that are unique, moments that will never come again, versus the time-looping edits which deliver other moments in which we are stuck in the repetitive grooves of addiction: the scene in which Asia (Asia Argento) opens a door and Blake's nodded-off body comes tumbling out across the floor, and the kitchen scene in which Scott, strung out, rambles insanely to Blake about needing apples, and wanting to buy "jet engines" to heat the house.

The nature of Blake's private music, and the way Van Sant hallows it cinematically by not cutting away, recalls what Forrester tells Jamal: "Why are the words we write for ourselves always so much better than the ones we write for others?" Private, invisible art is a source of subversive ecstasy, a Zen-like ecstasy of humility. It also recalls something that Artaud noted about Vincent Van Gogh: "Most of his canvasses were of moderate dimensions as though he had chosen them that way on purpose."[15] Humility comes through in Van Gogh's personal choices while creating paintings that few people ever saw in the painter's own lifetime. This sort of humility comes through in Blake, too, as well as his frustration and desperation, as if the music has finally become nothing but a way of overcoming temporarily (Artaud's prescription for "getting out of hell") and no longer requires an audience since it is "for" Blake alone. The meaning we find in it is tinted by the knowledge that this is the last of the last, the end: we want it to be a swan song, even if it isn't. In a short, fraught, brilliant life, even the off-handed crap becomes significant and worthy of hearing, if only as morbid evidence of how much the artist's death was gaining on his life at any given moment. Of course, the fact that these two performances are "invisible" as cultural products suggests, in a parallel metonymy of death, that Blake's days as a commodity are doomed, even as his artistry remains undiminished.

The persistent references to Blake as a Christ figure, as well as the use of loud, discordant church bells in the scene where Blake returns to the shed where he will die, recall Fassbinder's *Veronika Voss* (1981), another great film about a fading, heroin-addicted star who is driven to an ambiguous death. Veronika (Rosel Zech) is locked in a room by her evil doctor, without heroin but with "many, many sleeping pills"; a radio broadcast of an Easter service blares through Veronika's cell as she literally crawls up the wall; when enough time has passed for desperation to give way to resignation, she puts on lipstick and begins to swallow the bitter-tasting pills. The doctor and her lesbian lover immediately profit by Voss' death, moving into her antique-filled mansion. Both *Veronika Voss* and *Last Days* articulate the unique vulnerability of the addict, while finally leaving open the famous question: *did she jump or was she pushed?*

When Blake is found dead, Scott and Luke flee in terror to Los Angeles with their female groupie Nicole (Nicole Vicius). There is a sharp focus to what survives in the harsh current world of *Last Days*: it survives not because it is braver or more righteous, not because it deserves to, but because it makes fewer waves within a capitalist system that makes money from art and does not even need the artist anymore to do this. In the 60s it would have been unimaginable, from a human standpoint, that an artist could be worth more money, and easier to handle, dead than alive; today it is axiomatic. In *Last Days*, the queer figure bears the most risk, the most audacious challenge to the system, and who is driven under as a result — "*suicidé*," or suicided, a word coined by Antonin Artaud to denote a situation in which murder and suicide become indistinguishable, imposed on the dead subject by the continuous, grinding hostility of life. Blake finds a sinister post-it note on the refrigerator that reads, "The gun is in the bedroom closet," as if someone close to him were suggesting a way for him to end his life. This is how the self-given injunction to seek death is literalized and concretized through external objects: the cigar box in which Blake keeps his works; the milk he leaves out on the counter; the ominous ringing telephone whose bad news he already anticipates. These objects take more and more bites out of the possibility of time, revealing a definitive finitude that closes in and blocks Blake off. In part, he dies to revivify his hopes for an infinity that is necessary to his genius but increasingly impossible to imagine. This is why, as Artaud would say, he draws the negative attention of the suiciders. For Artaud, writing about Van Gogh, these suiciders were literal and ordinary "executioners" who came to the artist one day and killed him by saying: "we've had our fill of your genius, and as for the infinite, the infinite belongs to us."[16]

There is a distinctly spiritual element in Gus Van Sant's films. I would hesitate to call it religious, although I could understand why some viewers might see and feel a religious aspect to his work. The cloudscapes and Pietàs that we discussed in Chapter 2 point toward religious imagery, even though they often revise and secularize the context. But there is no need to secularize *spirituality*. It already has universal, secular forms: karma, the interrelatedness of all life, the soul, the conscience, the sense of responsibility to those who are weaker or less fortunate. In fact, this is one of the ways in which Van Sant fights for modernist meanings within a generally postmodern style and approach. In *My Own Private Idaho*, the reprobate Bob seems to "see God" in the moment of his death, although his calling out to God is inflected as a terrible question more than a certainty. Only the senile Jane Lightwork (Sally Curtice) makes anything of this, and the film leaves entirely open the question of whether God, as such, embraced or chastised the dying Bob. The more surprising interpretation would be if the down-and-out, mad, queer figures in Van Sant's films actually do find a spiritual place in death — a place denied them in life by a society which seeks to codify "grace" by such superficial markings as outward appearance or income level.

With its punning title (the "last days" of Blake's life, and the Biblical "end-time"), as well as its recurring references to Blake as a Christ figure, *Last Days* suggests Van Sant's broadest outreach to religion, but mediated by rock'n'roll, itself a kind of secular religion or mode of worship. However, by positing Blake as the second coming, the film asks us to consider what a hypothetical Christ would be, today, if he did return to human form and walk among us. Would he be, like Blake, crippled, addicted, half-mad, unkempt, talking to himself— unable to bear the weight of worldly pain and making his life a visibly disfigured sign of this inability? Would he, in fact, have to commit suicide, making explicit the implied significance of Christ's consent to be crucified?

The means of death are less important than the fact that Blake's "soul," after death, can ascend to its goal, out of body, out of time and space. This image, sometimes considered baffling, pretentious or silly by reviewers (Richard Corliss comes to mind), is necessary in order to deflate and redefine *Last Days'* abundant capitulations to postmodernist ungrounding. Everything quotidian is depicted as askew and splintered by multiple viewpoints; even Blake's death is all about angle — from the angle we are shown (a close-up of Blake looking slightly up and away), it is impossible to determine if he is overtaken by a sudden commitment to the idea of suicide, or if he has been surprised by an intruder (or a familiar) in the boathouse. Like Bob's deathbed scene, we do not know if this is an assault from a real presence, or the mind playing its druggy, stupefied tricks.

Thus, even dying is definitively ungrounded. And yet, the literal moment of ungrounding — when the soul rises up from the body — is presented "straight," as it were, as a kind of deserved miracle transpiring in a world that does not "do" miracles. It is here that we must learn to care about the fate of someone lost and doomed, when his removal from the world of immanence marks him as no longer labile and unstable, no longer subject to the grain of postmodern living. Life is steeped in thoughts and vain, secondhand representations of what death might be like, but death itself, the condition of being dead, because it occurs definitively outside of life and time, holds onto a transcendental, if inscrutable, meaning. In Van Sant's films, death is almost always the one thing that refuses to be postmodernized. The candlelight vigil and march for Harvey Milk is another instance of death instantiating a newfound and anti-cynical faith or hope. Life must be a constant avoidance of cliché, a roundelay of transvaluations; but death is the return to meanings, to absolutes. Cinema as séance is one of Van Sant's abiding conceptions, an attempt to reconstruct and interrogate the life that has wound down and out, and at the same time a conscious, formal respect for the fact that that life, in death now, no longer belongs to our illusions or our certainties about the real. What it knows casts a disfiguring shadow over our world, while never revealing itself; a haven of modernist absolutism bobbing in a sea of postmodern qualifications.

All roads lead to a kind of universal Rome, and so, in both parts of this book, we have arrived at the same place, a consistent theme raised by Van Sant's films. I am referring to a broad redefining of postmodernism, whereby we can acknowledge and affirm what was most essential about modernism, namely its liberating emphasis on unique personal ways of seeing, its search for ever newer and more comprehensive truths, and the concomitant decentralization of white, straight, male, European culture.

The question on my mind is this: why did history have to "end" as soon as it became *histories*? Why can't we absorb diverse multicultural viewpoints and experiences into a single "masterless master narrative," one which takes up simultaneous threads, decentered but balanced? Postmodernism's various crises — of meanings, groundings, certainties — seem to me a complex, coded, yet partly unconscious refusal to dignify the projects of social and political liberation, occurring roughly from the 1920s through the 1960s. Rather than conceiving, finally, an accurate, multi-tiered vision of history, where all things transpire in their own aura, their own meaning, giving and taking, we have shrugged off the possibility, or need, to confront historical truth at all, and taken refuge in defiant meaninglessness.

Put in simpler terms, just when people of color, women, and gays were beginning to offer their testimony as to what *their* histories have been, we have called an end to history itself. Like sore losers in a child's game, the predominant institutions of culture have preferred to gather up their marbles and go home, rather than welcome the challenge of this new leveling.

To be sure, this has been a tribute to the powerful and successful ways in which minorities have jammed the gears of racist, patriarchal, homophobic culture. By overcoming, our minorities have brought about a crisis in which the dominant culture is now faced with something that it needs to overcome. The dominant culture, however, is accomplishing that dubious overcoming by denigrating all meanings, all sacredness, or by radically sectioning them off from mainstream culture in the form of atavistic, fundamentalist bodies of dogma — themselves often an elaborate cover for lingering feelings of racism, sexism and homophobia.

Vattimo's recommendation of the weak or debilitated subject as a sort of default postmodernist position, a way of recuperating *any* degree of subjectivity albeit recognizably impaired, is echoed in Avital Ronell's theory that Zen-like transcendence is detectable, today, only through senselessness and an ironic, double-edged "idiocy" which passes for the sublime.[17] What is sacred now appears "through the lens of vulnerability. Not in the emanation of pride and beauty, but as their shattering. Broken and mangled, isolated by its suffering, the sacred in our day pulsates, if at all, weakly."[18] The truly benighted are the ones who *deny* the impossibility of meaning, and try to stave it off with unbearably clumsy gestures. And yet, there must be something beyond even these shrewd and nearly Voltairean truces with experience — if only because, as Ronell herself affirms, we are already "the evidence"[19] needed to prove that experience valid. Postmodernism, having reached the total impasse of a human existence which continues to feel, to love, to think, etc., even in the supposed waning of these attributes, will end, if it has not ended already, in an inevitable renewal of subjectivity. Causes will be found; histories will be expanded.

Of course, there is reason to believe that we are already moving beyond this impasse of postmodernism, to a place where the longing for human meanings that are both immanent and progressive can filter back into the mirror-play of fragmentation and ungrounding, and shine light into the prism, so to speak. Van Sant's films are essential for precisely this reason. They seem to build a bridge between the subversive upheavals of the 60s and the cool, self-negating Babel of our current time. They want to honor the survivors and the dead, and restore some lost dignity to living and dying. Van Sant has taken up challenges that few of us even realized were needed. He has sought ways of constructing nonlinear narratives, to overcome the tendency to see time either teleologically (modernism) or entropically (postmodernism). He has created films which veer into diverse, random, momentary viewpoints — all of them sincere and meaningful on their own, all of them reflective of the strength of modernist identities and the humble confusion of postmodernist ones, and of course, engaged in a struggle as yet ongoing, not completely won. But even when these identities triangulate and cancel each other out, as they do somewhat in *Last Days*, they speak to the important, if messy, need to bring disparate identities and viewpoints together into a multivalent history. These cross-cancellations — grunge rock replaced by R-&-B; female stardom eclipsing that of the male; queerness coming into and going out of fashion — are never manipulative, and never unfair to any of the identities involved.

The sometimes disorienting sense of simultaneity in Van Sant's films is an attempt to understand the world itself, on its own terms, and within a kind of ultimately totalizing vision that treats the conquered — poor people, people of color, street people, drug people, gays and bisexuals, young people, etc. — as prime movers of history, and as heroes.

The work of art must, then, become a process of helping to regenerate human history, even in an era where the ongoing movement of individual subjective history is (for various reasons) difficult to discern. This is because the work of art enables an individual, either artist or viewer or both, to discover his own true meaning in an act of transpropriation occurring between other works of art (intertextualities) and other phenomenological categories of existence, which remain recognizable even as they are blended.

The work of art, as Vattimo writes, "sets up historical worlds; it inaugurates and anticipates, as an original linguistic event, the possibility of historical existence...."[20] Barthes' somewhat anxious intuition, in *Writing Degree Zero*, that it was impossible to find original uses for language is counteracted only by the revelation of the personal, the previously secret, as a unique historical event. An example of this would be the moment in *Howl* when Ginsberg (well played by James Franco) tells the interviewer:

> The crucial moment of breakthrough came when I realized how funny it would be, in the middle of a long poem, if I said, 'who let themselves be fucked in the ass and screamed with *joy*!' instead of 'screamed with pain.' That's the contradiction of that line. An American audience would expect it to be pain.... It's an acknowledgment of the basic reality of homosexual joy....

And of course, Ginsberg calls attention to this precisely *as* an historic utterance.

The historic utterance, tied to the expression of identity and selfhood, to self-revelation, is always a jouissance, even if it is not specifically about sex (although, in this case, it is). But it is a jouissance that partakes of a sort of joyous duty to the self and its minoritized group, and to the self's position in history. Thus, it possesses a sense of purpose which mitigates against, if not entirely defeats, the nihilism of post-historical ungrounding. This is largely because, put in the simplest terms, it *is* a grounding, a way of claiming meaning, new inflections, new certitudes, for identities that are still testing the waters of public expression.

Mike (River Phoenix) and other down-and-out street denizens, including Gary (Rodney Harvey), erupt in furious dancing and yelling at the funeral of their friend Bob. If I had to choose one scene in all of Van Sant's cinema, I would say that this remains the most quintessential and evocative in the way it celebrates liberation as a kind of necessity or survival mechanism, a public blast of anarchy that is ultimately futile but which makes one feel as though one is bearing witness to a secret history.

This is why, if forced to choose one quintessential scene from a Van Sant film, my favorite would be the spontaneous cemetery protest near the end of *My Own Private Idaho*. Scott, in the middle of a staid, ritzy-looking group, his fiancée at his side, is burying his father. Within sight of them, in the same graveyard, Mike and the other street denizens are laying Bob to rest. Noticing that what Scott's group stands for is repression — repression of response, repression of truth and real identity — Mike leads his friends in an increasingly noisy wake, dancing and chanting, "Bob! Bob!" Sometimes this name is hurled like a curse at Scott's wealthy enclave; sometimes it becomes onomatopoeic noise. Of course, this is a protest, and though we understand that on one level it changes nothing (Mike must press on without his ex-lover, and dies soon after), it is emblematic of a hard-won victory. It is, finally, historic in the sense that I am trying to trace here. Even as it acknowledges postmodern fragmentation and elusiveness, it hearkens back to wonderfully frenzied moments from films of the 60s: it is like the beggars' banquet in *Viridiana* (or even *Beggars Banquet* by the Stones); it deeply exhales, like the long-delayed eruption of revolution in *If...*; and it evokes the panther-like physicality and sly menace of Lou Castel's performance in *Fists in the Pocket*. Finally, it bravely yokes sexual dissidence to a vision of class warfare which is truly visionary and still in need of exploration; it indicts the privilege of wealth as being identical to the privilege of straightness (in name only perhaps). It is, I believe, the most convincing portrait of revolution that U.S. cinema has managed to give, and no less so for being poignantly "unfinished" as a revolutionary gesture. A mood is changed, a moment; but not an entire era, not a system itself.

Robert Epstein refers to the reflexive way that the poem "Howl" marked a simultaneous turning-point for Ginsberg the man (he fully grew up, and set himself free, by writing it) and for Ginsberg's society (which expanded and became more open, more liberated).[21] Identity and time coalesce to name themselves and to name each other. This is why Epstein can title his documentary *The Times* (plural) *of Harvey Milk*. Milk's own life traces the same arc as the history of the gay rights struggle over the same period: from silence and isolation (Milk was closeted in his youth), to "piggybacking" the Civil Rights movement and the peace movement (Milk adopted a hippie look when he first moved to San Francisco), to increasingly bold attempts at public self-definition and unification (the rallies, the marches, the election night celebration, etc.), and finally to backlash and the eventual burnishing of the entire era with the halo of legend. In each stage, needless to say, a single image of Harvey is nearly always sufficient to conjure up not only who he was at any given time, but what the time around him was like, as well.

We see this phenomenon more clearly in "misfits," social outsiders. For them, time can change more drastically; can become, as Epstein observes, *times*. But this is not even a uniquely postmodernist development, this confluence of individual and collective experiential histories with art and with something that becomes apparent as a question of measuring, documenting and, indeed, "naming" passages of time. Vattimo refers to Heidegger's analysis of "the peasant's shoes in Van Gogh's painting — for they show cracks that are not to be seen, according to Heidegger, as a realistic representation of life in the fields, but rather as the presence of earthliness as lived temporality in the form of birth, ageing and death."[22] Time is not "realism," and cinematic "real time," which is already a false claim (since everything in a film has been set up in advance to fill a certain duration), always feels more surreal and artificial than the patterned edits which our eyes have become used to. Duration of any sort implies eternity, or at least eternity in metonymy, but it is falsified literally from the start because, as Deleuze points out, "eternity has no beginning."[23] What is arbitrary is not that chunks of real time extend and endure but that they begin *somewhere*. Thus, real time appears precisely as the *Verfremdungseffekt* which it is intended to be. It is not continuous time, but the end of time, mortality, which is evoked by unbroken set-ups and events unfolding in perpetuity.

We are familiar with place-names and what they invoke. But there are also time-names, although these have not been as rigorously codified. In a certain sense, they cannot be pinned down with the same exactitude. Yet, they often apply more deeply to current cultural productions. Again, Van Sant has understood how quickly and penetratingly visual and aural cues can connote entire eras. The Rudy Vallee song in *My Own Private Idaho*, playing under the scenes of the elderly John, Daddy Carroll, summons up a historical past in which gay life, for instance, was far more tentative, shiveringly romantic, and isolated. The music, combined with the images of the elderly man, produce what we could call a time-name. So does the inserted photograph of Sissy Hankshaw as an Edie Sedgwick–like fashion plate: the blonde bubble hair, the mascara, the miniskirt, the black and white of the photograph itself, all conjure Avedon and Warhol and even wider, more generalized aesthetic forms, "styles" or "looks." This, too, is a time-name.

Time-names are both individual and cultural-historical. They are partly what Vattimo refers to as "aesthetic consciousness," and whose synecdoche is the museum where disparate epochs and "tastes" are made to resonate with each other in a way that attempts to delineate the common aesthetic quality.[24] But the elderly John does not only represent the history of gay rights, but the arc of an individual man's life. The fashion photo does not only call out to a disparate decade of pop culture, but to an earlier time in Sissy's life: her youth. Thus, there are other time-names, which can also be codified, including adolescence, aging, etc. When we see an example of an adolescent, we are inescapably reminded of "adolescence" itself. It is not allegory, the turning of abstractions into physical symbols in real or imaginary space, but what I am calling a unique "time-name," in which the example does not lose the poignancy of realness even as it gains new dimensions in the abstract.

Likewise, the immediacy of the impression mitigates against the absolute meanings of allegory. We might all recognize the 60s, or an adolescent, but we do not all feel the same responses. Postmodernism highlights the grayness of interpretation even as it acknowledges that everything is reducible to a code that can be grasped on the surface of things. It is that triumph of human instinct which Deleuze has referred to as "a secret inner impulse,"[25] and which has played a role in philosophy and other pursuits of consciousness in the way that people become drawn into the subjects of their thoughts, the subjects of their lives, without first premeditating or even understanding why. If there is rigor or development, it comes as the dogged seeing-through-to-the-end of that early impulse — the conversion of impulse into history itself.

Perhaps this is, ultimately, how postmodernism has reconfigured the philosophy of history. In place of guiding absolutes, it has created a texture or warp, in which periods of recognizable time are articulated with great clarity of form and simultaneous amorphousness of intention or "content." Time-names, in a way that focuses on primal associations and instantaneous historical indexing, are the names we now give to history itself, that mutilated body which speaks to us only through images of perfect, intact skin; that ancientness which moves us now only through the thought of damaged and perishable youth. That human truth, which must first exist primarily as a secret in order, finally, to be expressed and believed.

Conclusion
Beyond "Private"

There's a thing Cleve Jones said early on. He said gay-rights activists, talking about straights who are sympathetic to the movement, will often say, "They're just like us—it's just the sex is different." And Cleve said, "It's actually quite the opposite—we're nothing like you, it's just that the sex is the same." And that's really true.—Sean Penn[1]

Whether I like it or not, or whether you like it or not, we are bound together forever. We are part of each other ... I think that what we really have to do is to create a country in which there are no minorities—for the first time in the history of the world.—James Baldwin[2]

Let me say something about the queer adoption of the phrase "my own private..." from the title of Van Sant's *My Own Private Idaho*. Not exactly meant as a slogan, this title is derived from a B-52's song, in which the accusation that some unnamed person is living in his or her "own private Idaho" is meant as a cheeky, 80s putdown from the New York art world to someone with (we can assume) Midwestern cultural values. It is hardly a praiseworthy thing to live in "your own private Idaho."

Van Sant alters the meaning greatly by owning this state as "*my* own private Idaho," and also suggesting that it stands for a kind of "double sexual life" enacted by the tentatively gay character, Mike. But in fact, even in spite of this, it is still far from being a hopeful or optimistic condition. As it applies to Mike, it essentially denotes a fantasy world that does not hold up to scrutiny in the light of day, a poetic paraphrase of his black-outs, broken heart, and eventual death. A "private Idaho" (perhaps like the "private island" which the long-suffering Marion Crane wants to go to in *Psycho*) is more like La-La Land than a good place to be, and not necessarily a valid substitute for living the life of a whole person in the world at large.

Moreover, the word "private" seems to have been misunderstood, striking a chord among gay viewers as a descriptor for gay desire itself. But this only evokes memories of the closet. By definition, something cannot be both "private" *and* a public act of radical insurrection or change. At the same time, "private" in this case means something more like private property rather than something secretive or hidden from view: the ideal of finding and having something that belongs to you exclusively, and cannot be taken away. Partly this is an expression of longing for being able to enjoy true love, lifelong companionship and commitment, traditionally difficult bets within many gay lives. It is also a utopian ideal of gay identity in general, in which we can be automatically accepted (this is my world too), or in which the affirmation of gay desire does not have to become a "big deal" in the social realm (disapproving straights will mind their own business and show tolerance), but one, at the same time, in which every choice we make (as gay spectators, as gay consumers) is magnified in sociopolitical importance — again, and ironically, the very opposite of something "private."

Rainer Werner Fassbinder's seminal reading of Douglas Sirk[3] laid the foundation for all current projects of queering mainstream cinema — and that essay was not actually queering so much as sexually forthright and subversive. It was radically liberating, but we have not progressed much beyond the groundwork that it laid down. Also, Fassbinder was actively engaged in producing radical new (queer) images, in his own films; his analysis of Sirk was not strictly theoretical, therefore, but proactive. The legacy for much academic queer theory, however, is often that we are stuck mining a sort of "eternal 1950s" for images of undetected queerness — images which usually cast us as hidden or pathologized. It sometimes seems as though we are more comfortable when elegantly decoding whispered queer messages far below the radar of straight mainstream culture rather than creating, or dealing with, wholly original works of queer art whose meanings might be crude albeit effective.

Of course, certain genres which happened to thrive during the 50s — musical, melodrama or women's picture, social comedy, horror/sci-fi film — have opened themselves quite readily to queer readings because they already question the social codes by which heteronormative institutions (marriage, family, citizenship) operate, and also because they invert traditional moral judgments (we often root for the monster in horror films) and aesthetic/moral judgments (musicals encourage us to applaud men who sing and dance). But what of the war film, or the western, which seem to preserve heteronormative codes in their very structures? Can these, too, become opened to gay desire? Of course they can, but this involves as much "straightening" of queerness as queering of straightness.

The alternative, of course, to queering the eternal 50s is to rigorously and honestly document queer existence as it is lived today. Here, "private" is again forced to become public. And of course, this is what some current queer cinema (if not queer theory) is already doing. Van Sant himself has recently produced a documentary on the ACT UP radical queer movement of the 80s, the single most devastating decade for gay men in modern times, and an era which still needs further memory-work and examination (if we can bear it). When we have established more of an absolute value for gayness (through transpropriations which will bring gay and straight worlds ever closer together, humanly the same albeit remaining different in their ways), then we can return to ungrounding, to postmodern readings of indeterminate texts (if we still want to) with the powerful advantage of experiential, rather than speculative, knowledge.

The only problem with this is the inevitable invisibility at either end of the spectrum, both in the repression and in the thorough, painstaking acceptance. When we queer the eternal 50s (and find ourselves missing, unaccounted-for, defeated, etc.) or when we present ourselves as having fully arrived within a reality that is coextensive with heteronormative reality, we disappear, at least as an element within society that can be visible, oppositional and empowered. Meanwhile, the goal of all our efforts is to gain more and more acceptance, and eventually to become appreciated not just in spite, but *because*, of the fact that we are gay. And thus, although we are not there yet, the cultural work of queering (queer theory in general) might no longer be necessary or relevant when we have finally achieved acceptance in a daily, experiential way. Will we be happy or sad at this prospect — to gain the life and lose the need for theory?

To the extent that the argument in this book is inspired by Sontag's rallying call for "an erotics of art," the future might entail not that we continue to queer the artifacts of culture but to directly experience works of art in a way that would justify the claim that queerness can be radical, subversive, against the grain — therefore never *completely* acceptable but always occupying an indefinable, shape-shifting fringe; making raids and interventions on dominant systems but always holding on to the rebel-cred that comes only in the margins.

Van Sant's films demand that we meet somewhere in the middle, that queerness become more masculine in form even as masculinity itself is queered. It is a complex back and forth, expressed often in the allegorical in-betweenness of adolescent males and females. In any event, the yearning for something "private" (as in furtive rather than as in all-mine) is at odds with the movement of queer history, in which the queer himself or herself is rapidly disappearing into a social order that reduces differences — we need for the private to be public, now more than ever, so that identities can remain maximally irreducible and substantiated. We need many more paths to follow, more open roads, not fewer ones. "My own private..." is not a slogan but an elegiac statement of mourning for what can and must never truly be, if we intend to promote more and more queer self-identification and self-revelation. It is the longing (far from being rare or unindulged) that one can happily live forever in any kind of closet.

Of all his peers, many of whom have been equally influenced by the 60s (Spike Lee and Richard Linklater immediately come to mind), Van Sant has arguably had the greatest impact in terms of creating a meaningful counterculture in our own time. *My Own Private Idaho* succeeded in negatively branding the smiley face logo and the catchphrase, "Have a nice day," as impossible pieces of denial, by superimposing them on the misery and doom of the hopelessly down-and-out. Largely because of Van Sant, I can never hear that phrase now without cringing at how it is the ultimate, generic expression of not really caring about others at all; although John Waters' fans will recall that this exact phrase is spat out sarcastically by Connie Marble (Mink Stole) as she dismisses a job-seeker in *Pink Flamingos* (1972). The meaning is clear. We can have a "nice day" but must go on stumbling through a shitty life. Indeed, one of the most persistent moods of Van Sant's cinema is the wary, envious, compassionate eye which it keeps on those forced to live in poverty within a wealthy nation; even this is less hardcore-political than inspired, at least in part, by erotic feeling. It is the same fevered, unwashed erotic heat which Harmony Korine finds in the backwater gulch of *Gummo* (1997) and which Larry Clark finds in barrios, trailer parks, and druggy squats.

However, Van Sant, it bears repeating, is far more chaste and sexually reserved than most current directors, especially queer ones. Even when he shows naked flesh, it is from a wistful distance and primarily involved with formal and emotional concerns. Thus, the shower scene in *Paranoid Park* is, on one hand, an exquisite, abstract treatment of the stream of water being transformed by slow-motion into a cascade of shimmering lights; and on the other hand, a revelation of Alex's complete psychological and emotional vulnerability after the train-yard accident. Young male nudity, often considered to be animalistic or antisocial by the popular media and feminist theorists, is never displayed aggressively in Van Sant's films, but always (when it is displayed) as the sign of a greater vulnerability.

Likewise, sex itself tends to be presented either as a disappointment (the much-anticipated deflowering in *Paranoid Park* which takes no more than thirty seconds), a burden (the painful penetration in *Mala Noche*), a poor substitute (the way heroin has usurped Bob's sexual libido in *Drugstore Cowboy*), and a weapon used to wound and control (Scott's bisexual activity in *My Own Private Idaho*; Suzanne's seduction of the teenage killer in *To Die For*). When two Van Sant characters are actually in love, or when at least one of them has true feelings for the other, the director almost never places them in bed together—a token, perhaps, of how deeply and painfully gay men know the feeling of unrequited, unfulfilled or discontinuous loves. The only exceptions to this are the scene where Sissy and Jellybean cuddle after sex in *Even Cowgirls Get the Blues*, and the domestic bliss of Harvey and Scott in *Milk*, the latter a real breakthrough in terms of how Van Sant was able to romanticize gay love and sex.

In a sexually explicit culture, is Van Sant's reticence a sign of refusal — the refusal to give the audience what it might want, or to depict sex as being more casual and unproblematic than it really is? People are hurt by sex in Van Sant's films, in large and small ways, and somewhat unfashionably so. Also, sex is linked, again and again, to commodities and drugs, unhealthy and dehumanizing fetishes. From *Mala Noche* onward, there is an iconoclastic insistence that the true goal is to rediscover a kind of innocence. In a distinctly American way, Van Sant's characters yearn for innocence—whether Blake dressing like a woman because it presumably feels less threatening and sexist, or the Gerrys speaking in their childlike glossolalia, or the older Walt "regressing" to a point where he can look up to the Mexican teenagers as heroes and father-figures.

In keeping with this iconoclastic, anti-commercial spirit, *Mala Noche* was nearly impossible to see for a long time; it seemed to fall through the cracks of an increasingly market-driven (indie) cinema. It had gay and Mexican heroes, it took place on Skid Row, no one was happy in the end. It wasn't until some twenty years later that it got a proper DVD release in the U.S. (as part of the Criterion Collection), and then it was as if the images had stayed fresh and vivid for having been vacuum-sealed in my memory. Of all the U.S. films I know, I think it is closest to what people always say about the Velvet Underground: not many people heard them when they were together, but everyone who did went out and started a band. It's a film that can hook you that way on a certain kind of personal, hand-made cinema. Watching *Mala Noche* again the other day, I was struck by something I should have noticed at the time but had never really paid attention to before, how the working-class clothes of Walt and the Mexican boys—flannel shirts and denim jeans— inspired the grunge look that came roaring out of Seattle only a few years later. It all seemed so inevitable and right when it was happening, that we were Gus Van Sant fans, and Nirvana fans, and Red Hot Chili Peppers fans, and.... Like any counterculture, we were too busy participating in it to think about how it was all coming together, or, indeed, to see when it might start to come undone.

There is no end to history. What is ultimately documented in Van Sant's films are messy, ambiguous feelings, phenomena which we are not sure we have properly even seen, though they have seemingly passed before our eyes. Can one-sided love be as poignant as it is in *Mala Noche* or *My Own Private*

Idaho? Can the primal erupt as definitively as it does in *Elephant, Paranoid Park* and *Gerry*, where murder is both conventionally wrong and nonetheless exhilarating, transformative, shamanistic? *Last Days* is an intense vision of the destiny of all original art, to become a sacrifice even to its fans and followers who are inevitably unworthy of it, and whose mediocrity it shows up. Blake's hangers-on, when they aren't picking his brain about how to promote their own music careers, use his music and cachet as a pretext merely to fuck: an act that is an exhilarating liberation of energy, on one hand, but also an inadequate, prosaic and even somewhat desecrating counterpoint to the largely unnoticed spectacle of Blake's disintegration. As in vampire films, Blake grows weaker and weaker to the point of death, while others feed off his dwindling life energy. *Last Days* makes the claim that the greatest art is not only beyond gender or straightforward personae, but beyond the human, not of this world.

But not of Interzone, either, which must finally emerge a capital of false liberation at best. Setting oneself free from Interzone is the uneasy task of every individual, and of every artist. Sometimes it is hard to leave its numbed security behind, and sometimes freedom from Interzone only means that it becomes un-localized, its power unleashed to infiltrate everywhere, so that anyplace can come to seem its temporary or permanent double. In the 20th century, drug literature has taught us that states of mind can feed autonomously off a thinker, that nightmares can return in broad daylight, precise and baffling. Van Sant is perhaps a drug filmmaker without drugs. Even after adopting a harsher stance toward depicting their use (for example, the cafeteria workers are on crack in *Elephant*'s doomed, dysfunctional high school) he remains in some ways enamored of what they represent to consciousness, the way they bend and alter time, the way they bring life and death into a kind of double helix, or a black hole that leads to another world, like the warp in Kubrick's *2001*.

It is possible to read the legendary and difficult ending of *2001* as a powerfully poignant metaphor for a certain kind of fame. The astronaut, played by Keir Dullea, has become a "star," and by the end of the film this meaning will be literalized, when he glows as a newly formed fetus in outer space. But for the time that he exists in the strange room — a mix of eighteenth century and space age — he is another kind of star: a notable, historic figure. Which is to say, a kind of prisoner under watch, an object of study, whispered about, venerated perhaps, also mocked and tormented. Just as he is forced to watch himself as another, aging through a series of changes, so public life tends to reward those who have traveled the farthest with the meager wages of a kind of non-life — a shrinking world, constant exposure, often intense existential loneliness — in exchange for a nearly infinite expansion of consciousness.

Chapter Notes

Preface

1. William Burroughs, *My Education: A Book of Dreams* (New York: Penguin Books, 1995), 103.
2. William Burroughs, *Interzone* (Ed. James Grauerholz; New York: Penguin Books, 1989), 33.
3. Quoted in Oliver Harris and Ian Macayden, Eds., *Naked Lunch @ 50: Anniversary essays* (Carbondale: Southern Illinois University Press, 2009), 61.
4. Harris and MacFayden, *Naked Lunch @ 50*, 236.
5. Ibid., 215.
6. Gary Indiana, interview with Gus Van Sant, http://bombsite.com.issues/back.
7. Graham Fuller, "Gus Van Sant: Swimming Against the Current," in Gus Van Sant, *Even Cowgirls Get the Blues & My Own Private Idaho* (London and Boston: Faber and Faber, 1993), vii.
8. Armistead Maupin, Interview with Gus Van Sant, *Interview*, www.interviewmagazine.com.
9. "No Cutting, No Stars, No Script: An Interview with Gus Van Sant," *Mala Noche* DVD (Madman, 2006).
10. John Robert Parrish, *Gus Van Sant: An Unauthorized Biography* (New York: Thunder's Mouth Press, 2001), xii.
11. Gus Van Sant, Interview with Madonna, *Interview*, www.interviewmagazine.com.
12. Quoted in Brian J. Robb, *River Phoenix: A Short Life* (New York: HarperCollins, Inc., 1994), 115.

Introduction

1. Susan Sontag, *Against Interpretation* (New York: Farrar, Straus and Giroux, 1966), 14.
2. Roland Barthes, *Camera Lucida: Reflections on Photography* (Trans. Richard Howard; New York: Hill and Wang, 1983), 6.
3. Robb, *River Phoenix: A Short Life*, 114–115.
4. Gianni Vattimo, *The End of Modernity* (Trans. Jon R. Snyder; Baltimore: The Johns Hopkins University Press, 1991), 118.
5. Ibid.
6. Ibid.
7. Ibid.
8. William Burroughs, *The Adding Machine: Selected Essays* (New York: Seaver Books, 1986), 1.
9. Barthes, *Camera Lucida*, 6 (It's worth noting that Bathes' book on photography was inspired by the act of mourning for a loved one, and his attempt, both successful and dissatisfying, to try to recapture her through looking at the photographs he had of her.)
10. Diane Arbus, *Diane Arbus: An Aperture Monograph* (New York: Aperture, 1972), 15.

11. Sam D'Allesandro, *The Wild Creatures: Collected Stories of Sam D'Allesandro* (Ed. Kevin Killian; San Francisco: Suspect Thoughts Press, 2005), 16.
12. Ibid.
13. Sontag, *Against Interpretation*, 10.
14. Ibid., 6.
15. Ibid., 7 and 13.
16. Ibid., 14.
17. Friedrich Nietzsche, *Beyond Good and Evil: Prelude to a Philosophy of the Future* (Trans. Walter Kaufmann; New York: Random House, Inc., 1966), 88.
18. Walter Benjamin, *Reflections: Essays, Aphorisms, Autobiographical Writings* (Trans. Edmund Jephcott; New York: Harcourt Brace Jovanovich, 1979), 190.
19. Warhol screenwriter Ronald Tavel said something along these lines: "You feel that films are very much history ... the most authentic history books we have. They record infallibly how people think, because when you watch them ... what you really watch is the flesh at work..." as quoted in Stephen Koch, *Stargazer: The Life, World & Films of Andy Warhol, Revised and Updated* (New York and London: Marion Boyars, 1991), 68–69. Films have made history the history of flesh, history made flesh. We watch films in order to *see* others, and perhaps become more like them, more at one with them, in a kind of addiction of identification. Indeed, after Trent Reznor's influential single, "The Perfect Drug" (1997), this conception of love as a narcotic has become more or less commonplace and mainstream.
20. D'Allesandro, *The Wild Creatures*, 83.
21. Sontag, *Against Interpretation*, 8.
22. Ibid., 12–14.
23. Ibid., 13.

Chapter 1

1. DVD liner notes, *The Films of Kenneth Anger Volume II* (Fantoma, 2007).
2. In *Milk*, Van Sant quietly revels in the fact that Harvey Milk's camera store, Castro Camera, served as political headquarters and epicenter of the San Francisco gay rights movement. In the front of the store, cameras were sold and customers got their developed pictures back; in the back of the store, "behind the curtain," activists were planning how to change the world. Photography was not in contest with the aims of real life, but acting in tandem with them, helping, too, in the outreach and universalization which is necessary in any program of political action. On the commentary of Criterion's DVD edition of the documentary, Robert Epstein's *The Times of Harvey Milk* (1984), photographer and Milk colleague Daniel Nicoletta states that the very first, impromptu "queer film festival" took place in that backroom of Castro Camera, which was "not only their campaign headquarters but very much a community center."
3. Sontag, *Against Interpretation*, 5.
4. Van Sant himself has specifically invoked the model of the diorama as one closely connected to the way he specifically re-stages real life events in his own films, as "a sculpture of the event [which is. supposed to be a representation of the event and in that way a celebration of the event." This important statement is made in "Celebrating Harvey Milk: Two Films, One Legacy," a documentary which appears as a bonus feature on the 2011 Criterion DVD of Robert Epstein's *The Times of Harvey Milk* (1984), an inspiration for Van Sant and screenwriter Dustin Lance Black when they made *Milk*.
5. In "The Limits of Intertextuality" (first published in 1983), Nicholas Zurbrugg writes: "Perhaps the most revealing tension in Barthes's writing is that between his efforts to create more or less analytical systems that deny the existence of the author and dismantle texts into as many codes as he had currently invented, and his conflicting compulsion to locate loopholes within these systems for symptoms of authorial presence and originality..." (*Critical Vices: The Myths of Postmodern Theory*; International: G + B Arts, 2000, 18). Zurbrugg does two things in this essay with which I wholeheartedly agree: he points to a link between Barthesian intertextuality and the literary cut-ups practiced mainly by William Burroughs; and he deplores the way that "Barthes's followers seem to lack their master's breadth of vision, and only 'live with' his ideas by reducing them to a dogmatic, quite un–Barthesian vision that tranquilizes the ten-

sions within Barthes's teachings by ignoring them" (ibid., 18). In retrospect, it seems clear that the essay "The Death of the Author" (1968; later collected in *Image-Music-Text*; trans. Stephen Heath; New York: Hill and Wang, 1977) was strategic on Barthes' part, to promote the role of the critic as a creative agent, a prime mover, over and above any writers he happened to be criticizing; no text was privileged in and of itself, until and unless some sharp-eyed critic came along to deconstruct it. This led to a widespread practice in which the critics' vision could blissfully supersede the author's, or even the given elements of a text itself; and yes, this practice has often been abused, and given rise to solipsistic analyses. Barthes himself was perhaps at his most interesting when *focusing* on authors, as he did at every stage of his career: Racine, Sade, Baudelaire, Cy Twombly, etc. I, too, believe that the strategies presented in "The Death of the Author" can, and should, be adapted to work in tandem with authorial-minded criticism. The author is not so much dead as ghostlike, in the sense of transparent: intertextualities are points where the author can be "seen through," so to speak. In general I am more interested than Zurbrugg in the productive possibilities of non-originality as exemplified in the instances of what I am calling "queer intertextuality." For further investigation into Burroughs' synchronicity with the French deconstructionists and proponents of intertextuality-theory, see Robin Lydenberg, *Word Cultures: Radical Theory and Practice in William S. Burroughs' Fiction* (Urbana: University of Illinois Press, 1987).

 6. DVD commentary track by Kenneth Anger, *The Films of Kenneth Anger II* (Fantoma DVD, 2007).
 7. Mikhail Iampolski, *The Memory of Tiresias: Intertextuality and Film* (Trans. Harsha Ram; Berkeley, Los Angeles, and London: University of California Press, 1998), 40.
 8. Burroughs, *The Adding Machine*, 62.
 9. Harris and MacFayden, *Naked Lunch @ 50*, 112.
 10. Sigmund Freud, *The Schreber Case* (Trans. Andrew Weber; New York: Penguin Books, 2003), 58–59.
 11. Ibid., 57.
 12. Ibid., 56.
 13. Ibid., 53 (double emphasis in the original text).
 14. Tinckom's book, *Working Like a Homosexual: Camp, Capital, Cinema* (Durham and London: Duke University Press, 2002), takes as its point of departure a comment from a former M-G-M production assistant stating that as a director Vincente Minnelli "was not a man who was a dictator. He tried to do it in a soft and nice way. He worked in let's say ... I don't know whether you will understand what I say.... He worked like a homosexual." (35)
 15. Indiana, ibid.
 16. Alan Sinfield, *Gay and After* (London: Serpent's Tail, 1998), 33–34.
 17. In *Homos* (Cambridge, Mass., and London: Harvard University Press, 1995), Leo Bersani relates this anecdote: "At a gay and lesbian conference ... a lesbian colleague complained that my talk marginalized women. Since much of what I said had to do with gay men's sexuality and, more specifically, with gay men's love of the cock, her entirely accurate comment became entirely puzzling when voiced as a complaint." (8)
 18. Iampolski, *The Memory of Tiresias: Intertextuality and Film.*, 79–80.
 19. David Thomson, *The New Biographical Dictionary of Film: Updated and Expanded* (New York: Alfred A. Knopf, 2011), 993.
 20. Anne Waldman (Ed.), *Out of This World: The Poetry Project at the St. Mark's Church-in-the-Bowery, An Anthology 1966–1991* (Foreword by Allen Ginsberg; New York: Crown Publishers, Inc., 1991), 109.
 21. Ibid., 586.
 22. Avital Ronell, *Stupidity* (Urbana and Chicago: University of Illinois Press, 2002), 125.
 23. Ibid., 110.
 24. Fuller, "Swimming Against the Current," xliv–xlv.
 25. Walt Curtis, *Mala Noche & Other "Illegal" Adventures* (Portland: Bridge City Books, 1997), 216.
 26. Phil Stanford, *Portland Confidential: Sex, Crime, and Corruption in the Rose City* (Portland: West Winds Press, 2004), 15.
 27. DVD commentary track, *Psycho* (Universal, 1999).
 28. Gerald Peary, "Gus Van Sant — Elephant," http://geraldpeary.com/interviews.

29. Curtis, *Mala Noche & Other "Illegal" Adventures*, 219.
30. DVD commentary track by Van Sant and Matt Dillon, *Drugstore Cowboy* (Artisan Home Entertainment, 1999).
31. Chris Holmlund and Cynthia Fuchs, editors, *Between the Sheets, In the Streets: Queer, Lesbian, Gay Documentary* (Minneapolis and London: University of Minnesota Press, 1997), 159.
32. Ibid., 161.
33. Ibid., 162.
34. Roland Barthes, *Writing Degree Zero* (Trans. Annette Lavers and Colin Smith; New York: Hill and Wang, 1999), 88.
35. Burroughs sometimes explicitly denied any link between the cut-up and the surrealists' automatic writing, and even affirmed that cut-ups were fully conscious and not unconscious at all; but he also called it "blind prose," and in many cases he is clearly speaking of things that only come to conscious awareness after being concealed by the great nemesis, "the Word" (the un–cut-up word). For an excellent overview of Burroughs' cut-up experimentation, see Marianne DeKoven, "William Burroughs: Any Number Can Play" (pp. 161–182, *Utopia Limited: The Sixties and the Emergence of the Postmodern*; Durham and London: Duke University Press, 2004).
36. William Burroughs, *The Burroughs File* (San Francisco: City Lights, 1991), 56.
37. Ibid.
38. William Burroughs, "Origin and Theory of the Tape Cut-Ups," *Break Through in Grey Room* (Sub Rosa, 2001).
39. Ibid.
40. Burroughs, *The Adding Machine*, 19.
41. Barthes, *Writing Degree Zero*, 27.
42. Burroughs, *The Adding Machine*, 53.
43. DeKoven, *Utopia Limited*, 166.

Chapter 2

1. This is not to say that Van Sant is the only modern director who has made artistic use of cloudscapes and time-lapse cinematography. Notably Derek Jarman used these to glorious effect in *The Garden* (1990), to show the passing of historical epochs and to highlight the fragility of life on earth. The talented James Marsh signals a certain indebtedness to both Jarman and Van Sant by using time-lapse clouds in-between the 19th century and modern passages of his stunning *Wisconsin Death Trip* (1999).
2. Iampolski, *The Memory of Tiresias: Intertextuality and Film*, 108.
3. Barthes, *Writing Degree Zero*, 50.
4. Ibid.
5. Ibid.
6. Ibid., 49.
7. Ibid., 51.
8. Charles Baudelaire, "L'Albatros," in *Les Fleurs du Mal* (Paris: Flammarion, 1991), 61–62.
9. Barthes, *Writing Degree Zero*, 51–52.
10. Ibid., 49.
11. Nietzsche, *Beyond Good and Evil*, 82.
12. Hart Crane, *The Poems of Hart Crane* (Edited by Marc Simon; Liveright: New York, 1986), 44.
13. Barthes, *Writing Degree Zero*, 41–49.
14. Ibid., 42.
15. Koch, *Stargazer*, 19.
16. Ibid., 60.
17. Davies, *Trash: A Queer Film Classic*, 128.
18. Jonathan Crary, *Techniques of the Observer: On Vision and Modernity in the Nineteenth Century* (Cambridge, Mass., and London: MIT Press, 1992), 139.

Chapter 3

1. Burroughs, *My Education*, 132.
2. Burroughs, *The Adding Machine*, 20.
3. Quoted in Vattimo, *The End of Modernity*, 169.
4. Kenneth Goldsmith (Ed.), *I'll Be Your Mirror: The Selected Andy Warhol Interviews, 1962–1987; Thirty-Seven Conversations with the Pop Master* (New York: Carroll & Graf Publishers, 2004), 7.
5. Mark Stevens and Annalyn Swan, *De Kooning: An American Master* (New York: Random House, Inc., 2006), 359.
6. Ibid., 359–360.
7. Ibid., 360.
8. Ibid., 359.
9. Burroughs, *The Adding Machine*, 20–21.
10. This prop is identified in the credits as having been borrowed from John Woo: in the world of current thrillers, this is somewhat like borrowing a pistol from John Ford in the 40s to make a Western.
11. DVD commentary track, *Psycho*, ibid.
12. The presence of this green motif is confirmed, but not explained in so many words, by Van Sant and actress Anne Heche in the DVD commentary track of *Psycho*.
13. DVD commentary track, *Psycho*, ibid.
14. Iampolski, *The Memory of Tiresias: Intertextuality and Film*, 2.
15. Burroughs, *My Education*, 49.
16. Burroughs, *The Adding Machine*, 9.
17. Sebastian Stoppe, *Original und Fälschung?—Hitchcocks Psycho und das Remake von Gus Van Sant* (GRIN Verlag: 2002), 12 (my translation).
18. Ibid., 15 (my translation).
19. Ibid., 15 (my translation).
20. DVD bonus feature, "Psycho Path," *Psycho*, ibid.
21. DVD commentary track, *Psycho*, ibid.
22. Stoppe, *Original und Fälschung?*, 12 (my translation).
23. DVD bonus feature, "Psycho Path," *Psycho*, ibid.
24. DVD commentary track, *Psycho*, ibid.
25. Tinckom, *Working Like a Homosexual*, 102.
26. DVD bonus feature, "Psycho Path," *Psycho*, ibid.
27. DVD commentary track, *Psycho*, ibid.
28. In Brookner's documentary, *Burroughs* (Citifilms, 1983), Burroughs says: "In a prerecorded universe the only things that are not prerecorded are the prerecordings themselves."

Chapter 4

1. Nicholas Garnham, *Fuller* (New York: Viking Press, Inc., 1972), 89.
2. Burroughs, *My Education*, 6.
3. Fuller, "Swimming Against the Current," xxx.
4. Burroughs, *My Education*, 33.
5. Ibid., 79.
6. William Burroughs, *Exterminator!* (New York: Penguin Books, 1981), 55.
7. Ibid., 55.
8. Ibid., 56.
9. Ibid.
10. Ibid., 61.
11. Gus Van Sant, Interview with Madonna, *Interview*, www.interviewmagazine.com (online archives).
12. Fuller, "Swimming Against the Current," xxxviii.
13. I have explored this idea of "fatherness" as a chosen relation between unrelated men in my first book, *Male Bisexuality in Current Cinema: Images of Growth, Rebellion, and Survival* (Jefferson, NC: McFarland, 2011).

14. Cooper, *Smothered in Hugs*, 15.
15. Van Sant, *Even Cowgirls Get the Blues & My Own Private Idaho*, 108.
16. Ibid., 117.
17. Ibid., 126.
18. Fuller, "Swimming Against the Current," xxxix.
19. Freud, *The Schreber Case*, 55.
20. Diane Wakoski, *Virtuoso Literature for Two and Four Hands* (Garden City, New York: Doubleday & Company, 1975), 27–29.
21. Curtis, *Mala Noche & Other "Illegal Adventures,"* 34–35.
22. Gus Van Sant, *Pink* (New York: Anchor Books, 1998), 224–225.

Chapter 5

1. Aired on BookTV, 4/28/2012.
2. Vattimo, *The End of Modernity*, 9.
3. Ibid., 3.
4. Ibid., 9.
5. DeKoven, *Utopia Limited*, 17.
6. Ibid., 290.
7. Vattimo, *The End of Modernity*, 4.
8. Ibid.
9. Ibid.
10. Ibid., 37.
11. Dr. Lucius T. Outlaw (Jr.), *On Race and Philosophy* (New York and London: Routledge, 1996), 18.
12. Ibid., 19.
13. Ibid., 29.
14. Vattimo, *The End of Modernity*, 12.
15. Ibid.
16. Forrester's sharp-angled, cavernous apartment is one of the great sets of modern cinema, defined by the problem of its lighting: either natural in daytime or, diurnally, by dim, isolated lamps which drop shadows on bunkers of books stacked deep with dust; the antique crystal-teardrop chandelier in the central room, like a proverbial white elephant or embarrassment of riches, goes pointedly unused.
17. DeKoven, *Utopia Limited*, 185.
18. Ibid.
19. Ibid., 229.
20. Ibid., 237.
21. Ibid., 290.
22. Outlaw, *On Race and Philosophy*, 30.
23. Ibid., 53.

Chapter 6

1. D'Allesandro, *The Wild Creatures*, 157.
2. Fuller, "Swimming Against the Current," ix.
3. D'Allesandro, *The Wild Creatures*, 54.
4. Goldsmith, *I'll Be Your Mirror*, 128.
5. Tinckom, *Working Like a Homosexual*, 87.
6. Goldsmith, *I'll Be Your Mirror*, 128–129.
7. Ibid., 129.
8. Tinckom, *Working Like a Homosexual*, 181.
9. Thomas Hine, *The Rise and Fall of the American Teenager* (New York: Harper Collins, 1999), 63.
10. Ibid., 53.

11. Ibid., 8.
12. Ibid., 10.
13. Ibid., 275.
14. Goldsmith, *I'll Be Your Mirror*, 95.
15. Hine, *The Rise and Fall of the American Teenager*, 19.
16. Ibid., 51.
17. Ibid., 15.
18. Goldsmith, *I'll Be Your Mirror*, 134.
19. Hine, *The Rise and Fall of the American Teenager*, 46.
20. Ibid., 47.
21. William Burroughs, *Naked Lunch: The Restored Text* (Eds. James Grauerholz and Barry Miles; New York: Grove Press, 2001), 128–129.
22. D'Allesandro, *The Wild Creatures*, 56.
23. Arthur Rimbaud, *Oeuvres Complètes* (Librairie Gallimard, 1954), 220 (my translation).
24. Paul Burston, *What Are You Looking At? Queer Sex, Style and Cinema* (London: Cassell, 1995), 31.
25. Michael De Angelis, *Gay Fandom and Crossover Stardom: James Dean, Mel Gibson, and Keanu Reeves* (Durham and London: Duke University Press, 2001), 9.
26. Ibid., 9.
27. Burston, *What Are You Looking At?*, 34.
28. Ibid.
29. Cooper, *Smothered in Hugs*, 25.
30. De Angelis, *Crossover Stardom and Gay Fandom*, 15.
31. Ibid., 4.
32. Cooper, *Smothered in Hugs*, 21–22.
33. De Angelis, *Crossover Stardom and Gay Fandom*, 205.
34. Ibid., 188–190.

Chapter 7

1. Dante, *La Vita Nuova* (Trans. Barbara Reynolds; Harmondsworth and New York: Penguin Books, 1978), 73.
2. Jean-Paul Sartre, *Baudelaire* (Trans. Martin Turnell; New York: New Directions, 1967), 25–26.
3. Dante, *La Vita Nuova*, 80–81.
4. Crary, *Techniques of the Observer: On Vision and Modernity in the Nineteenth Century*, 107.
5. Ibid., 109.
6. Sartre, *Baudelaire*, 28.
7. Ibid., 30.
8. *Tous les garçons s'appellent Patrick* (*All Boys Are Named Patrick*, 1957) is an early short film directed by Jean-Luc Godard, with a screenplay by Eric Rohmer, in which two young women, best friends, are talking about their new boyfriends, both named Patrick. They think they are describing two different men; but he turns out to be the same in the end.
9. Dante, *La Vita Nuova*, 32.

Chapter 8

1. Arbus, *Diane Arbus*, 10.
2. Walt Whitman, *Specimen Days & Collect* (New York: Dover Publications, Inc., 1995), 108.
3. Ibid.
4. Ibid., 60.
5. Ibid., 37.
6. Ibid.

7. Ibid., 108.
8. Nietzsche, *Beyond Good and Evil*, 92.
9. So indelible is actor Alex Frost in the role of Alex that I experienced a shiver seeing him among the soldier characters in *Stop-Loss* (2008), in which a scene of bored young veterans taking target practice on various household items seems like an homage to the gun violence of Van Sant's *Elephant*.
10. Garnham, *Fuller*, 104.
11. Arbus, *Diane Arbus*, 10–11.
12. Ibid., 3.
13. Daringly, Van Sant teases out a nearly subliminal subplot in which Milk becomes susceptible to White through a kind of hopeful or faulty "gaydar." Harvey's staff repeatedly warns him off trying to cozy up to White, but Milk defends his conservative colleague: "Dan White is just uneducated, we will teach him." Savvy Cleve Jones (Emile Hirsch), Milk's right hand man, gently chides Milk: "Is it just me or is he cute?" Although Milk denies that he is attracted to the straight White, his staff continues to press him on whether or not there is some attraction there. Milk says, tipping his hand, "I think he may be one of us ... I know what it's like to live that lie. I can see it in Dan's eyes, that fear and pressure." His staff stifles their groans at this, seeing the situation more clearly, it seems, than Harvey does. Is this a rationalization? Is Milk seeing what he wants or hopes to see? Is this his fatal hubris, that he can "educate," convert or somehow change Dan? Appearing on a local TV talk show with White, Harvey stresses their teamwork as fellow Supervisors, making the broad joke, "Dan and I are in bed together ... politically speaking," which makes Dan cringe and look askance. This is not to say that Milk is asking to be killed, or that he even participates in his own slaughter; but it complicates his character as a gay pioneer, traveling down an uncharted road and needing to sort through his own baggage as he goes. Milk is not painted as "perfect," according to those moral standards which tend to obsess straight people. And just as *Milk* is a radical biopic simply for exploring its famous subject's sexual relationships (usually off-limits when filmmakers are trying to construct a "serious" portrait of a public figure), so Harvey becomes a figure not only of gay power and gay pride but of lingering self-esteem issues and the romantic tendency to idealize love from a distance (or perhaps the love of a straight man). In any event, it is a very subtle motif within the film, albeit one which returns in a number of scenes.
14. For reasons known only to himself, but perhaps having to do with the Trotskyist idea of permanent revolution, Jarman seems to be constructing a visual slogan here that states: "Fuck Caravaggio," the subject of his previous film.

Chapter 9

1. Burroughs, *Interzone*, 72.
2. Harris and MacFayden, *Naked Lunch @ 50*, 31.
3. Burroughs, *Interzone*, 147.
4. Harris and MacFayden, *Naked Lunch @ 50*, 116.
5. Burston, *What Are You Looking At?*, 167.
6. These shots, following people as they walk, also correspond, in Van Sant's films from *Gerry* onward, to similar shots in Béla Tarr's *Satan's Tango* (1994), making comprehensible the possibility that the Hungarian Tarr is also commenting on the idea of surveillance and persecution in certain communist nations: similar to internalized homophobia, a kind of paranoia of one's own freedom (mobility), instigated by actual repression and victimization.
7. Burroughs, *Interzone*, 59.
8. Ibid., 76.
9. Nietzsche, *Beyond Good and Evil*, 42.
10. Kurt Hemmer has reached a similar conclusion: "...Burroughs' concern about his personal freedoms, supported by colonial control in Tangier, superseded any sympathy with Moroccan nationalism. This is in keeping with Burroughs' feeling that individual freedoms are more important than national autonomy, especially if such nationalism is itself oppressive to personal rights.... As Burroughs wrote *Naked Lunch*, the resistance to imperialism in Tangier forced its way into his novel but was met with the desistance occasioned by his sexual desire. Tangier was

a place where Burroughs could indulge his sexual desire for young boys, who were plentiful and cheap, without arousing the animosity of local authorities, who seemed to maintain a relatively laissez-faire attitude toward the sexual proclivities of the expatriate population" (Harris and MacFayden, *Naked Lunch @ 50*, 66–67).

11. Burroughs, *The Adding Machine*, 143.
12. William Burroughs, *Early Routines* (Santa Barbara: Cadmus Editions, 1982), 11–12.
13. Harris and MacFayden, *Naked Lunch @ 50*, 77.
14. Davies, *Trash: A Queer Film Classic*, 21.
15. "But [hustlers and transvestites] have wholly dissociated actual desire and their actual bodies. Sexual identity is in that sense [the sense of fulfillment] forbidden." (Koch, *Stargazer*, 123).
16. Davies, *Trash: A Queer Film Classic*, 54. A complete and unbiased socioeconomic study of the Warhol scene still needs to be made: Warhol came from a blue-collar upbringing (hence the conceit of making art in something called a "factory"), but his art earned a lot of money and he moved in wealthy circles; the Factory itself was a "classless society," in that people from all different backgrounds found their way there. Although a number of Factory artistes came from wealthy families (in fact most bohemian scenes throughout history have been dominated by the slumming sons and daughters of the rich, who have access to power at the bottom as well as the top of the social order), wealth actually guaranteed popularity *there* far less than qualities such as charisma, exhibitionism, and of course raw talent. Class distinctions that surely would have mattered in the rest of the world seemed to dwindle away under the effects of drugs and chronic performativity. This is one of the things that made the Factory seem so dangerous at the time; inside its walls no one could really distinguish anymore the kind of social markers (ones of gender as well as economic status) that seemed to hold society at large "together." Nor was Warhol himself even safe, as his near-murder in 1968 attests. Perhaps, in a state of constant revolution, the normative barrier between revolution and reaction becomes as paper-thin as the walls of a cheap hotel.
17. D'Allesandro, *The Wild Creatures*, 113.
18. Ibid., 114.
19. Ibid., 115.
20. Ibid.
21. Ibid.
22. Ibid.
23. Ibid., 116.
24. Ibid.
25. Sontag, *Against Interpretation*, 290.
26. Harris and MacFayden, *Naked Lunch @ 50*, 95.
27. Ibid., 165.
28. Burroughs, *Naked Lunch: The Restored Text*, 132.
29. Harris and MacFayden, *Naked Lunch @ 50*, 71.
30. Brookner, *Burroughs*, ibid.
31. Burroughs, *Interzone*, 47.
32. Ibid., 49.
33. Ibid., 54.
34. Ibid., 74–75.
35. Ibid., 67.
36. Harris and MacFayden, *Naked Lunch @ 50*, 27.
37. Burroughs, *Naked Lunch: The Restored Text*, 130.
38. Burroughs, *Interzone*, 69.
39. Ibid., 65.
40. Ibid., 40.
41. Ibid., 66.
42. Ibid., 77.
43. Ibid., 78.
44. Ibid.
45. Wesley Morris, "Cosmic 'Elephant': high school existential," Boston Globe, 11/14/2003, www.bostonglobe.com.

46. Ibid.
47. D'Allesandro, *The Wild Creatures*, 83.
48. Nietzsche, *Beyond Good and Evil*, 41.
49. Burroughs, *Interzone*, 78.
50. Nietzsche, *Beyond Good and Evil*, 42.
51. Ibid., 54.
52. In Brookner's documentary, he disapproves of his son, William Burroughs, Jr., giving money to a panhandling wino.
53. Burroughs, *Interzone*, 70.
54. Garnham, *Fuller*, 97.
55. D'Allesandro, *The Wild Creatures*, 17.

Chapter 10

1. Gilles Deleuze, *Spinoza: Practical Philosophy* (Trans. Robert Hurley; San Francisco: City Lights, 1988), 45.
2. Antonin Artaud, *Artaud Anthology* (Ed. Jack Hirschman; San Francisco: City Lights, 1965), 157.
3. Vattimo, *The End of Modernity*, 11.
4. "Who Killed *Winter Kills*?," bonus feature, Winter Kills DVD (Anchor Bay, 2003).
5. Artaud, *Artaud Anthology*, 143.
6. Ibid., 138.
7. Ibid., 135.
8. "Celebrating Harvey Milk: Two Films, One Legacy," ibid.
9. Ibid.
10. Robert Epstein, *The Times of Harvey Milk* (1984).
11. "Celebrating Harvey Milk: Two Films, One Legacy," ibid.
12. Fritz Lang and Jean-Luc Godard, *The Dinosaur and the Baby* (1967).
13. Robert Epstein, Deborah Hoffmann, and Daniel Nicoletta, DVD commentary, *The Times of Harvey Milk*, ibid.
14. Artaud, *Artaud Anthology*, 149.
15. Ibid., 142.
16. Ibid., 161.
17. Ronell, *Stupidity*, 207.
18. Ibid., 206.
19. Ibid., 208.
20. Vattimo, *The End of Modernity*, 126.
21. DVD commentary, *Howl* (Oscilloscope Laboratories, 2010).
22. Vattimo, *The End of Modernity*, 126.
23. Deleuze, *Spinoza: Practical Philosophy*, 63.
24. Vattimo, *The End of Modernity*, 122.
25. Deleuze, *Spinoza: Practical Philosophy*, 129.

Conclusion

1. Mark Binelli, "Sean Penn: The *Rolling Stone* Interview," *Rolling Stone* (February 19, 2009), 50.
2. Quoted in DeKoven, *Utopia Limited*, 238.
3. Rainer Werner Fassbinder, "Imitation of Life: On the Films of Douglas Sirk," *The Anarchy of the Imagination: Interviews, Essays, Notes* (Eds. Michael Töteberg and Leo A. Lensing; trans. Krishna Winston; Baltimore and London: The Johns Hopkins University Press, 1992), 77–89.

Bibliography

Andreas, Jörg. *Gefangen [Locked Up]*. Cazzo, 2004.
Anger, Kenneth. *The Films of Kenneth Anger Volume I*. Fantoma DVD, 2007.
─────. *The Films of Kenneth Anger Volume II*. Fantoma DVD, 2007.
Arbus, Diane. *Diane Arbus: An Aperture Monograph*. New York: Aperture, 1972.
─────. *Magazine Work*. New York: Aperture, 1984.
Artaud, Antonin. *Artaud Anthology*. Ed. Jack Hirschman. San Francisco: City Lights, 1965.
Barthes, Roland. *Camera Lucida: Reflections on Photography*. Trans. Richard Howard. New York: Hill and Wang, 1983.
─────. *Image-Music-Text*. Trans. Stephen Heath. New York: Hill and Wang, 1977.
─────. *Writing Degree Zero*. Trans. Annette Lavers and Colin Smith. New York: Hill and Wang, 1999.
Baudelaire, Charles. *Les Fleurs du mal*. Paris: Flammarion, 1991.
Benjamin, Walter. *Reflections: Essays, Aphorisms, Autobiographical Writings*. Trans. Edmund Jephcott; Ed. Peter Demetz. New York and London: Harcourt Brace Jovanovich, 1979.
Bergman, Ingmar. *Nattvardsgästerna [Winter Light]*. Svensk Filmindustri, 1963.
─────. *Persona*. Svensk Filmindustri, 1966.
Bersani, Leo. *Homos*. Cambridge, Mass., and London: Harvard University Press, 1995.
Binelli, Mark. "Sean Penn: The *Rolling Stone* Interview." *Rolling Stone*. February 19, 2009.
Bogdanovich, Peter. *The Last Picture Show*. Columbia, 1971.
Brickman, Paul. *Risky Business*. Geffen Company, 1983.
Brookner, Howard. *Burroughs*. Citifilmworks, 1983.
Broomfield, Nick. *Kurt & Courtney*. Strength Ltd., 1998.
Burroughs, William. *The Adding Machine: Selected Essays*. New York: Seaver Books, 1986.
─────. *Break Through in Grey Room*. S.I.: Sub Rosa, 2001.
─────. *The Burroughs File*. San Francisco: City Lights, 1991.
─────. *Early Routines*. Santa Barbara: Cadmus Editions, 1982.
─────. *Exterminator!* New York: Penguin Books, 1981.
─────. *Interzone*. Ed. James Grauerholz. New York: Penguin Books, 1989.
─────. *My Education: A Book of Dreams*. New York: Penguin Books, 1995.
─────. *Naked Lunch: The Restored Text*. Eds. James Grauerholz and Barry Miles. New York: Grove Press, 2001.
─────, and Gus Van Sant. *The Elvis of Letters*. TK Records, 1985.
Burston, Paul. *What Are You Looking At? Queer Sex, Style and Cinema*. London: Cassell, 1995.
"Celebrating Harvey Milk: Two Films, One Legacy." DVD bonus feature, *The Times of Harvey Milk*. Criterion Collection, 2011.
Clarke, Alan. *Elephant*. BBC Northern Ireland, 1989.
Cooper, Dennis. *Smothered in Hugs: Essays, Interviews, Feedback, and Obituaries*. New York: Harper Collins, 2010.
Crane, Hart. *The Poems of Hart Crane*. Ed. Marc Simon. New York: Liveright, 1986.
Crary, Jonathan. *Techniques of the Observer: On Vision and Modernity in the Nineteenth Century*. Cambridge, Mass., and London: MIT Press, 1992.
Curtis, Walt. *Mala Noche & Other "Illegal" Adventures*. Portland: Bridge City Books, 1997.

D'Allesandro, Sam. *The Wild Creatures: Collected Stories of Sam D'Allesandro*. Ed. Kevin Killian. San Francisco: Suspect Thoughts Press, 2005.
Dante. *La Vita Nuova*. Trans. Barbara Reynolds. Harmondsworth and New York: Penguin Books, 1978.
Davies, Jon. *Trash: A Queer Film Classic*. Vancouver: Arsenal Pulp Press, 2009.
De Angelis, Michael. *Gay Fandom and Crossover Stardom: James Dean, Mel Gibson, and Keanu Reeves*. Durham and London: Duke University Press, 2001.
DeKoven, Marianne. *Utopia Limited: The Sixties and the Emergence of the Postmodern*. Durham and London: Duke University Press, 2004.
Deleuze, Gilles. *Spinoza: Practical Philosophy*. Trans. Robert Hurley. San Francisco: City Lights, 1988.
Epstein, Robert. *The Times of Harvey Milk*. Black Sand Productions, 1984.
_____, and Jeffrey Friedman. *Howl*. Werc Werk Works, 2010.
Epstein, Robert, Deborah Hoffman, and Daniel Nicoletta. DVD commentary, *The Times of Harvey Milk*. Criterion Collection, 2011.
Fassbinder, Rainer Werner. *The Anarchy of the Imagination: Interviews, Essays, Notes*. Eds. Michael Töteberg and Leo A. Lensing. Trans. Krishna Winston. Baltimore and London: The Johns Hopkins University Press, 1992.
_____. *Veronika Voss*. Roxy Film, 1981.
Fogle, James. *Drugstore Cowboy*. New York: Bantam-Doubleday-Dell Publishing Group, Inc, 1990.
Franco, James, Robert Epstein, and Jeffrey Friedman. DVD commentary, *Howl*. Oscilloscope Laboratories, 2010.
Freud, Sigmund. *The Schreber Case*. Trans. Andrew Weber. New York: Penguin Books, 2003.
Fuller, Graham. "Gus Van Sant: Swimming Against the Current," in Gus Van Sant, *Even Cowgirls Get the Blues & My Own Private Idaho*. London and Boston: Faber and Faber, 1993.
Garnham, Nicholas. *Fuller*. New York: Viking Press, Inc, 1972.
Goldsmith, Kenneth (Ed.). *I'll Be Your Mirror: The Selected Andy Warhol Interviews, 1962–1987; Thirty-Seven Conversations with the Pop Master*. New York: Carroll & Graf Publishers, 2004.
Griffith, D. W. *The Avenging Conscience*. Biograph, 1913.
Harris, Oliver, and Ian MacFayden (Eds.). *Naked Lunch @ 50: anniversary essays*. Carbondale: Southern Illinois University Press, 2009.
Haynes, Todd. *Far From Heaven*. Focus Features, 2002.
Hine, Thomas. *The Rise and Fall of the American Teenager*. New York: Harper Collins, 1999.
Head, Steve. "An Interview with Gus Van Sant." http://movies.ign.com. October 22, 2003.
Hetherington, Tim, and Sebastian Junger. *Restrepo*. Outpost Films, 2010.
Hitchcock, Sir Alfred. *Psycho*. Universal Pictures, 1960.
Holmlund, Chris, and Cynthia Fuchs (Eds.). *Between the Sheets, In the Streets: Queer, Lesbian, Gay Documentary*. Minneapolis and London: University of Minnesota Press, 1997.
Howard, Ron. *Parenthood*. Imagine Entertainment, 1989.
Hunter, Tim. *River's Edge*. Arcade Enterprise, 1986.
Iampolski, Mikhail. *The Memory of Tiresias: Intertextuality and Film*. Trans. Harsha Ram. Berkeley, Los Angeles, and London: University of California Press, 1998.
Indiana, Gary. "Interview with Gus Van Sant." BOMB #45. Fall 1993.
Jarman, Derek. *Blue*. Basilisk Communications, 1993.
_____. *The Garden*. Basilisk Communications, 1990.
_____. *Jubilee*. Megalovision, 1978.
_____. *The Last of England*. Anglo International Films, 1988.
Koch, Stephen. *Stargazer: The Life, World & Films of Andy Warhol, Revised and Updated*. New York and London: Marion Boyars, 1991.
Kubrick, Stanley. *2001: A Space Odyssey*. MGM, 1968.
Lang, Fritz, and Jean-Luc Godard. *The Dinosaur and the Baby*. INA, 1967.
Lewis, Everett. *Lucky Bastard*. Breaking Glass Pictures, 2009.
Lydenberg, Robin. *Word Cultures: Radical Theory and Practice in William S. Burroughs' Fiction*. Urbana: University of Illinois Press, 1987.
Marsh, James. *Wisconsin Death Trip*. BBC, 1999.

Mendes, Sam. *Jarhead*. Universal Pictures, 2005.
Minnelli, Vincente. *An American in Paris*. MGM, 1951.
Morris, Wesley. "Cosmic 'Elephant': high school existential." *Boston Globe*, www.bostonglobe.com. November 14, 2003.
Moverman, Oren. *The Messenger*. Oscilloscope Laboratories, 2009.
Nietzsche, Friedrich. *Beyond Good and Evil: Prelude to a Philosophy of the Future*. Trans. Walter Kaufmann. New York: Random House, Inc. 1966.
"No Cutting, No Stars, No Script: An Interview with Gus Van Sant." *Mala Noche* DVD. Madman, 2006.
Nyswaner, Ron. *The Prince of Pennsylvania*. Columbia, 1988.
Outlaw (Jr.), Dr. Lucius T. *On Race and Philosophy*. New York and London: Routledge, 1996.
Parrish, John Robert. *Gus Van Sant: An Unauthorized Biography*. New York: Thunder's Mouth Press, 2001.
Peary, Gerald, "Gus Van Sant — Elephant." http://geraldpeary.com/interviews.
Peckinpah, Sam. *The Wild Bunch*. Warner Brothers/Seven Arts, 1969.
"Psycho Path," featurette. *Psycho* DVD. Universal, 1999.
Richert, William. *Winter Kills*. Winter Gold Productions, 1979.
Rimbaud, Arthur. *Oeuvres Complètes*. Paris: Librairie Gallimard, 1954.
Robb, Brian J. *River Phoenix: A Short Life*. New York: Harper Collins, Inc.,1994.
Ronell, Avital. *Stupidity*. Urbana and Chicago: University of Illinois Press, 2002.
Rossen, Robert. *Lilith*. Columbia, 1964.
Sartre, Jean-Paul. *Baudelaire*. Trans. Martin Turnell. New York: New Directions,1967.
Schlesinger, John. *Midnight Cowboy*. Florin Productions, 1969.
Sinfield, Alan. *Gay and After*. London: Serpent's Tail, 1998.
Sokurov, Aleksandr. *Otets i syn [Father and Son]*. Nikola Film, 2003.
Sontag, Susan. *Against Interpretation*. New York: Farrar, Straus and Giroux, 1966.
Stanford, Phil. *Portland Confidential: Sex, Crime, and Corruption in the Rose City*. Portland: West Winds Press, 2004.
Stevens, Mark, and Annalyn Swan. *De Kooning: An American Master*. New York: Random House, Inc, 2006.
Stoppe, Sebastian. *Original und Fälschung?— Hitchcocks Psycho und das Remake von Gus van Sant*. GRIN Verlag, 2002.
Tarr, Béla. *Sátántangó [Satan's Tango]*. Mozgókép Innovációs Társulás és Alpativány-Von Vietinghoff Filmproduktion, 1994.
Thomson, David. *The New Biographical Dictionary of Film: Updated and Expanded*. New York: Alfred A. Knopf, 2010.
Tinkcom, Matthew. *Working Like a Homosexual: Camp, Capital, Cinema*. Durham and London: Duke University Press, 2002.
Valls, Andrew (Ed.) *Race and Racism in Modern Philosophy*. Ithaca and London: Cornell University Press, 2005.
Van Sant, Gus. *The Discipline of DE*, 1978.
_____. *Drugstore Cowboy*. Avenue Pictures Productions, 1989.
_____. *Elephant*. HBO Films, 2003.
_____. *Even Cowgirls Get the Blues*. New Line Cinema, 1993.
_____. *Even Cowgirls Get the Blues & My Own Private Idaho*. London and Boston: Faber and Faber, 1993.
_____. *Finding Forrester*. Columbia, 2000.
_____. *Gerry*. Epsilon Motion Pictures, 2002.
_____. *Good Will Hunting*. Be Gentlemen Limited Partnership, 1997.
_____. Interview with Madonna. *Interview Magazine*, www.interviewmagazine.com.
_____. *Last Days*. HBO Films, 2005.
_____. *Mala Noche*. MK2 Productions, 1986.
_____. "Mansion on the Hill," episode in *8*. LDM Productions, 2008.
_____. "Le Marais," episode in *Paris, Je T'Aime*. First Look Features, 2006.
_____. *Milk*. Focus Features, 2007.
_____. *My Own Private Idaho*. New Line Cinema, 1991.
_____. *Paranoid Park*. MK2 Productions, 2007.

_____. *Pink: A Novel*. New York: Anchor Books, 1998.
_____. *Psycho*. Universal Pictures, 1998.
_____. *Restless*. Columbia, 2011.
_____. *To Die For*. Columbia, 1995.
Van Sant, Gus, and Matt Dillon. DVD commentary, *Drugstore Cowboy*. Artisan Home Entertainment, 1999.
Van Sant, Gus, Anne Heche, and Vince Vaughn. DVD commentary, *Psycho*. Universal, 1999.
Vattimo, Gianni. *The End of Modernity*. Trans. Jon R. Snyder. Baltimore: The Johns Hopkins University Press, 1991.
The Velvet Underground. *The Velvet Underground & Nico*. Polydor, 1967.
Vicari, Justin. *Male Bisexuality in Current Cinema: Images of Growth, Rebellion and Survival*. Jefferson, NC.: McFarland, 2011.
Wakoski, Diane. *Virtuoso Literature for Two and Four Hands*. Garden City, New York: Doubleday & Company, 1975.
Waldman, Anne (Ed.). *Out of This World: The Poetry Project at the St. Mark's Church-on-the-Bowery, An Anthology 1966–1991*. New York: Crown Publishers, Inc., 1991.
Warhol, Andy. *The Chelsea Girls*, 1966.
_____. *Empire*, 1964.
Weber, Bruce. *Broken Noses*. Kira Productions, 1987.
Welles, Orson. *Mr. Arkadin*. Filmorsa, 1955.
Whitman, Walt. *Specimen Days & Collect*. New York: Dover Publications, Inc., 1995.
"Who Killed *Winter Kills*?" Bonus feature, *Winter Kills* DVD. Anchor Bay, 2003.
Zurbrugg, Nicholas. "The Limits of Intertextuality: Barthes, Burroughs, Gysin, Culler" in *Critical Vices: The Myths of Postmodern Theory*. International: G + A Arts, 2000.

Index

Numbers in **_bold italics_** indicate pages with photographs.

Abraham, F. Murray 122
Acker, Kathy 130–131
Affleck, Ben 104
Affleck, Casey 95, 148, **_149_**
Allen, Woody 153
Alton, John 41
American History X 46
An American in Paris 29–30, 40
Anderson, Gail-Nina 3
Anderson, Paul Thomas 152
Andersson, Bibi 148
Anger, Kenneth 10, 20, 22, 32, 77, 128, 138
Annie Hall 153
Anonymous 101
Apollinaire, Guillaume 16
Araki, Gregg 28, 42
Arbus, Diane 12–13, 159, 165–169
Argento, Asia 216
Artaud, Antonin 201, 203, 216, 217
Avedon, Richard 224
The Avenging Conscience 50, 52

Back to the Future 87
Baker, James Robert 42
Baldwin, James 16, 226
Barr, Roseanne 166
Barthes, Roland 9, 12, 16, 43, 47, 53–54, 58, 59, 221, 233n, 234n
Bass, Saul 65
Baudelaire, Charles 149–150
Beatty, Warren 74
Bedelia, Bonnie 144
Beethoven, Ludwig van 76, 161
Beggars Banquet 223
Benjamin, Walter 15–16, 112, 114
Bergman, Ingmar 72, 148, 156
Berry, Stephanie 117
Bersani, Leo 235n
Birney, Frank 83
Björnstrand, Gunnar 72, 148
Black, Dustin Lance 4, 234n
Blue 148, 156
Boddie, Ken 108
Bogarde, Dirk 153

Borgnine, Ernest 37
Bottoms, Sam 99
Bottoms, Timothy 99, **_100_**
Bowie, David 31
Boyz II Men 214
Bridges, Jeff 201
Brokeback Mountain 5
Broken Noses 131, **_136_**, 137–140
Brolin, Josh 88, **_171_**
Brookner, Howard 237n, 242n
Broomfield, Nick 205, 206
Brown, Rob 21, **_121_**
Browne, Jackson 28
Bryant, Anita 5
Buñuel, Luis 57, 170
Burroughs, William 1, 11, 21, 24, 25, 26, **_43_**, 44–45, 46–48, 62, 67–68, 80–87, 111, 125, 134, 173, 180–184, 189–191, 192–197, 234–235n, 236n, 237n, 240–241n
Burroughs, William, Jr. 242n
Burrowes, John "Mike" 108
Burston, Paul 140, 141, 181

Callas, Maria 130
Campbell, John 141
Caravaggio 176–177
Caron, Leslie 29
Carter, Grace 107
Caselli, Chiara 92
Castel, Lou 223
The Chelsea Girls 185
Un Chien Andalou 170
Christensen, Benjamin 86
Citizen Kane 201–202
Clark, Larry 159, 229
Clarke, Alan 32–34, 40
Clarkson, Patricia 212
Cobain, Kurt 29, 41, 215–216
Connery, Sean 47, 118, **_121_**
Cooeyate, Doug 21, **_139_**
Cooper, Dennis 141, 142–143
Corliss, Richard 218
Cottrell, Mickey 129
Crane, Hart 58

247

Cross, Joseph 88
Cruise, Tom 132–133, 135
Curtice, Sally 218
Curtis, Walt 40–41, 97

Dallesandro, Joe 129, 184–185
D'Allesandro, Sam 13, 128, 129, 134, 186–187, 195, 199
Damon, Matt 33, 55, 104, 148, *149*
Dangerous Game 31
Dano, Paul 152
Dante 146–147, 158
David and Lisa 153–154
Davis, Brad 46
Dawson, Rosario 152
Dean, James 28, 143
De Angelis, Michael 140, 143
Deats, Danyi 23
Dekker, Desmond 30
de Kooning, Willem 62–63
DeKoven, Marianne 48, 113, 123–124, 236n
Deleuze, Gilles 201, 224, 225
De Mornay, Rebecca 133
Despair 153
Deulen, Eric 37
Dillon, Matt 21, *43*, 94, *95*
The Discipline of DE 81–87, 170
DJ Spooky 3
Doyle, Christopher 76, 107
Driver, Minnie *55*, 89
Drugstore Cowboy 6, 15, 21, 23, 30, 31, 35, 36, 41, 42, *43*, 44, 51, 56–57, 60, 95–96, 102, 156, 170, 181, 192, 196, 198, 199, 209, 229
Dullea, Keir 150, 153–154, 231
Dyer, Richard 10
Dymkoski, Dale 101

Eden Lake 151, 153
8 135
Eisenstein, Sergei 22
Elephant (1988) 32–34, 36–40, 54
Elephant (2002) *12*, 32, 36, 41, 58–60, 86, 96, 99–100, *100*, 101–102, 103–104, *103*, 105, 140, 161–164, 169–170, 172–173, 175, 179, 189, 195, 198, 199, 231, 240n
The Elvis of Letters 48
Emerson, Eric 185, 186
Empire 59–60
Epstein, Rob 205, 206, 223, 234n
"Erased de Kooning" 62–63
Even Cowgirls Get the Blues 6, 15, *17*, 17, 18, 21, 27, 55–56, 101, 129, 163, 165–168, *167*, *168*, 198, 199, 200, 230

Far from Heaven 212–213, 215
Fassbender, Michael 152
Fassbinder, Rainer Werner 11, 46, 130, 153, 157, 227

Father and Son 105–106, 110–111
Fellini, Federico 57
Ferrara, Abel 31
Ferréol, Andrea 153
Finding Forrester 21, 47, 117–125, 140, 208–209
Finklea, Carrie 103, *103*
Fists in the Pocket 223
Fitzgerald, Glenn 208
Fogle, James 95
Ford, John 237n
Forster, Robert 66
Foster, Ben 175
Franco, James 101, *207*, 221
Freud, Sigmund 25–26, 93
Friedman, Jeffrey 206
Frost, Alex 37, 240n
Fuller, Graham 35–36, 100–101, 128, 198
Fuller, Samuel 198
Funeral Rites 169

Garcia, Jerry 21, 214–215
Garnham, Nicholas 80
Gates of Heaven 28
Gavin, John 69
Gefangen 46
Genet, Jean 46, 169, 173, 181
Gerry 21, 64, 146–158, 149, 193, 198, 210, 231, 240n
Ginsberg, Allen 206, 210, 221, 223
Giorno, John 185
Glover, Crispin *17*, 101, 141
Go 153
Godard, Jean-Luc *207*, 239n
Good Will Hunting 31–32, *33*, *55*, 89, 104–105, 131, 157, 196, 210
Gordon, Kim 215
Grace, April 117
Graham, Heather 56
Green, Scott 108, 211
Griffith, D.W. 50, 52
Gummo 229
Gysin, Brion 44

Haas, Lukas 211
Harold and Maude 28
Harrelson, Woody 175
Harvey, Rodney *222*
Häxan 86
Hayenga, Jeff 144
Haynes, Todd 46, 212–213
Haysbert, Dennis 212
Heche, Anne 65, *70*, 75, 237n
Heidegger, Martin 9–10, 224
Hemmer, Kurt 240–241n
Hetherington, Tim 173
Hine, Thomas 132, 133
Hirsch, Emile 240n

Index

Hitchcock, Sir Alfred 40, 63–64, 76
Hitler, Adolf 162–164, 169, 179, 203
Holden, William 37
Hopkins, Bo 37
Hopper, Dennis 28
Hopper, Henry 13, *14*
Horton, Robert 180, 193
Howl 206–207, *207*, 214, 221
Hurt, John 27, 129
Hussey, Andrew 184
Huston, John 208

Iampolski, Mikhail 24, 29
In a Year with Thirteen Moons 108
Invasion of the Body Snatchers (1956) 156

Jarhead 175–176
Jarman, Derek 42, 148, 156, 176–179, 236n, 240n
Jeffryes, Treva 21
Johnson, Ben 99
Jones, Cleve 205, 226
Jones, George 76
Joy, Nicholas 212
Junger, Sebastian 173

Kase, Ryo 39
Keaton, Diane 153
Keegan, Kari 145
Kelly, Gene 29
Kennedy, Pres. John F. 204, 205
Kesey, Ken 155
Kidman, Nicole 94
Kier, Udo 52, 166
Koch, Stephen 60, 234n, 241n
Korine, Harmony 214, 229
Krauss, Ruth 32
Kubrick, Stanley 61, 150, 151, 231
Kurt & Courtney 205–206, 215

Last Days 15, 21, 31, 41, 170, 192, 198, 205, 206, 211–219, *213*, 221, 231
The Last of England 176–179
The Last Picture Show 99
Lavrov, Fyodor 105
Leachman, Chloris 99
Lee, Spike 229
LeGros, James 56
Leitch, Ione Skye 23, 141
Let's Get Lost 138
Levant, Oscar 29
Lewis, Everett 101
Lilith 74
Linklater, Richard 229
Liu, Dan 108
Lockhart, Calvin 152
Love Story 27
Lucky Bastard 101
Lydenberg, Robin 235n

Lynch, David 16, 152
Lynch, Kelly 56

MacFayden, Ian 189
Macy, William H. 66, *72*
Madigan, Amy 144
Madonna 30–31
Mahler, Gustav 6
Mala Noche 5, 6, 21, 36, 40–44, 50–51, *55*, 55, 91, 92–93, 94, 96–98, 101, 102, 109, 111, 134, 137, *139*, 140, *188*, 190–191, 194, 199, 204, 229, 230
Malloy, Matt 96
Malone, Dorothy 156
"Mansion on the Hill" 135
"Le Marais" 29–30, 40
Margolin, Janet 154
Marsh, James 236n
McConnell, Elias *12*, 29
McFarland, John 86, *100*
McKinney, Lauren 36
Mendes, Sam 175
The Messenger 175, 176
Metty, Russell 41
Midnight Cowboy 60, 128
Miles, Barry 181
Miles, Vera 75
Milk 4–5, 6, 85, 88–89, 101, 105, 129, *170*, 172, 197, 198, 205, 206, 210, 230, 234n, 240n
Milk, Harvey 4, 7, 199, 205, 219, 223, 234n
Miller, Jake 108
Mineo, Sal 27
Minnelli, Vincente 27, 29, 235n
Minsker, Andy *136*, 137–139
Mishima, Yukio 27
Mr. Arkadin 204
Mitchell, Joni 138
Mohr, Jay 153
Momsen, Taylor 108
Monge, Ray 41, *188*
Monroe, Marilyn 204, 205
Moore, Julianne 74, 212
Mori, Paola 204
Morris, Erroll 27, 156
Morrissey, Paul 128–129, 184–185
Mortensen, Viggo 69, *70*

Neo Boys 42
Nevins, Gabe 36, *110*
Neymyshev, Aleksei 105
Nicholson, Jack 104
Nico 28
Nicoletta, Daniel 234n
Nietzsche, Friedrich 15, 56, 62
Norton, Edward 151
Nyswaner, Ron 131, 144

O'Connor, Sinead 31
Outlaw, Dr. Lucius T. 116, 124

Palin, Sarah 5
Paquin, Anna 21
Paranoid Park 36, 58–60, 86, 105, 107–111, *110*, 140, 182–183, 192, 199, 200, 229, 231
Parenthood 142
Paris, Je T'Aime 29
Parker, Charlie 29
Parstein, David 46
Pärt, Arvo 154
Pasolini, Pier Paolo 5, 57, 130–131
Peckinpah, Sam 37, 39, 40, 57, 171
Penn, Arthur 171
Penn, Sean 6–7, *171*, 206, 226
Perkins, Anthony 27, 73–74, 77, 79, 203
Perry, Frank 154
Persona 148, 156
Phoenix, Joacquin 94, *95*
Phoenix, Rain 15, *168*
Phoenix, River 6–7, 9, 10, 11, *222*
Pink 106–107
Pink Flamingos 229
Pitt, Michael 31, *213*, 215
Plateau, Joseph 147
Poe, Edgar Allan 120
Point Break 141
Poison 46
The Prince of Pennsylvania 144–145
Promised Land *33*
Psycho (1960) 48, 63–79
Psycho (1998) 40, 48, 54, 62–79, *70*, *72*, 102, 156, 199, 210, 226
Puryear, Jordan 212

Quaid, Dennis 212
Querelle 46

Rauschenberg, Robert 62–63
Razbash, Aleksandr 105
Rebel Without a Cause 28
Reed, Lou 158, 215
Reeves, Keanu 11, 23, 56, 89, 131, 140–145, *158*
Reilly, Kelly 152
Remar, James 24
Restless 13, *14*, 27–28, 39, 40, 57, 86, 157
Restrepo 173–175, 176, 178
Reznor, Trent 234n
Rhymes, Busta 118
Richert, William 89, 201, 202, 207–208
Rimbaud, Arthur 81, 139
Risky Business 132–133, 135
River's Edge 23, 141
Roebuck, Daniel 23
Rohmer, Eric 239n
Ronell, Avital 34–35, 220
Rooney, Mickey 10

Rossen, Robert 74
Running on Empty 9

Sadoul, Georges 147
Sànchez, Jaime 39
Sartre, Jean-Paul 146, 149–150
Schlutt, Marcel 46
Scorpio Rising 10, 11, 22, 23, 24
Scorsese, Martin 104
Scott-Heron, Gil 2–3
Sedgwick, Edie 165, 224
Shakespeare, William 80, 89, 138
Shapiro, Ken 83
Shchetinin, Andrei 105
Shilts, Randy 4
Simanga, Dr. Michael 112
Sinfield, Alan 28
Sirk, Douglas 156, 157, 227
Skarsgaard, Stellan 89
Smith, Elliott 31–32
Smith, Jack 129
Sokurov, Aleksandr 105–106, 110
Sontag, Susan 9, 11, 13, 14–15, 16, 17–18, 114, 188, 228
Specimen Days 159–161
Spengler, Volker 153, 156
Stack, Robert 156
Stand by Me 9
Stanford, Phil 32
Stole, Mink 229
Stone, Oliver 4
Stop-Loss 240n
Stoppe, Sebastian 73–74, 75
Streeter, Tim 41
Superstar, Ingrid 130

Tarr, Béla 240n
Tavel, Ronald 234n
Tchaikovsky 106
There Will Be Blood 152
The Thin Blue Line 156
Thomas, Thaddeus A. 213, *213*
Thomson, David 32
Thurman, Uma *17*, 55, *167*
The Times of Harvey Milk 205, 206, 207, 223, 234n
Tinckom, Matthew 27, 77, 130, 235n
To Die For 36, 91, 94, *95*, 170, 229
Troupe, Tom 89
25th Hour 151
2001: A Space Odyssey 61, 150–151, 231
Tyson, Nathan 103, *103*

Ulliel, Gaspard 29

Vallee, Rudy 224
Van Gogh, Vincent 216, 217, 224
Vattimo, Gianni 9–10, 19, 112–116, 202, 220, 221, 224

Vaughn, Vince 65, *72*, 73–74, 78
Velàzquez 155
The Velvet Underground 134, 158, 214
Veronika Voss 217
Verow, Todd 101
Vicius, Nicole 217
Viridiana 223
von Sydow, Max 72

Wakoski, Diane 96
Ward, Fred 144
Warhol, Andy 26, 59–60, 62, 76, 79, 129, 130, 133, 185, 224, 234n, 241n
Wasikowska, Mia 13, *14*
Waters, John 32, 129, 130, 229
Weber, Bruce 122, 131, *136*, 137–140, 159
Welles, Orson 202, 204
Whitman, Walt 159–161
Wild at Heart 152

The Wild Bunch 37–40, 100
Williams, Robin 4, 89
Williamson, Jay "Smay" 107
Winter Kills 201–204, 208, 209
Winter Light 72
Wolf, Scott 153
Wood, Ed 66
Worden, David 83
Written on the Wind 156
Wyatt, Justin 42
Wynette, Tammy 76

Yorty, Don 34
Young, Sean *17*, 101

Zabriskie, Grace 53, 152
Zech, Rosel 217
Zurbrugg, Nicholas 234–235n

www.ingramcontent.com/pod-product-compliance
Ingram Content Group UK Ltd.
Pitfield, Milton Keynes, MK11 3LW, UK
UKHW041917140426
5217IPUK00013B/194